Familiar Strangers, Juvenile Panic a

Familiar Strangers, Juvenile Panic and the British Press

The Decline of Social Trust

James Morrison
Robert Gordon University, Aberdeen, UK

First published 2016 by
PALGRAVE MACMILLAN

The author has asserted their right to be identified as the author of this work in accordance with the Copyright, Designs and Patents Act 1988.

Palgrave Macmillan in the UK is an imprint of Macmillan Publishers Limited, registered in England, company number 785998, of Houndmills, Basingstoke, Hampshire RG21 6XS.

Palgrave Macmillan in the US is a division of Nature America, Inc., One New York Plaza, Suite 4500 New York, NY 10004-1562.

Palgrave Macmillan is the global academic imprint of the above companies and has companies and representatives throughout the world.

ISBN: 978–1–137–52994–7 (HB)
ISBN: 978–1–349–95845–0 (PB)
EPUB: 978–1–137–52996–1
EPDF: 978–1–137–52995–4
DOI: 10.1057/9781137529954

Distribution in the UK, Europe and the rest of the world is by Palgrave Macmillan®, a division of Macmillan Publishers Limited, registered in England, company number 785998, of Houndmills, Basingstoke, Hampshire RG21 6XS.

Library of Congress Cataloging-in-Publication Data
Names: Morrison, James, 1971–
Title: Familiar strangers, juvenile panic and the British press: the decline of social trust / James Morrison, Robert Gordon University, Aberdeen, UK.
Description: Houndmills, Basingstoke, Hampshire ; New York, NY: Palgrave Macmillan, 2016. | Includes bibliographical references and index.
Identifiers: LCCN 2015037087 | ISBN 9781137529947 (hardback)
Subjects: LCSH: Children—Crimes against—Great Britain. | Abused Children—Great Britain. | Juvenile delinquents—Great Britain. | Trust—Great Britain. | Anxiety—Great Britain. | Children—Press Coverage—Great Britain.
Classification: LCC HV751.A6 M67 2016 | DDC 362.760941—dc23
LC record available at http://lccn.loc.gov/2015037087

A catalog record for this book is available from the Library of Congress

A catalogue record for the book is available from the British Library

Typeset by MPS Limited, Chennai, India.

For my mum and dad

Contents

List of Figures

Acknowledgements

The author would like to thank staff, parents and pupils at St Luke's Primary School, Whitehawk Primary School and Hanover Community Association, Brighton, for help with focus group research. Thanks also to the 30 journalists who gave their time to speak so openly about their work (you know who you are), and Dr David Rogers at Kingston University for being so supportive of this research – both intellectually and financially.

1
Trust, Risk and Framing Contemporary Childhood

Panics about the risks faced by children are nothing new. A wealth of literature testifies to a long British tradition of problematizing the status and condition of childhood – with news media, politicians, police and other key definers repeatedly voicing (or consciously whipping up) deep-seated societal neuroses about juvenile vulnerability. Threats, we are continually reminded, come in any number of forms: everything from mundane household objects (Hood et al., 1996; Kelley et al., 1997), to injury and sickness (Hier, 2003, 2008) to drug treatments specifically designed to *protect* children from ill health (Mason & Donnelly, 2000; Evans et al., 2001; Ramsay et al., 2002; Boyce, 2007) can present potential dangers to the wellbeing of the young. All the while, kids are continually at risk of being preyed upon by an omnipresent rogues' gallery of malevolent deviants. Among the most feared 'folk-devils' (Cohen, 1972) is a baleful figure straight out of the Brothers Grimm: the predatory paedophile who threatens to poach unsuspecting innocents as they play, walk to school or pop around the corner to visit friends (Fritz & Altheide, 1987; Best, 1990; Jenkins, 1992; McNeish & Roberts, 1995; Valentine, 1996a, 1996b, 1997a, 1997b; Valentine & McKendrick, 1997; Gentry, 1988; Scott et al, 1998; Kitzinger, 1999; Gallagher et al., 2002; Meyer, 2007). Then there are *familiar* strangers: half-known figures we encounter as we go about our daily lives. This amorphous array of individuals encompasses everyone from more obviously suspicious loners and eccentrics to neighbours, shopkeepers or fellow parents with whom we are on nodding terms but whose benign exteriors might one day turn out to mask diabolical intent.

Concerns about deceitful and untrustworthy familiar strangers pollute our perceptions of childhood in other respects, too. If there is one lesson to be drawn from the extensive academic literature on media-fuelled

1

'moral panics', which began with Stanley Cohen's seminal 1972 study of the feeding frenzy over 1960s clashes between Mods and Rockers, it is that the discourse of juvenile risk very often has the boot (so to speak) on the other foot. While dominant day-to-day risk narratives about children tend to focus on younger juveniles, framing them as actual or potential *victims* – as this book demonstrates – an equally powerful, if slightly less prominent, secondary discourse caricatures older kids (typically dubbed 'youths' or 'teenagers') as *threats* (Fishman, 1978; Hall et al., 1978; Davis, 1980; Pearson, 1983; Valentine, 1996a). In recent years, this has been articulated as a problem of 'antisocial behaviour' (ASB): a highly politicized term which, though not theoretically confined to the young, is closely associated with them (Farrington & Coid, 2003; Squires & Stephen, 2005; Solanki et al., 2006; Rodger, 2008; Squires, 2008; Waiton, 2008). There are, then, clear contradictions at work in the way perceptions of childhood are constructed (and *reconstructed*) in Britain today. And, as in the parallel discourse around 'victims', many juvenile malefactors typically identified as 'threats' surface in the guise of familiar strangers: from playground bullies (Valentine, 1996a; Jago et al., 2009) to the loitering 'hoodies' blighting our shopping malls (Lett, 2010) and the troublesome offspring of our noisy neighbours. A key argument of this book is that this moral ambivalence about the position of children (a term that will, from now on, be applied to anyone under the age of 18) both *shapes* the way juveniles are commonly discussed (in the media, by our law-makers and law-enforcers – and by ourselves) and *is perpetuated by* these popular framings. Whatever its origins or causes (subjects explored at length in coming chapters), a self-reinforcing juvenile panic seems to have taken root in late-modern Britain, with the very concept of childhood now viewed through a distorted prism which foregrounds risk and menace over all other aspects of children's lives (and selves). This confused and conflicted social construction is reflected in every arena of discursive life – from our snatched conversations in the dinner queue or at the school gates to our exchanges on Facebook and other social media, to the speeches of politicians and judges and (perhaps especially) reports and commentary in the news.

Fuzzy and contradictory positioning of childhood as a state of, simultaneously, innate goodness and untamed badness – of children themselves as both potential victims *and* threats – became a running thread throughout the various levels of empirical research carried out for this study. A trainee nursery worker from a low-income working-class background who participated in a series of focus groups designed to explore the rationales underpinning parental decisions about how much freedom to allow their children – and the roots of safety fears that informed their behaviour – was one of several interviewees who contrasted the secure world in which she grew up with the more dangerous one of today. She recalled how 'when I was younger, my mother said, "there are some people that are bad, so don't talk to strangers"', while 'nowadays ... it [the threat] don't even have to be a stranger – it can be a kid in your class that ... has brought a knife to school'. Alluding to a story 'in the news' about 'children stabbed ... in class with scissors', she concluded, 'for some reason, as a culture we've got more violent'. A volunteer teaching assistant with three children in the same group summed up the consensus by evoking nebulous, all-encompassing fears about 'the risks out there' and 'what could happen in life' if children were permitted too loose a rein. These views were widely shared by mothers in a parallel focus group recruited from a middle-class postcode area in the same city. 'It feels like an *angrier* world', observed a special needs worker with three children, while a former teacher articulated a widely shared feeling that it had become harder to trust individuals one met 'through' one's children – including other *parents*. Recalling an encounter with a mum she 'hadn't met before' who 'came up to me in the playground and said, "can my son come out for the day?"', she admitted, 'at the back of my mind ... I'm thinking, "I know absolutely zero about this person"'. And the risks posed by the world that today's children inhabit are far from confined to external threats, according to these parents: kids are also capable of harming *themselves*. 'Friends' may 'get distracted' and cause 'accidents and stuff', observed a working-class mother-of-four, who fretted about her primary school-aged children injuring themselves by fooling around outdoors with mates. The eldest son of a middle-class midwife remained a source of worry in his teens – chiefly because she suspected he 'dabbles in smoking pot and stuff with his friends'. Questions of trust, then – a subject to which we return throughout this book – loomed large in the willingness (or *unwillingness*) of parents to permit their children to socialize independently in ways that, most conceded, they once had themselves. And feelings of distrust and suspicion were intimately bound up with not only their perceptions of the social environment at large (and potential dangers it presented) but also their degrees of confidence about the trustworthiness of *their own* children – to heed warnings, to only stray so far, to take specified routes home, even to behave civilly and responsibly towards *others*.

This widespread perception of today's social world as a scarier, more disconcerting, place than it once was – one becoming progressively *more* menacing over time – not only emerged from focus groups. Perhaps unsurprisingly – given that media coverage of child abductions, murder and abuse was frequently cited as a key source of such anxieties – it was heavily reflected in another key strand of research: a month-long textual analysis of routine newspaper narratives and online reader discussion threads accompanying them. The most widely covered 'child victim' stories invariably revolved around children being terrorized by familiar strangers – with multiple reports about a girl finding her mother murdered by a 'hair fetish fiend' (e.g. 'Teen's Horror', Nash, 2011, p. 11) posing as a benign next-door neighbour and a fast-food takeaway manager who lured schoolgirls to his bedsit to abuse them in exchange for money. The next most prominent category ('child threats') also emphasized the menace of familiar strangers, through a litany of stories about teenage hoodies and unruly schoolchildren. Common to all these cautionary tales was an undercurrent of emphasis on questions of trust – with the most extensively reported story of the whole period aptly symbolizing this in the form of a 'hybrid' narrative positioning juveniles as both victims *and* threats. This hinged around the trial of a callous teenager who murdered his girlfriend by bashing her over the head with a rock, and abandoning her dead body to go and watch television with friends. In the lengthiest article about this case – a double-page spread, published in *The People* (Jeffs, 2011, pp. 16–7) – the youth was framed as a classic familiar stranger, with the victim's uncle remembering him as 'an ideal teenager' who was 'from a church-going family, academically gifted – everything you could want for your own daughter'.

As the extensive interviews with journalists also conducted for this study demonstrate, the 'scarier word' paradigm promoted by newspapers is a highly commercially motivated discourse: a form of 'market-driven journalism' (McManus, 1994) that sensitizes and exploits popular fears about juvenile risk and threatening familiarity for monetary gain. But, as with all such phenomena, it would be glib to suggest that news producers are engaged in a simple process of myth-making, with no basis in reality. If that were the case, the discourse would lack the 'salience' (Critcher, 2003) it clearly holds not only for audiences but practitioners themselves. Journalists interviewed appeared to view the world as scarcely less threatening than parents, grandparents and children themselves imagined it. As one tabloid assistant news editor put it, 'when I was a kid ... we were shit scared of our granddad', whereas 'now, "I'm a granddad, I go on the street, and I'm shit scared of the children and, in fact, *my own* grandchildren"'. This view 'in some ways

... reflects social reality', he argued – in that 'there *has* been a change'. For a broadsheet feature writer, by contrast, the heightened profile of stories focusing on juvenile risk and threat – particularly those involving familiar strangers – is less a reflection of an overblown media obsession with child abuse and murder than a largely positive development which, in recent years, has helped expose denials of the past. Today's world may be *no more* dangerous for the young than it used to be, but the reason we are now aware that child abductions and murders, when they occur, are 'almost always' committed by 'someone they know' (however vaguely) is because of '20 years of reporting of these kinds of cases'. Indeed, these words echo a sentiment voiced by the founding father of moral panic theory, Cohen himself, who used a recent address to a Moral Panics in the Contemporary World conference to argue in favour of the deliberate construction of 'positive panics' analogous to 'anti-denial movements' and 'consciousness-raising' campaigns of the 1960s (Cohen, 2010, p. 1) – to *counteract* precisely the same elite agendas that framed earlier panics. Nonetheless, whatever *justifications* there may be for the dominance of media narratives positioning juveniles as, alternately, victim and threat (or prey and predator), it is hard to escape the conclusion that we are living through a prolonged period in which all of us – from families agonizing over how to regulate their children's daily activities to journalists and policy-makers who rush to portray every new alarming case as evidence of a growing pattern and need to act – are so extraordinarily sensitized to issues of juvenile risk that we are gripped by panic. But what *form* of panic is this? What are its root *causes* – and, perhaps most importantly, what does the fact we are experiencing one tell us about the state of our society generally? It is to these questions, one by one, that this book turns.

News media and panics about threatened childhood and youth disorder

Before examining the shifting theoretical paradigms about what constitutes a panic – and the various forms they can take – it is important to introduce some real-world context. Precisely what *evidence* is there to support the contention that Britain has become locked in a mind-set of juvenile panic? In addressing this question, we will consider what might best be likened to 'two sides of a coin': the popular positioning of children as (actual or potential) victims on the one side, and threats on the other. By way of justifying this conceit – which is central to this book – it is worth noting that the paradoxical nature of today's dual (and, as we shall see, far from mutually exclusive) problematization of children has itself been the subject of growing academic attention since the 1990s – with several scholars arguing that the underlying motives behind it are ideological. Like historical portrayals of Mods versus Rockers (Cohen, 1972) and teenage muggers (Hall et al., 1978), the conflicted images of childhood consistently conjured up by Britain's elite(s), according to Goldson (1997, p. 5), reflect 'the emergence and consolidation of moral anxieties and reactionary political concerns', while Scraton (1997, p. x) sees them as providing 'popular legitimation for authoritarian interventions' by politicians, judges and police. For Scott et al. (1998, p. 1), such 'contradictions' represent a tension between 'two conceptualizations of children': as both 'active, knowing, autonomous individuals' and 'passive, innocent dependants'. Yet, beyond *identifying* this contradiction, and speculating about possible reactionary motives behind it – largely by cross-referencing key events, like the 1993 murder of toddler James Bulger by two 10-year-old boys, to subsequent draconian policies and legal judgments – few studies have offered satisfactory explanations as to *how and why* such a perceived sea change in conceptualizing childhood should have occurred when it did. Too little emphasis has been placed on the media's role in constructing/ reinforcing this discourse; their reasons for doing so (ideological and/ or commercial); and the extent to which news narratives influence the reactions of politicians, control agencies, public and juveniles themselves. All these dynamics will be addressed, to a greater or lesser degree, as we attempt to anatomize this double-sided juvenile panic.

One side of the coin: child safety and the great 'parenting panic'

Recent studies have identified clear evidence of significant increases in parental protectiveness. An influential Policy Studies Institute monograph found the average 'home habitat' of a British eight-year-old – the area within which he/she is allowed to wander at leisure – shrank to one-ninth of its former size between 1971 and 1990 (Hillman et al., 1990), with the number of children walking to school alone at this age plummeting from 80 to nine per cent. Revisiting this study two decades later, the PSI found children's independence had diminished further – with the overall proportion of primary-aged pupils walking home from school unaccompanied plummeting from 86 to 35 per cent between 1971 and 1990, before dropping to one in four by 2010 (Shaw et al., 2013). Separate studies for the Children's Play Council (Children's Play Council, 2006, and Gleave, 2008), Children's Society (2007) and National Trust (National Trust, 2008, and Moss, 2012) paint similar pictures.

Meanwhile, a 1995 Barnardo's survey found that seven out of ten parents judged their neighbourhoods unsafe, with half saying they would never let their children play out unsupervised (McNeish & Roberts, 1995). Ninety-five per cent of parents interviewed for another study admitted restricting their activities due to safety fears (Valentine, 1996b).

Approaching their subject from a socio-geographical perspective, both PSI studies combined comparative longitudinal surveys of official data on 'children's independent mobility' with focus group interviews in both England and Germany to identify why parents were restricting their children's outdoor activities. Both concluded that the extent of parental protectiveness was significantly greater in England, with parents primarily concerned about their children being run over (a threat exacerbated, potentially, by increases in school-run traffic *stemming* from resultant over-protection). The former cited road safety figures demonstrating that, while three-quarters of junior schoolchildren were allowed to cross roads unaccompanied in 1971, this had dropped to barely half by 1990. As a result, the number of children killed on roads nearly halved in that period, but the volume of traffic doubled. Road safety fears have since been highlighted by Lansdown (1994), Valentine (1996a, 2004), Grayling et al. (2002), and Jago et al. (2009). That traffic fear broadly qualifies as a panic (albeit not a strictly *moral* one) is supported by government statistics showing that between 1977 and 1987 child death rates on Britain's roads dropped from six to less than four per 100,000 (Hillman et al., 1990), despite evidence of continued parental sensitization to the prospect of their children being killed or injured. BBC news programme *Frontline Scotland* identified a similar degree of ignorance about the true scale of this threat north of the border, reporting a survey in which eight out of ten respondents said they believed accidents involving juveniles had increased in the previous 20 years. In truth, the number run over in that period had fallen by 60 per cent (as cited in Furedi, 2001). As official government figures demonstrate (e.g. Department for Transport, 2014), the prospect of serious or fatal road accidents is a *genuine* threat to children – at least compared with other concerns examined in this book. However, it does not axiomatically follow that the *extent* of parental anxieties about speeding vehicles is justified. The argument is not that no threat exists (when it clearly does), but rather that parents' perceptions of the *likelihood* of their children being injured or killed on the roads are out of all proportion to the probability of this happening. In 2013 (the latest 12-month period for which statistics were available at time of writing), the number of children seriously injured by vehicles fell year on year by 13 per cent, to 1,932, while the number of under 15-year-olds killed on the roads dropped to 48, down from 61 in 2012 – continuing a long-term trend interrupted only by a fleeting blip two years previously (Ibid.).

Of greater significance to this book, however, is the fact that several of Hillman, Adams and Whitelegg's interviewees also mentioned 'fear of molestation' as a reason for their protectiveness (Hillman et al., 1990, p. 24) – with concerns about girls being attacked particularly marked (Ibid., p. 32) and parents of older children more worried about 'stranger-danger' than traffic (Ibid., p. 30). The authors' identification of this as a growing concern from the 1970s onwards chimes with a historical overview by Meyer locating the point at which the media 'discovered' paedophilia in the growing 'problematization of child pornography and homosexuality' during that decade (Meyer, 2007, p. 9). Research has also identified a fear of 'bullies' and older children (Valentine, 1996a; Jago et al., 2009), pointing to a partial overlap with the flipside of the parental panic: the youth ASB furore. Worries about extra-familial sexual threats to children have repeatedly emerged from empirical research since the 1990s – a point at which Meyer sees the discourse on paedophilia undergoing a 'conceptual shift' away from 'child sexual abuse as a problem *of* the family' (as epitomized by the 1980s scare about an alleged Cleveland child sex ring) to 'a problem *outside* the family' (Meyer, 2007, p. 9). 'Strangers' emerged as the chief fear of 950 out of 1,000 parents surveyed in 1993 by children's charity Kidscape, while the same concern topped the Barnardo's study (McNeish & Roberts, 1995) and Valentine's questionnaire of 400 parents with primary-aged children (Valentine, 1996a). The word 'paedophile' – and images of 'people getting' children – arose unprompted from qualitative interviews with 24 Bristol parents by Jago et al. (2009, p. 474). Meyer lists similar findings from successive MORI polls, principally surveys conducted at pinch-points after the high-profile murders of eight-year-old Sarah Payne and ten-year-olds Holly Wells and Jessica Chapman in 2000 and 2002 respectively. In a poll published shortly after the former incident, 78 per cent of parents said they believed contemporary society was more dangerous for children than previously (MORI, 23 July 2000), while seven out of ten voiced similar sentiments after the Soham killings (MORI, 19 September 2002). Intriguingly, the fact that the latter crime involved an archetypal *familiar* stranger (Ian Huntley, the boy-friend of Maxine Carr, a classroom assistant who worked with the girls) seems to have escaped those responding to the 2002 poll – further evidence that concerns about *literal* stranger-danger contrast starkly with the actual scale of this problem in society. Studies by La Fontaine

(1994), Grubin (1998), Corby (2000) and Pritchard and Bagley (2001) all cite data confirming most paedophilia occurs within families – with strangers responsible for as few as one in five cases (Grubin, 1998). Similarly misinformed have been widespread media-stoked fears about child murder, post-Bulger: between 1988 and 1999 (a period overlapping with the panic that that case provoked) the number of murders of under 16-year-olds fell from four to three per million, with stranger killings falling from 26 to eight per million (Furedi, 2001). *Frontline Scotland* similarly found a stark disjunction between the extent of fears about child murder and the reality of the situation there: three-quarters of respondents believed stranger-danger killings had risen, but there had been no discernible statistical change either way in 20 years (Ibid.).

Once again, it is *not* this book's intention to portray child abuse or abduction as imaginary crimes – or anything less than horrific when they occur. However, what it *does* argue is that – as many studies have demonstrated (e.g. Best, 1990; Grubin, 1998) – such criminal activities thankfully remain far rarer than media representations, and popular perceptions, would have us believe. Moreover, they tend to overwhelmingly take place in contexts and settings when children should be at their safest: in institutionalized care, in the company of adults in positions of *loco parentis* and, most disturbingly of all, in their own homes (e.g. La Fontaine, 1994; Grubin, 1998; Corby, 2000; Pritchard & Bagley, 2001; Horvath et al., 2014). And, if the various (long-overdue) reports published in recent years into longstanding and historic paedophilia cases (e.g. Berelowitz et al., 2013; Gray & Watt, 2013; Horvath et al., 2014; Bedford, 2015; Jay, 2015) have anything more far-reaching to tell us about our society, it is this: far from being a curse of our times, systematic sexual abuse has occurred, often under the radar but sometimes in plain sight, for decades. If there is any overriding *positive* to today's juvenile panic, then, it is that our growing sensitization to child abuse might make us less likely to repeat the collective denials of the past on occasions when such crimes do take place. Conversely, what the devastating evidence for *historic* incidents (e.g. Berelowitz et al., 2013; Gray & Watt, 2013; Horvath et al., 2014; Bedford, 2015; Jay, 2015) also tells us is that perceptions repeatedly aired in focus groups, discussion threads and newspapers that the world today is *more* dangerous than previously are fundamentally misplaced.

Pinpointing the origins of today's parenting panic

As the literature discussed so far demonstrates, it is beyond dispute that the *causes* of parental anxieties about child safety boil down to fears about stranger-danger, traffic accidents and, to a lesser extent, victimization by older juveniles. So, too, is the fact that the first two concerns amount to panics. What is less clear from any existing study, however, is the *sources* of these panics: in short, from where do our fears *derive*? Several studies have sought to demystify particular parental panics by locating them in *time* – providing contextual explanations of social circumstances in which they arose. De Young (1998) identified the stimulus for America's early 1980s 'Satanic day-care' panic as wariness felt by the growing numbers of mothers entrusting their maternal roles to childcare providers so that they could enter employment, while Best (1990) cited economic insecurity as a key factor contributing to the salience of a 1980s flap about missing children. But few studies have attempted (let alone managed) to trace *causal* relationships between perceptions of child risk and news messages – or, indeed, other information channels. McDevitt published an exhaustive longitudinal survey analysing an apparent correlation between stories about child abuse/ neglect published in American metropolitan daily newspapers over a 25-year period and subsequent reporting of such crimes to statutory agencies. She found that, while complaints increased over time, they did so *concurrently* – casting doubt over any hypothesis that heightened media coverage *prompted* people to report offences. The upward trend in abuse allegations, she concluded, might have been due to 'economic downturns and other widespread societal changes rather than media attention', while initial rises in news coverage and offence reporting may have been sparked by government initiatives (McDevitt, 1996, p. 261). Yet her research did not *disprove* an effects hypothesis: while news coverage and filing of abuse claims appeared to go hand in hand, the latter had not come first. More importantly, in identifying national policy changes as likely causes of these two trends, McDevitt failed to enquire why such changes had occurred, and to what extent they might themselves have been prompted by media pressure. As Cohen (1972), Hall et al. (1978) and Fishman (1980) have observed, crime crackdowns repeatedly flow from intense media focus on issues. By concentrating on formal reporting of alleged abuse to the authorities, to the exclusion of any other behavioural effects of news coverage, McDevitt (1996) also left open the question of whether the combination of policy changes, heightened media interest and increased complaints about maltreatment she identified might have impacted on family rituals – something impossible to ascertain through content analysis. Circumstantial evidence for media effects drawn from interviews conducted by Boyce (2007), Reilly (1999) and others in relation to other risk anxieties involving children suggests that qualitative approaches to investigating the causes (and consequences) of abuse fears may be fruitful – and, to this end, their work has closely informed the approach taken here.

Of those who have narrowed their research to focus on stranger-danger – rather than wider definitions of child abuse, including incest – only Meyer (2007) has come close to anatomizing this panic, by considering its historical roots and looking at both news representations of paedophilia and public responses to it. Laudable though her study is, however, it has limitations – notably the absence of interviews with journalists to bolster her case for distorted coverage based on scattered comments from focus groups and content analysis. In addition, Meyer's scrutiny of media texts confined itself to two (polar opposite) national papers: *The News of the World* and *The Guardian*. And while she rightly saw in focus groups a device for elucidating 'the reasons behind concern' about paedophiles 'and its "contradictions"' in ways questionnaires cannot (p. 13), her groups almost entirely comprised middle-class and aspirational 'upper working-class' participants. Moreover, she concerned herself primarily with the problematization of *paedophilia*, rather than *childhood*. And while she made passing reference to the double-edged nature of the juvenile panic – the tendency to perceive children as both victims and threats – she focused solely on the former. In addition, in cross-referencing her focus group findings with her content analysis she concluded that the news had 'a power to incite fears, in some people, and shape practices as well as opinions' (p. 29). Yet, if she did elicit anecdotal evidence of such effects from interviews, she did not explicitly quote these.

The other side of the coin: the youth ASB panic

Just as recurring child safety fears have generated considerable academic literature since the 1980s, concerns over juvenile delinquency have also seen periodic spikes in scholarly interest. The resurgence of studies focusing on youth justice and (mis)behaviour in the 1990s coincided with a renewed political focus on these issues. The Major and Blair governments' embrace of hazily defined concepts of antisocial behaviour led to zero-tolerance policies and extensive news coverage. ASB was crystallized as a concept in New Labour's Crime and Disorder Act 1998, which introduced antisocial behaviour orders (ASBOs): civil penalties imposing conditions on the movements of anyone judged by police/local authorities to have behaved 'in a manner that caused or was likely to cause harassment, alarm or distress to one or more persons not of the same household' (Great Britain. *Crime and Disorder Act 1998*).

While nearly two-thirds of ASBO recipients were adults, 36 per cent of those receiving them between 1999 and 2013 were juveniles (Ministry of Justice, 2014). And various spin-off measures specifically targeted children and teenagers – ranging from curfews and parenting orders to dispersal zones and alcohol disorder zones. Mr Blair also formalized bottom-up initiatives already used by some communities to self-police by introducing new state-sponsored agents at grassroots level, including police community support officers (PCSOs) and neighbourhood wardens.

The hyperactive political reaction to ASB – at a time of widespread (media-endorsed) consensus about the need to tackle violent criminals – followed years of supposedly sustained youth disorder. The early 1980s and 1990s recessions had witnessed civil unrest in inner-city areas, notably Brixton and Toxteth, with unemployed youths engaged in running battles with police. Following periodic outbreaks of football violence during the 1980s, by the 1990s 'joy-riders' had become a favourite youth folk-devil (Groombridge, 1998). Viewed against the background of haunting CCTV images of ten-year-old Robert Thompson and Jon Venables luring two-year-old Bulger to his death on a Merseyside railway track, their antics were depicted less as exuberant (if lawless) expressions of rebellion articulated in previous generations by Mods or Punks than alarming symbols of a cancerous moral decay among juveniles – and, by implication, their parents (Scraton, 1997; Squires & Stephen, 2005; Millie, 2008; Rodger, 2008; Waiton, 2008; Burney, 2009). What ensued was a textbook '"law-and-order" panic' (Hall et al., 1978, p. 288). Youth justice policy began abandoning the liberal, rehabilitative approach adopted previously – with Mr Blair explicitly blaming 'permissive' social attitudes of the 1960s and 1970s for fostering indiscipline (Blair, 2002). Yet the true scale of antisocial activity bore little relation to claims made by screaming headlines. A 2004 analysis of British Crime Survey data by Tonry found that the actual incidence of the 'problematic behaviours' targeted by Home Secretaries Michael Howard and Jack Straw was 'flat or falling' until 1998 – the year ASBOs were introduced (Tonry, 2004, p. 19). As for one commonly cited behaviour, vandalism, incidents fell by 19 per cent between 1995 and 2005–06, despite its remaining a consistent topic of news discourse (Walker et al., 2006). Longitudinal content analysis of newspapers stretching back 20 years from the mid-2000s found that, while the term 'antisocial behaviour' appeared in only 'a couple of articles a year' during the 1980s, in January 2004 alone it was mentioned more than 1,000 times (Waiton, 2006). This reflects New Labour's emphasis on ASB: the number of ASBOs issued rose from

322 in the first two years to peak at 13 times that number (4,122) in 2005. The growing obsession of politicians and media with ASB therefore displayed all the disproportion of conventional moral panics.

Towards anatomizing the 'ASB panic'

Where panics begin and end remains debatable. Of particular dispute are those, like the endlessly resurfacing furores over delinquency, originating in widely held perceptions of societal problems observable to many in everyday life. Just as, for example, periods of economic decline see elites endlessly recycling images of the feckless poor as 'scroungers' (Golding & Middleton, 1982) – arguably to distract attention from deeper social problems – so, too, do they scapegoat rootless youth for deep-seated structural issues that successive administrations have failed to address. As with 'scroungers', the durability of teenage yob or hooligan archetypes rests on their recognizability to other citizens – many of whom encounter people who (at least superficially) fit the mould far more regularly than *socially distant* deviants like the tax-evading rich. While any anatomy of today's rolling youth panic should acknowledge the increasing preoccupation with the moral degeneracy of Britain's urban poor under Mr Major (Waiton, 2008), it arguably began in earnest with Mr Blair's election in May 1997. His government's 'invention' (Millie, 2008, p. 3) of ASB rested on a definition embracing a 'wide spectrum' of behaviours, ranging from 'serious criminal violence and persistent ongoing intimidation' to 'minor' infringements like dropping litter (Mackenzie et al., 2010, p. i). But though it took politicians to articulate the simmering, occasionally explosive, dysfunctions of (largely socially excluded) youngsters as threats from an antisocial 'other' (Wilson & Kelling, 1982), the appealing nature of New Labour's policies was testament to an already widespread belief that this problem existed. A 2010 Home Office-commissioned review of all post-1995 English-language research into public perceptions of ASB found considerable evidence identifying younger people, women and 'those with prior victimization experiences (both real and vicarious)' as groups likely to have 'high perceptions of ASB' (Mackenzie et al., 2010, p. iii). To the extent that there was *already* a sentiment among ordinary citizens (particularly residents of deprived areas) that youth misbehaviour was worsening, then, the ASB flap strongly resembled other bottom-up panics cynically exploited by politicians, including elite-sponsored discourse about 'scroungers'.

Indeed, some evidence suggests that, long before governments turned the spotlight (back) onto ASB, people were already adjusting their routines to minimize the risk of encountering such behaviour – whether by changing routes to work or sidestepping clusters of youths on street corners (Mackenzie et al., 2010). But what effect have successive ASB policies introduced since the 1990s, and news coverage flowing from/ encouraging them, had on wider social attitudes? Though piecemeal, there is some evidence to suggest that ASB's heightened media and policy visibility has (at least) *reinforced* public perceptions of youth disorder. We know of several instances of bottom-up panicking about it: in 2005, Kent's Bluewater shopping centre captured national headlines by becoming the first major retail outlet to ban anyone wearing hooded tops ('hoodies') and baseball caps obscuring their faces (www.bbc.co.uk, 2005). Although ASB was already high on the Blair government's 'Respect' agenda by the time this community-level initiative took place, others – including various local bylaws introduced to curb under-age drinking and other nuisances (*Local Government Chronicle*, 1996) – occurred at times when it was a moot point as to who was driving the ASB crackdown: ministers, councils or grassroots moral entrepreneurs. As for the question of how *individuals* adapt their routines to avoid encountering ASB, empirical evidence for wide-scale behavioural responses to the perceived threat remains minimal. Teenagers interviewed for a British Youth Council/Youth Net report into young people's attitudes towards the ASB debate repeatedly alluded to feeling discriminated against. Likening the media's perpetuation of antisocial stereotypes to a reverse 'ageism', they accused journalists of encouraging their elders to eschew them (Wisniewska et al., 2006, p. 20). Intriguingly, of fragmentary anecdotal evidence for *pro*-social actors adjusting their habits in response to concerns about *anti*social ones, much involves parental protectiveness. As well as recording focus group concerns about stranger-danger, Jago et al. (2009, p. 5) elicited comments about fears of 'older children'. In a holistic study embracing semi-structured interviews with parents of eight- to 11-year-olds in northern England, questionnaires of 400 parents, ethnographic work with police community support officers and group interviews with teenagers – though omitting media analysis – Valentine (1996a, pp. 590–1) cited parental concerns about 'other, violent, children' as a key driver for restrictions imposed by parents. Relating this to then ongoing public discourse about the Bulger case, she elided:

> I argue that contemporary parents perceive their own children to be innocent and vulnerable (angels) whilst simultaneously representing other people's children as out of control in public space and a threat to the moral order of society (devils). (Valentine, 1996a, pp. 581–2)

As always, *explosive* societal reactions are more visible than day-to-day ones, though – and perpetrators of youth disorder have often been subject to vigilante responses. Perhaps most famously, the trial of Venables and Thompson witnessed aggressive protests from vengeful locals, and such was the ferocity of the death threats they received before and after conviction that their identities (and those of their parents) were changed on their release from prison to prevent them being hunted down. Indeed, as Hall et al. showed in *Policing the Crisis* (1978), hate-mail has long been a behavioural manifestation of public revulsion towards violent crime. In terms of evidence for more *direct* media effects on public perceptions of youth ASB, several studies have implicated TV-watching in fostering impressions that violent juvenile crime is rising when it is not, with news programmes singled out repeatedly for blame (O'Connell, 1999; Goidel et al., 2006; Dixon, 2008). However, research focusing on the media's role in stoking fear of violent crime has mostly adopted a top-down perspective – concentrating on news *construction* to the exclusion of audience *reception* (Fishman, 1978; Hall et al., 1978). Excepting Cohen (1972) on Mods versus Rockers, much of the work done to elucidate the media's influence on popular perceptions of youth ASB has been drawn from general literature on fear of violent crime/disorder. And patterns emerging from this have been wildly contradictory – with, variously, TV blamed over papers for cultivating fears of personal risk among viewers, particularly residents of high-crime neighbourhoods (Doob & MacDonald, 1979; Gerbner et al., 1979; Dowler, 2003); papers alternately credited and blamed over TV for having the strongest agenda-setting effect on crime perceptions (Sheley & Ashkins, 1981; Heath & Gilbert, 1996); and women, white people and/ or pensioners identified as the groups most susceptible to panicking about crime, despite being its *least* likely victims (Liska & Baccaglini, 1990; Chiricos et al., 1997).

Moreover, as the Home Office review emphasizes, no study has yet been conducted to measure media effects on perceptions of ASB *per se* (Mackenzie et al., 2010) – another oversight that this book aims to help rectify. Might not the variable 'interpretations' (Ibid., p. i) different individuals put on the sight of youth gatherings – and the 'lay heuristics' (Ibid., p. 8) on which others base their disproportionate fears about risks of victimization – be partly shaped by media-constructed images? Moreover, few studies have explicitly addressed the ASB panic at all, and none has adequately *anatomized* it – by synthesizing empirical research into its construction, transmission and reception. Scraton (1997) published a collection of papers on the subject, explicitly relating it to earlier panics about youth disorder. Most of these, however, merely collated arguments drawn from secondary literature. In a later collection, Squires (2008) updated the discourse by casting the spotlight on New Labour's initiatives – but this book, too, contained scant primary research and little emphasis on the media's role in framing the panic. Of the two other key studies – Squires and Stephen's *Rougher Justice: Antisocial Behaviour and Young People* (2005) and Waiton's *The Politics of Antisocial Behaviour: Amoral Panics* (2008) – only the former contains any empirical research to speak of. Although it provides a useful insiders' view of youth responses to the ASB agenda – and a shrewd examination of deviancy amplification – given the authors' status as criminologists its primary focus is on public policy, rather than media influence. In the end, only a multi-level research design combining textual analysis and interviews with both news-makers and audience members can fully illuminate the dynamics of how images of antisocial children are constructed, reproduced and responded to – just as getting to grips with the construction and perpetuation of disproportionate fears about child *vulnerability* requires similarly triangulated analysis. In illuminating the interplay between elite(s), news sources, media and audiences, this book aims to elucidate the relative balance of influence between top-down and bottom-up societal forces in perpetuating our current state of juvenile panic.

From periodic panics to 'permanent' panicking: lessons from the literature

Research into panics can be traced through successive phases. These reflect not only the changing times in which studies have been conducted, but changing conceptualizations of the *nature* of panics wrought by the shifting sands of society, economy and culture. While early monographs on panics conceived of them as discrete 'periods' occurring 'every now and then' (Cohen, 1972, p. 9), in the 40 years since Cohen popularized the term '*moral* panic' [author's italics] to describe a disproportionately alarmist societal response to a perceived outbreak of deviant behaviour by a sub-group threatening society's 'values and interests' (Ibid.), it has become increasingly fashionable to speak of more ongoing, even continuous, forms of panic – often relating to fears about vague, inanimate, even unspecified environmental, technological and public health risks as much as more classically *personified* menaces of old. Occupying the most significant intermediate position in this evolution of thinking about panics, meanwhile, was a succession of influential studies published from the late 1970s onwards that saw moral panics as increasingly *serial* (rather than *periodic*) phenomena: bursts of popular outrage that the elite 'control-culture' that Cohen identified would repeatedly orchestrate to mobilize public opinion in favour of punitive law-and-order measures and, ultimately, the establishment and consolidation of an underlying neoliberal hegemony (Hall et al., 1978). A key challenge for this book, then, is to locate Britain's *contemporary* juvenile panic in the context of these shifting currents of thinking about the causes, nature and consequences of panics. What does the corpus of existing literature offer us as we try to diagnose the origins and characteristics of our particular panic? More precisely, how does this panic *relate to* (and *differ from*) any number of earlier juvenile panics? Before endeavouring to answer these questions, we start with a brief overview of various ways in which panics have previously been interpreted by researchers, and the key phases in conceptualizing them through which thinking has evolved.

'Periodic' panics

When Cohen published his seminal study of the 1960s furore surrounding Mods and Rockers, the concept of moral panics was novel. Identifying the *existence* of such panics, and labelling them as such, was ground-breaking enough, but suggesting that the iconic folk-devils of his age represented merely the latest in a succession of rebellious youth sub-cultures – and that their forebears had *also* sparked bouts of panic – was more significant (1972, p. 9). Cohen's deviants – who, significantly for our purposes, included (older) juveniles – were identified not as an isolated, let alone entirely new, phenomenon but, crucially, the latest manifestation of a *periodic* panic about hooliganism. In this case, the wave of perceived youth disorder occurred at a time when the post-war liberal consensus still broadly prevailed. But, while the precise cultural context of this particular moment was certainly distinct, the explosions of media and political opprobrium that manifested (and magnified) a sense of juvenile panic represented, to students of history, an all-too-familiar *fin de siècle* reassertion of decent dominant societal values. Far from being a singular, never-repeated occurrence signalling the final breakdown of post-Victorian civilization, the cries of moral outrage voiced by alarmist headlines in Brighton's *Evening Argus* and the *Daily Telegraph*, and the fierce condemnations by judges, politicians and 'moral entrepreneurs' (Becker, 1963, p. 147) echoing them, were of a piece with those that had sporadically occurred during discrete flaps about delinquency since Elizabethan times (Pearson, 1983).

But Cohen's cogent analysis of the links between these periodic panics went beyond merely identifying their common focus on the offensive behaviour of wayward youths: it pinpointed the secret of their *success*. Whenever panics *succeeded*, he argued, this was primarily because claims-makers manning the barricades – from bishops and politicians to journalists and concerned citizens – were able to seize the imaginations of 'the majority in any given society' by appealing to their notions (however unconscious) of a shared 'consensus about reality' (Cohen & Young, 1973, p. 431). Goode and Ben-Yehuda (1994) later developed this idea to emphasize the significance of specific *points in time* when panics arise – arguing that the reason one 'problem issue/group' is targeted over another is because it presents a salient scapegoat onto which wider lay concerns (and/or political frames) of the moment can be displaced. Both views concur that a *successful* panic must pit society's respectable, law-abiding majority against a disrespectful, lawless other – namely 'those who are abnormal, who deviate or who present problems to the dominant value system' (Cohen & Young, 1973, p. 431). Should it be necessary for 'mass media' and/or control-culture to 'manufacture' this 'other' – as some have implied (Ibid.) – so be it, but if the images it popularizes chime with audience members' *own* experiences and/or pre-existing prejudices then the panic itself (and the consensus it mobilizes around the need to bring deviants to heel) will prove more enduring. This notion of the 'successful' panic as a mutually reinforcing collision between individuals' direct or vicarious real-world experiences/observations and 'the world' as news media and other key definers portray it – as a *meeting of minds* between public, news-makers, politicians and law-enforcers – remains a useful model for understanding the dynamics of contemporary panics, and informs much of the theorizing in this book.

Serial panics: the rise of the 'law-and-order' society

It was another 'awakening' of (dormant) 'lay public attitudes' that, for Hall et al. (1978, p. 137), enabled elite forces – government ministers, judges, the police – and their media accomplices to manipulate a succession of then recent panics about *disparate* forms of youth deviancy to *collectively* symbolize a cancerous 'crisis' of values and identity in early 1970s Britain. That the long-lasting consequences they argued (all too presciently) would flow from this – the construction of a *redefined*, 'law-and-order' (Ibid., p. 288) consensus – ultimately occurred is significant here in two key respects. Firstly, it set the scene for the socioeconomic, and wider cultural, backdrop against which our contemporary juvenile panic is unfolding: an environment in which British civil society is collectively 'policing' a 'crisis' of perceived juvenile vulnerability and/ or deviancy. Secondly, Hall et al. fired the opening salvo in what would become the next phase of the study of panics: the recognition that *periodic* panics were increasingly being supplanted by *serial* panics that conflated superficially similar, but often fundamentally distinct, outbreaks of 'lawlessness' as intrinsic symptoms of *the same* underlying social ills. Hall et al. were not alone in identifying this pattern. Through the near-contemporaneous writings of US academics Fishman (1978) and Gerbner et al. (1979, 1980), it was also possible to infer that such fear-of-crime panics were being happily fomented by the agents of an increasingly assertive new order that today would be termed neoliberalism. The emerging thesis was that panics were now *primarily* the 'constructs' of elite forces determined to embed and preserve their 'hegemony' (Gramsci, 1971), as opposed to explosions of popular alarm about authentic social concerns opportunistically 'hijacked' by those elites. To Hall et al. (1978, p. 29), this tactic of systematic 'ideological displacement' reached an early apotheosis in the (largely bogus) panic about 'mugging' by black youths that they outlined in *Policing the Crisis*. They traced the roots of this supposed epidemic to sensationalist tabloid reports *anticipating* the arrival of the phenomenon from the USA – reports eagerly exploited by politicians and police to justify an authoritarian crackdown. The cynically manipulated mugging scare was, they argued, an object lesson in how elites presiding over inherently unequal social conditions purposely emphasize 'the wrong things' (Hall et al., 1978, p. vii). Using their policy levers and the media, they distract the public with a 'sensational focus' – thereby 'hiding and mystifying the deeper causes' of society's problems (Ibid.). And the mugging panic, the book argued, was no isolated phenomenon. Rather, it crystallized a growing sense among certain (socially conservative, if economically liberal) sections of society 'that the "British way of life"' was 'coming apart at the seams' (Hall et al. 1978, p. viii): or, to quote a recent political catchphrase, that it was 'broken' (Thorp & Kennedy, 2010). Moreover, if 'mugging' was symptomatic of creeping moral decline, so, too, was this sickness signified by deviant behaviours identified in other, then recent, panics about the 'steadily rising rate of violent crime' (Hall et al. 1978, p. vii) – *including* those around Mods and Rockers (Cohen, 1972) – not to mention various menaces still persisting at the point Hall et al. were writing, notably 'unofficial' industrial action (Hall et al., 1978, p. 274). As we shall see, this theme of a Britain that has 'gone to the dogs'[1] is being consciously exploited by newspapers in relation to the panic on which this book pivots.

For their part, Gerbner et al. (1979, 1980) used a series of influential 'Cultivation Theory' studies to argue that 'heavy exposure' to television crime drama and sensational news bulletins was sensitizing audiences to the possibility of becoming crime victims themselves – suggesting such media effectively instilled dominant ideological norms among (in their case) the US populace. Though this reading of their focus group data was swiftly contested by Hirsch (1980, 1981) – who found patterns indicating that the high levels of sensitization they identified could be attributed to the fact that their subjects lived in ghettoized, high-crime areas where mugging or murder presented plausible dangers – the position that the original researchers took only reinforced an increasingly influential current of academic opinion that panics were being mobilized for hegemonic ends. And while Gerbner et al. (1979 and 1980) were interpreting *audience* responses to narratives about street violence, Fishman (1978) was observing the *genesis* of sensational crime narratives from the inside, by reporting for a New York-based newspaper involved in concocting a 'crime-wave', in complicity with local law enforcement agencies and self-promoting city hall politicians. After a supposed spate of attacks on older people had bedded into the media narrative, polling organization Harris obligingly added a new category to its periodic crime surveys – 'crimes against the elderly' – and found that fear of such incidents had seeped into the public consciousness. Six out of ten respondents surveyed in 1977 believed that assaults on pensioners had increased and half of over 50-year-olds felt 'more uneasy on the streets' than a year previously (Ibid., p. 532). As at the height of Britain's mugging scare, these fears defied reality: despite stoking the panic by including more examples of such crimes on the newswires that it 'fed' journalists, the New York Police Department's own data showed a 19 per cent year-on-year drop in the number of elderly people murdered (Ibid.). While levels of other crimes against the elderly (including robbery and grand larceny) had risen, so had those against younger people (Ibid., pp. 532–3).

Though all three of these key studies – each preoccupied, at some level, with youth deviancy – portrayed panics as increasingly serial (rather than sporadic) phenomena, Fishman's was characterized by a subtle but important difference in the degree of *ideological* complicity he saw in the media's relationship to the overarching establishment. While Hall et al. explicitly labelled newspapers 'secondary definers', with police, politicians and 'the state' cast as 'primary' actors, for Fishman any elite 'ideology' propagated by America's media in spreading the myth of a street crime epidemic was more an *inadvertent* side-effect of commercially driven news organizations' pragmatic over-reliance on sources equipped to deliver steady flows of pre-packaged raw material to fill their pages and bulletins than any expression of a *deliberate* desire to promote the political status quo. Fishman argued that cosy arrangements between journalists and official sources did institutionalize dominant ideologies in media organizations – but only because the nature of routinized material used in reports was itself ideological, having been generated by elite agencies with vested interests in 'disseminating bureaucratic idealizations of the world' (Fishman, 1980, p. 154). Whatever the media's *intent*, however, the overwhelming consensus to emerge from many late 1970s studies was that one *effect* of its institutionalized working relationships with the authorities was to promote serial panics reinforcing ideologically normative representations of society that bolstered the interests of (incumbent or aspiring) elites. As with Cohen, this second key phase in the study of panics offers important pointers to unravelling the nature and dynamics of today's juvenile panic. Most notably, it presents intriguing clues about the motivations and mechanics that contribute to constructing and promoting panic discourses – questions that Chapters 4 and 5 address, in disentangling the *ideological* factors impinging on media narratives from the *commercial* ones.

From sick society to 'risk society': the rise of impersonal panics

If the overwhelming academic tendency of the late 1970s was to view contemporaneous panics as instruments of top-down elite oppression – tools for maintaining power by pitting society's law-abiding majority against multifarious (manufactured) enemies within – post-1980s panics have generally been characterized as more *bottom-up*. Whereas conventional 'moral' panics were typified by their demonization of identifiable folk-devils seen as threats to civil society, many (grassroots) panics that erupted towards the end of the Cold War focused on generalized, often nebulous, concerns relating to forces more powerful than individual governments, multinational companies or even political systems – ranging from public health worries about new drug treatments or medical conditions to the prospect of technological, environmental or nuclear catastrophe. The dominant intellectual idea to emerge from this reconceptualization of panics was that of 'risk' (Giddens, 1990, 1991) and the 'risk society' (Beck, 1992 [1986]), which posited that, in the post-industrial age, 'hidden' (often inanimate) threats unleashed by the process of modernity itself – 'bads', rather than 'goods' – were supplanting fears related to visible, personifiable folk-devils whose principal challenge to the established order was deviation from society's moral norms. Some years later, Bauman (2000) would build on these ideas in suggesting that late-modern Western societies had entered an era of 'liquid modernity' – a post-globalization epoch in which traditional social systems/community structures were destined to seem increasingly distant, if not absent, and day-to-day interactions between global citizens more fluid and unstructured. In this atomized world, devoid of peer-group, hierarchical or moral certainties of the past, individuals might be notionally more liberated and self-determining than before – but the (enforced) independence granted (and *expected of*) them would ultimately leave them feeling isolated and vulnerable. The *individualization* of society envisaged by this strain of academic thinking was accompanied by a suggestion that (perceived) risk – and, crucially, *management* of risk – was also being individualized, rather than subject to the community-wide barricade-building emblematic of conventional moral panics. Reflecting this paradigm, there has been a tendency for many *specific* panics manifested since the 1980s to take the form of concerns about threats to individuals' physical and mental wellbeing deriving from technology, the environment and Man's interference with (and misuse of) both. These latter-day flaps – variously described as 'risk anxieties' (Ungar, 2001) or 'moral regulation' issues (Hunt, 1999), rather than *panics* – embrace everything from the mid-1980s hysteria over the spread of AIDS (Rocheron & Linne, 1989; Weeks, 1989; Kitzinger, 1993; McRobbie & Thornton, 1995; Miller et al., 1998; Eldridge, 1999; Critcher, 2006b) to those over the human form of 'Mad Cow Disease' (CJD) (Reilly, 1999) and the measles, mumps and rubella (MMR) vaccine (Mason & Donnelly, 2000; Evans et al., 2001; Ramsay et al., 2002; Boyce, 2007). If problematic behaviours are associated with any or all such anxieties they are, primarily, individuals' disinclination (or refusal) to look after themselves (and/or their associates) – rather than *other people's* readiness to do them harm. The human agency involved in these moral regulation situations, then, has little to do with problem behaviours of deviant sub-groups – errant elements whose conduct must be regulated by society as a whole – but with behaviours that (mostly) pose little risk to anyone but those indulging in them, particularly ones relating to 'issues in the health category' (Critcher, 2009, p. 30).

While the prevalence and persistence of such risk anxieties/moral regulation issues in one sense points towards the emergence of an irrational worldview, it is worth pausing briefly to consider the (perhaps not immediately obvious) *positive* – even *counter-hegemonic* – features of some such panics. Goode and Ben-Yehuda (2009, p. 133) have emphasized the importance of peer-to-peer 'rumour' in spreading (even originating) some panics, while others identify instances of panicky conduct by citizens *defying* official lines promoted by elites. Indeed, recent history is littered with risk anxieties that defied elite efforts to instil calm but were ultimately vindicated by the facts. In Britain, newspapers reporting on the salmonella 'epidemic' (Reilly, 1999), BSE crisis (Ibid.), 'Gulf War syndrome' (Showalter, 1997) and the MMR scare (Mason & Donnelly, 2000; Boyce, 2007) campaigned *against* official lines – fostering widespread public doubts about the efficacy of politicians' pronouncements which, in all but the last case, proved justified. In these instances, the media's overriding adherence to normative news values – buffeted by interventions by experts better equipped to assume the mantle of primary definers than conventional elite sources – trumped any deference to politicians or police in determining the (enlightened) angles they pursued. The fact that qualified experts often publicly dispute politicians' preferred narratives creates space for a wider range of claims-makers to air their views. Significantly, this 'broader range of voices' – if applied to more conventional *moral* panic situations – can empower folk-devils, who can increasingly 'contest the setting of moral boundaries' (Ungar, 2001, p. 277). In describing the *process* by which campaigners asserted themselves as primary definers in relation to the AIDS debate, by 'working with the media and providing highly professional "sound-bites"', McRobbie and Thornton (1995, p. 270) implicitly likened the gay lobby's strategy to the manner in which elite bureaucracies routinely shape the news agenda by spoon-feeding it (ideologically loaded) information (Fishman, 1978, 1980; Sumpter, 2000). Gay campaigners demonstrated, they argued, how folk-devils can 'fight back' (McRobbie & Thornton, 1995, p. 270) – a factor they and de Young (1998) also used to explain the *collapse* of panics directly relevant to this book, including the demonization of British single mothers and US 'Satanic day-care' providers.

What studies of some recent panics have exposed, then, is not only the inadequacy of official narratives (and counter-narratives) as a means of opening up or closing down panic discourses but the fact that – contrary to Hall et al.'s vision of a monolithic elite control-culture – elites are sometimes *split*. One reason why a popular panic might succeed *in defiance of* official denials – or grassroots resistance might *thwart* elite-engineered panics – is because different branches of the establishment disagree with one another. And this has never happened as often as in this increasingly insecure age, in which the pace of technological and environmental change is proving all but impossible for anyone to predict, let alone control. During the debates about genetically modified (GM) foods (Eldridge, 1999) and BSE (Reilly, 1999; Evans et al., 2001), for instance, there were clear disparities between advice offered by different teams of scientists and lobbying interests in the first case and the UK government and European Union in the second. In other words, there was no consensus – elite or otherwise – among those assessing the safety of GM products and British beef. Reflecting on such bottom-up concerns from a global perspective, Habermas argued in *Between Facts and Norms* (1996 [1992], p. 381) that the proximity of the 'civil-social periphery' to laypeople gave it the 'advantage of greater sensitivity in detecting and identifying new problem situations' than 'the political centre'. It was, he argued, *grassroots* pressure – not top-down governmental action – which saw 'great issues' like gender inequality, climate change and global economic injustice 'force their way into newspapers and interested associations, clubs, professional organizations, academies, and universities' (Ibid.). Similarly, 'great issues of the last decades' – like atomic energy and Third World poverty (Ibid., pp. 381–2) – had entered the 'public sphere' through discourse initiated by wider 'civil society'. This was a point that Cohen (2010) would later echo in his call for 'positive panics' to be mobilized to root out 'hidden' social ills. It is as much in the context of these *anti-denial* 'panics' as the (more) conventionally *hegemonic* ones of old that today's social media-fuelled anxieties about children must be interpreted and understood.

Birth of the 'permanent' panic

While the 'risk society' (Beck, 1992 [1986]) and 'liquid modernity' (Bauman, 2000) concepts offer obvious explanatory frameworks for the melange of pre-millennial panics about technological, environmental and public health issues, they also have much to contribute to the debate about the (once more) evolving nature of panics in the 2000s. The past decade or more has seen the re-emergence of all manner of conventional *moral* panic narratives – not least those revolving around perceived threats posed to and (in some cases) *by* juveniles. So how do we account for this resurgence of interest in moral deviancy, and how might it relate to the wider discourse about social atomization and risk? As a starting point, there is much to be said for Hier's argument (2003, 2008, 2011) that, far from only having something to say about technological and environmental scares, the concept of risk *lends* itself to generating traditional-style moral panics. Taking as his locus the potent concept of the 'stranger' as an outsider figure signifying fear, Hier argues that Beck's era of 'reflexive modernization' (1992 [1986]) is one in which traditional moral certainties break down, to be replaced by situations in which *everyone* (not just the excluded 'other') *becomes* a 'stranger' to everybody else. In such circumstances it is increasingly necessary, in the interests of social cohesion, for societal/community leaders who remain to distinguish between 'everyday stereotypes of the stranger on the one hand and the enemy on the other' (Hier, 2003, p. 18) – in so doing, promoting social concerns focusing on, say, unruly teenagers or predatory paedophiles, with all the appearance of moral panics. Likewise, in the age of 'light modernity' and 'software capitalism' Bauman (2000, p. 116) sees as supplanting the 'heavy modernity' (Ibid., p. 114) of the preceding 'hardware era' (p. 113), today's community-less individuals are liable to come into (physical or virtual) contact with any number of 'strangers' (pp. 94–109) in their day-to-day interactions. Today Bauman's forecast seems more prescient than ever: as our daily exchanges with other people (and those of our children) increasingly take place online – in an intangible digital cloud encompassing social media, email, SMS text messages and Skype calls – we can chat, and even meet *face to face*, individuals on the other side of the world as easily as we once (exchanged pleasantries over the garden fence) with our neighbours (but now seldom do). These faintly familiarizing encounters with strangers have become part of our daily lives, and if ever there was a social environment in which fear of familiar strangers might take root and flourish, it is surely this – generating suspicion towards everyone from loosely *known*, but ultimately *unknowable*, acquaintances recognizable to us from the peripheries of our own social circles to hooded youths hanging out menacingly on our street corners.

But, as well as reviving and reinventing the spectre of the sinister stranger, this time as a personification of simmering fears about almost everyone we encounter, the risk-infused panic narratives of post-millennial Britain arguably go beyond the microcosm, by continuing to embrace more *distantly* threatening, macro-level concerns identified by Beck (1992 [1986]) – which, in this post-9/11, post-crash age, extend to Islamist terrorism or the collapse of the global financial system. It is this *montage* of disparate, overlapping and *ongoing* fears – some personifiable, others not – that emerges from much recent thinking on panics and, as we shall see, the (heavily mediated) discourse around which this book pivots. As Waiton puts it (2008), the first discrete, then serial, moral panics of the past have been usurped by 'amoral' panics, encompassing everything from classic morality-related issues to a continual whirlwind of risk-based anxieties. Many of these, in the end, are fears pertaining to questions of how families, law enforcement agencies, courts, politicians and/or individual citizens 'regulate' both public and private behaviour to minimize risk to others. Moreover, panics in the *plural* have arguably been supplanted by generalized, unending panic in the *singular*: as Waiton argues (specifically in relation to fears about youth ASB), we no longer encounter the '*occasional* moral panic', but are collectively locked into a 'permanent state of panic' (Waiton, 2008, p. 10). It is this notion of 'permanent panic' – a self-perpetuating societal neurosis about *omnipresent* risks and threats, both animate and inanimate – that provides our immediate arena of debate.

Questions of trust and security

All of which returns us to questions of trust. If, as this book argues, late-modern Britain is characterized by a social environment in which we are all perpetually worried about our children coming to harm at the hands of others – or older juveniles (especially other people's) harming us – does it follow from this that we no longer trust each other? And, if this is the case, what might this breakdown in social capital be telling us about the state of our society – and how it *views* itself – generally? A recurring theme in both parent focus groups was the sense that people who initially seem benign are not always as harmless as they appear. Concern about devious sexual perverts masquerading as conscientious schoolteachers or nursery workers, or 'plausible'[2] and 'manipulative'[3] acquaintances disguising ulterior motives to befriend children, were voiced repeatedly by both sets of mothers. This sense of *threatening familiarity* ran like a red thread through discussions, reappearing in the context of safe-seeming settings rendered suddenly menacing (the village where mother and daughter Lin and Megan Russell were slain by a lurking psychopath; the holiday apartment from which Madeleine McCann vanished) and in the middle-class mothers' recognition that 'classic' stranger-danger is less commonplace in society than abuse by familiars. The simmering air of suspicion permeating many exchanges fits with Beck's (1992 [1986]), Hier's (2003) and Bauman's (2000) visions of late-modern societies as ones in which we are *all* strangers to *each other*. It is also strongly consistent with evidence for a long-term decline in social trust documented in recent studies both by scholars and non-government organizations (NGOs) – some highlighting the erosion of confidence in the ability of governments and other institutions to minimize risk (e.g. Cvetkovich & Lofstedt, 2013), but most emphasizing a general collapse in *interpersonal* trust, attributable (in large part) to the social inequality and economic insecurities characteristic of liberal free-market societies like Britain's (*European Values Study Group and World Values Survey Association,* 2006; Hall, 1999; Harper, 2001; Li et al., 2005; Llakes, 2011; OECD, 2001). According to a 2001 report by the Centre for Educational Research and Innovation, the proportion of UK residents professing to 'generally trust others' plunged by half – from 60 to 31 per cent – between 1959 and 1995 (OECD, 2001, p. 101). Levels of general trust towards 'other people' had dropped a further percentage point by 2005, compared to the relative stability of 'social market' countries like France and the Netherlands – and in clear contrast to dramatically more trusting Scandinavian 'social democratic' societies (Llakes, 2011, p. 3). These findings reflect longer-term trends identified by Rothstein and Uslaner (2005, p. 45), who have used statistical tests to show that 'the causal direction' between socioeconomic inequality and declining social trust 'starts with inequality'.

While middle-class mothers countered some of their concerns about the trustworthiness of other adults with periodic declarations about feeling 'safe' in their neighbourhood[4] and that 'more people are nice than horrid'[5], working-class mums often complained of intolerant neighbours and the general erosion of community ties on their estate over time – though, significantly, they acknowledged that some locals still looked out for others. The groups were united, however, in expressing unease about what Putnam (2000, pp. 136–7) labels 'thin trust': a willingness to give the 'generalized other' outside one's immediate social circle (the man in the park or the parent of a child's friend) the benefit of the doubt. For middle-class parents, worries about trust also seemed bound up with feelings – related to their status as working mothers – that late-modern living was more 'frantic'[6] than when they were growing up. 'Life is just more *hurried*', added the midwife, because 'when I was younger ... you would have been allowed to walk to school at eight, because you would have been calling for a friend, and ... your mum would have known their mum, whereas now everyone's just dashing round in cars going to work ... so you don't know all the mums in the class'. While the media were repeatedly cited as a source of the worries both sets of parents raised, concerns about pressure from parenting literature also repeatedly surfaced in middle-class discussions – contributing to a sense that these hard-working mums felt constantly buffeted by entreaties to do the right thing for their children as they struggled to attain a healthy work-life balance. Connotations of guilt detectable in some comments reflected underlying tensions in late-modern Britain exposed in other recent studies between women's desire (or need) to build careers while striving to continue juggling traditional maternal responsibilities. According to a 2011 Social Issues Research Council study, the proportion of British mothers in employment rose from 43 to 68 per cent between 1973 and 2011. In qualitative interviews, mothers confessed that time they spent away from their children – at work or indulging in 'me time' – left them feeling 'towards the "extremely guilty" end of the scale' (Social Issues Research Centre, 2011, p. 15). Guilt was especially marked among mothers aged 30 to 44 – a range into which all but one middle-class mum fell (or had until recently). This emotion was associated with 'going back to work', 'spending so much time there' and daring to enjoy their jobs (Ibid.). Pressure to work was raised more than once by middle-class mothers – with the special needs worker and writer both complaining about social expectations that they should multitask. Conflicting stresses they identified included the former's contention that 'the way we are now with our children' had 'changed', in that 'nowadays mums feel they have to play with their kids, and entertain them'. Similarly, the hostel worker felt 'totally at the mercy of what people think' about whether 'your child's okay walking to school on their own', while the midwife criticized 'the amount of books available – and websites', that led to parents constantly 'analysing themselves'.

Studies have also linked work pressures (for men *and* women) to feelings of economic insecurity – another recent British trait, according to research. Since 2003, the annual British Social Attitudes survey has consistently found that more than twice as many UK adults would rather continue working the same amount of time they currently do than lose a penny in wages by cutting their hours – with 64 per cent of respondents confirming this in 2010, against 28 per cent who said they would consider doing less (National Centre for Social Research, 2010). Set against other BSA findings, this reflects a feeling of general employment insecurity consistent with the introduction of flexible labour markets and the recent British/global recession. Asked how easily they could find a similar or better job with another employer, more than half of adults questioned in 2010 replied that this would be 'difficult' or 'very difficult', with only 27 per cent saying it would be 'easy' or 'very easy' – compared to a 47–42 per cent split in 2005. Since 2008 (National Centre for Social Research, 2008), the survey has also identified growing pessimism among adults about their likely financial comfort in retirement, with six out of 10 respondents saying they 'worry a lot' about their 'standard of living' as pensioners, and only 15 to 18 per cent (2008 and 2010 respectively) claiming to be unconcerned. *Prima facie*, such economic insecurity was much higher among working-class focus group mothers – all reliant, at least partly, on state benefits at a time when Britain's government was cutting the welfare budget. However, while a running theme of their discussions was financial hardship, middle-class mums clearly experienced monetary pressures, too (albeit relatively), as their concerns about consumerist norms demonstrated. Moreover, the fact that all were working, and in responsible professional posts they had only reached after years of training, rendered the guilt factor – to which they repeatedly alluded (if obliquely) – more acute for this group. For all their distinguishing characteristics, though, one commonality shared by almost all mothers was some degree of reliance on extra-familial childcare. And, given the generalized undercurrents of social suspicion already identified, it is perhaps unsurprising that specific attention should be drawn to worries about child abuse by individuals in *loco parentis* – nursery workers, teachers or other children's parents. Such fears have clear antecedents, notably in America's early 1980s 'Satanic day-care panic', so convincingly dismissed by de Young (1998) as a fiction of Christian evangelicals, over-zealous social workers and, most significantly, a generation of stressed mothers acclimatizing to working life for the first time.

Gaps in the literature

The existing literature, then, offers a useful springboard from which to begin this study, in terms of research, context and explanation. Yet there remain notable gaps – and it is the business of *joining the dots*, both methodologically and interpretively, on which we primarily focus. While there has been no shortage of creditable studies focusing on individual panics – and the media's complicity in fuelling them – only a handful, to date, have empirically examined the flow of ideas between elites, sources, news organizations/journalists and audience members *in the round*. Most have dwelt on one or two levels of the process of ideational exchange which creates and sustains panics. Studies like those by Morley (1976) and Edwards (1979) of the media's treatment of striking workers; Hall et al. (1978) of mugging; Chiricos, Eschholz and Gertz (1997) of street violence and drug crime; Fritz and Altheide (1987) and Best (1990) of missing children; and Ost (2002) of internet child pornography all rely heavily on using textual analysis of news output to *infer* its agenda/bias – and its impact on audiences. The nearest any come to proving the relationships that they identify between elite/con-servative/neoliberal discourse and news content on the one hand, or media messages and audience reception on the other, is Edwards' citing of government statistics relating to the actual incidence of industrial action (lower than reports suggested); Chiricos et al.'s use of official figures confirming Americans' fear of violent crime was out of proportion with its true scale; and Best's use of opinion-poll data to demonstrate an apparent media effect on public perceptions of child vulnerability. In addition to Gerbner et al.'s disputed (1979, 1980) data sets focusing on the effects of 'heavy exposure' to crime-related television, a separate study by Dowler (2003) found an apparent correlation between fear of crime and exposure to violent dramas, but little evidence that such anxieties were heightened by *news* consumption. Whichever interpretation is right, most of these studies approached panics from outside-in perspectives – *inferring* intentionality behind media texts and/or effects from content. Others adopted an inside-out approach to examine panic generation, by conducting newsroom ethnographies and/or interviewing journalists. The best of these (Fishman, 1978; Ericson et al., 1987) illuminate the organizational practices of reporters and editors – with some incorporating textual analysis alongside participant-observation. But few examine the tripartite equation of news sourcing/creation and 'encoding' of ideology in content (Hall, 1980); decoding/interpretation; and any *effects* the media have on audience members' attitudes/actions. To this extent, both textual analysis and ethnographic/interview approaches to studying the media's role in panics can also be described as top-down: neither can satisfactorily evaluate the presence/extent of any *effects* content so encoded has on audience members. Conversely, many noteworthy studies focusing on media-relayed demonization stories – for example Hartmann and Husband on immigrants (1971) and Meyer on paedophiles (2007) – illuminate the *reception* end of the media food chain, but exclude the processes by which stories are *constructed*. Again, any steps they take to elucidate *intentions* behind media messages are largely inferred from textual analysis.

The problems of adopting too outside-in *or* inside-out a methodology while researching panics can be demonstrated by a closer critique of two key texts. Even if one accepts Hall et al.'s contention that most moral panics (in their era at least) are/were elite-engineered, they relied on *inferring* the media's intentions, after the event, through textual analysis of newspaper headlines, editorials, stories and features. They also adopted a highly selective structuralist approach – cherry-picking articles focusing on 'mugging', rather than systematically categorizing *all* press items involving youth, including those with different emphases. In so doing, they laid themselves open to accusations of selectivity – a charge previously levelled at Hall over his 1973 analysis of coverage of the 1967–69 student protests (Curran, 1976). On its own, textual analysis is also problematic as a means of gauging the extent to which media output affects (let alone *effects*) the spread of panics, by influencing audience perceptions/reawakening latent anxieties. Hall et al. extended the scope of texts they analysed to include a selection of letters sent by readers to newspapers during the mugging panic and to parents of convicted offenders involved in one infamous incident. Beyond this, they obtained no first-hand evidence of audience *responses* to stories, either from interviews or independent surveys. This conspicuous omission prevented them from fully anatomizing their chosen panic – in so doing, justifying their contention that it was elite-engineered. Moreover, as Hall himself argued (1980), the fact that a message is 'encoded' in a particular way does not guarantee this is how it will be 'decoded' by audience members – let alone that they will uncritically accept the worldview it presents. In relation to fear of crime – a subject of direct relevance to his 1978 study – a holistic mix of content analysis, official statistics and audience questionnaires led Roshier to conclude that, while the press did, indeed, portray 'a consistently biased impression of crime and criminals', there was 'little evidence' to suggest this was 'very influential' on public opinion (1973, p. 51) Conversely, Fishman experienced the construction of a panic contemporaneously and at first hand – interviewing journalists and observing them as they sourced information and wrote it up while working as a reporter alongside them. However, convincing though his thesis might be that it is journalists' *working practices* – and the sources they depend on – that determine 'news ideology' (1980, p. 18), he was as guilty as Hall et al. of failing to test the impact of their narratives on audiences. Given the absence of any textual analysis to speak of in his 1978 study – barring a fleeting tot-up of crime-related stories published during his research period – he did not demonstrate that what *resulted* from the news-creation process he observed was content *embodying* this ideology. The absence of substantive textual analysis, coupled with Fishman's self-proclaimed lack of interest (Ibid., p. 531) in interviewing audiences, lays him as open to accusations of failing to test the *effects* of his media-stoked panic as Hall et al. For these reasons, Fishman's work falls short of the multi-level approach required to *anatomize* a panic.

And just as few researchers have produced empirical studies which 'join the dots' between elites, news sources, media and audiences, fewer still have conducted *contemporaneous* research into the societal forces responsible for generating, promoting and escalating panics.

The handful of studies that examine the emergence and proliferation of unfolding panics tend to focus on one or two levels of the panic process – with Young (1971) and Cohen (1972) concentrating on their impact on the public and folk-devils themselves, and Fishman (1978) and Machin (1996) investigating the news construction end of the equation. Few studies have anatomized panics by investigating all the following: the means by which panics first come about; how/by whom they are spread, amplified and/or transformed; and the extent to which, at least in the short term, they can be said to affect the attitudes/behaviours of social actors. In their seminal ethnographies, Cohen and Young went some way towards squaring this circle, but they did so more than four decades ago – in a profoundly different media environment. To illustrate, the Brighton *Evening Argus* newspaper that Cohen (selectively) content-analysed is today merely the *Argus*: nominally still a 'paper', but one placing as much emphasis on its online operation, and inviting its 'audience' to both comment on and contribute to its output, as its (increasingly infrequent) print editions. Back in 1972, few could have anticipated the complex dynamics of today's audience-directed multimedia news environment – one in which content can be uploaded to news sites by audience members themselves live from the scene of a story, and readers engage in 'conversations', both between themselves (on discussion threads) and with journalists (for example, via Twitter).

It is in the spirit of both updating these classic panic studies and addressing the (at times, sizeable) gaps in their research designs that this book has adopted a multi-level methodological approach. In order to identify and explore the mental frames through which today's families view childhood – and the various factors (including, but not confined to, media influence) that inform parental decisions about the regulation of children's freedoms – it draws on findings from two parallel sets of focus groups: one recruited from a working-class postcode area of Brighton; the other from a nearby middle-class area. As other researchers have demonstrated (e.g. Hall, 1980; Morley, 1980; Kitzinger, 1993, 1999; Lunt & Livingstone, 1996; Boyce, 2007; Meyer, 2007), a great virtue of focus groups over other audience research tools – for example, questionnaires or individual interviews – is that they generate discussions resembling real-world water-cooler (or, in this case, school-gate) conversations through which people collectively negotiate their views of social reality and process what they have read/seen/heard (directly or indirectly) in the news. In the words of Hansen et al. (1998, p. 258), focus groups enable researchers to 'observe how audiences make sense of media *through conversation and interaction*'. The group discussion setup also made it possible to add a further layer of interpretation to material gleaned from audience members, by using caption-writing exercises based on the 'news-game' approach pioneered by the Glasgow University Media Group to explore their levels of engagement with – and recall of – media narratives (Philo, 1990, 1993; Kitzinger, 1993). Moreover, the intergenerational composition of the groups convened for this study – three in each area, comprising mothers, grandmothers and children respectively – had the virtue of illuminating *changing* patterns of parental protectiveness, and *fluctuations* in levels of concern about juvenile safety (and misbehaviour) *over time.*

To determine whether it was justified to define the dominant media discourse around children as a panic ('moral' or otherwise), a month-long textual analysis of articles printed across the spectrum of the British press – from red-tops to broadsheets – was conducted in August 2011. This was accompanied by analysis of discussion threads published beneath the online versions of all articles in the sample portraying juveniles as either or both 'victims' and 'threats'. The value of this analysis was twofold: to supplement findings from focus group discussions that revealed something about the way media discourse is decoded and (at an immediate level) responded to; and, more importantly, to inform our understanding of the ways that some members of today's audiences not only *react* to news narratives but help *construct* them – by publishing their own views, experiences and (from time to time) eyewitness testimony. The fourth and final level of research strategy was a series of qualitative, semi-structured interviews with 30 local and national press journalists – including several whose work was sampled by textual analysis. This was designed to illuminate the processes by which dominant news-frames about children come about, and explore the balance between the various forces (commercial, ideological, etc.) conspiring to shape such normative discourses. As with focus group participants, interviewees were encouraged, wherever possible, to 'narrativize' their responses (Hollway & Jefferson, 2000, p. 35) – drawing on personal anecdotes and experiences to provide deeper explanations of their rationales for adopting particular viewpoints, framing devices and behaviours.

By analysing the interplay between all the key players involved in mobilizing concerns about children in contemporary Britain, then, this book hopes to have gone some way towards explaining the myriad dynamics at work in sustaining what is arguably an *endemic* juvenile panic – and, especially, the role newspapers play in this process. Long ago, while collaborating on their classic collection *The Manufacture of*

News (1973), Cohen and Young contemplated producing a bogus press release warning of a putative new form of deviancy, in an experiment to locate Britain's 'moral panic button' (Young, 2010). The spark that ignites (or *reignites*) a successful panic in the public sphere may be as elusive as ever, but this book aims to help clarify the balance of influences that elites, news sources, journalists and audiences play in fanning the flames. Before embarking on our analysis of juvenile panic in the *present*, however, it is important to cast our eyes, fleetingly, over the past. No common narrative or dominant discourse – whatever its subject – appears overnight, as if conjured out of a puff of smoke. Is Britain's latter-day preoccupation with the nature of childhood – and with problematizing it as a state of, alternately, innate vulnerability and wild abandon – an idiosyncratic, historically specific, phenomenon? Or does it have parallels, even direct precedents, in earlier times? If so, what clues might these offer us as we unravel the complexities of how a juvenile panic discourse has come to be rooted and continually reinforced in the present – and, more importantly, what this discourse actually *means* as an embodiment (or projection) of the state of our society? It is to this question that we first turn.

2
'Worthy' vs 'Unworthy' Children: Images of Childhood through Time

If anything can be said for certain about the images of children that emerge from history it is that, contrary to the conclusions of some earlier theses (Aries, 1962), there is no linear narrative charting the evolution of ideas about the young – and no clear transition from an age when conceptualizations of childhood did not exist to one in which they did. Childhood was not 'invented' (Cunningham, 2006) or 'discovered' (Aries, 1962; Sommerville, 1990) at some imagined point between the early Middle Ages and the Enlightenment. Sources ranging from an early Mesopotamian tablet lamenting that 'children no longer obey their parents' (ibid., p. 15) to Anglo-Saxon king Aethelstan's ordinance exempting thieves aged 15 and younger from harsh punishments reserved for their elders (Heywood, 2001, p. 14) suggest that juveniles have been distinguished from adults, across continents, for millennia.

This is not to say that ideas about childhood have always been consistent. Although clear similarities can be discerned between the ways in which wildly disparate societies raised, taught and disciplined children (and portrayed them in culture and the arts), the levels of regard and respect paid to juveniles have fluctuated repeatedly. The writings of Locke represented a revival of Erasmus's teachings precisely because in the 150 years separating their major treatises on education there were prolonged periods when the latter's progressive beliefs were out of favour. And, however far back we detect a 'sentimentalizing' of childhood – for example, in Christian documents as early as St Jerome's letters on girls' education of 400 CE (Cunningham, 2006, p. 59) – only in the cosseting of the Victorian era does this affection appear to have bloomed into full-fledged 'ideology' (ibid., p. 41). As Heywood observes (2001, p. 30), the 'cultural history of childhood' may have key 'turning points', but it also 'meanders over the centuries' – with the result that 'a child might be thought of as depraved in the early 20th century as well as in the Middle Ages'. But while precise conceptions of childhood (and where it starts and ends) may have varied from one civilization/epoch to another, one aspect of how children are perceived and depicted has remained remarkably constant: ambivalence. From theological and pedagogic arguments about the value or futility of teaching children right from wrong (let alone anything else) that vexed moralists and thinkers throughout the Medieval period to the implicit distinctions between 'worthy' and 'unworthy' juveniles lacing 18th and 19th century discourse, juxtaposing 'sacralized' innocents (Zelizer, 1985, pp. 184–5) with 'delinquent' urchins (King, 1998), visions of childhood have been repeatedly polarized by one and the same society. The 'contradictory nature of ideas and emotions' about children, as Heywood puts it (2001, p. 32), can be seen 'running like a red thread through the historical literature'.

A central argument of coming chapters is that 21st century Britons remain as conflicted as our ancestors were about the concept of childhood: we simultaneously idealize and smother children, yet are wary of their wilder traits. These two conflicting perspectives, as we shall see, set up implicit distinctions between good and bad children; younger and older children; and, perhaps especially, *our own* children and *other people's*. Just as the fragmentary cultural deposits bequeathed us by earlier societies testify to an enduring human legacy of divided emotions towards the young, a paradoxical positioning of juveniles as (at one and the same time) 'angels and devils' (Valentine, 1996a) still plays out in popular discourse today – fuelled by double-sided representations to be found, consistently, in the news media.

The ambiguous child

Contradictory portrayals of children not only have deep historical roots, but also a tendency to manifest themselves in a variety of (sometimes overlapping) ways. In attempting to unpick the different aspects of this ambivalence, we will begin by analysing the overarching, centuries-long conundrum about what might be termed the *condition* of childhood – in crude terms, the nature–nurture debate – before addressing a succession of related polarities that have emerged from societies' efforts to distinguish between different *states* of childhood, or *types* of children. By examining various oppositions that have surfaced through time, this chapter aims to offer contextual pointers that might illuminate the origins and nature of today's juvenile panic.

Nature versus nurture

One of the few near-constants of the story of childhood down the ages is the tension between conceptions of the young as symbols of purity on the one hand and sinfulness on the other. Evidence of conflicting ideas about whether children enter the world in a state of innate innocence or savagery stretches back to antiquity (Sommerville, 1990), but the debate arguably crystallized with the emergence of the Medieval concept of 'original sin' (Cunningham, 2006, p. 29) and a wider discourse about 'nature' versus 'nurture'. While rationalists argued that juveniles could be improved through sound parenting and schooling (nurture), Christian purists maintained that their underlying nature(s) meant they were destined to remain indelibly stained until adulthood (Sommerville, 1990). Within the second camp, however, there were further shades of opinion – with some arguing that the rite of baptism could cleanse the young of 'infant depravity' (Shahar, 1990, p. 55) and set them on the path to redemption. Insights into the evolution of the nature–nurture debate can be gleaned from two principal bodies of evidence: published pronouncements of philosophers, moralists and politicians, and the documented behaviour towards children of individuals, families and authorities. Early theologians like St Augustine are credited with first articulating the original sin concept – an enduring idea that would beget a long line of adherents, from Roman Catholics through Calvinists and Puritans to John Wesley, who implored parents to 'break the will' of their untamed offspring (Sommerville, 1990, p. 145). But the secular concept it opposed – that of young children as empty vessels that could be tipped either way through socialization – had its origins in much earlier writings. When Locke likened the minds of the very young to 'soft wax' which could be moulded into model citizens, he invoked a metaphor all but identical to that used by Erasmus and, 500 years earlier, the enlightened Christian philosopher Anselm of Canterbury – who had argued that, although mothers fulfilled a primary role in rearing their children and giving them their 'world-picture', infants were as yet *too* soft and wax-like to be fashioned at all (Shahar, 1990, p. 115). Similarly, Locke's use of the term *'tabula rasa'* (Cunningham, 2005, p. 73) drew on ideas that can be traced back to ancient Greece, notably Pelagius's 'clean slate' (ibid., p. 29) and Aristotle's 'blank tablet' (Sommerville, 1990, p. 142).

The nature–nurture debate underscored discussion about whether children should be (formally or informally) educated – and, if so, by whom, how and in which disciplines. Although there is evidence that future leaders were tutored in philosophy and science in antiquity, and there was some debate about the value of teaching children as early as the 12th century (Berkvam, 1983), the little we know about this suggests that moralists were still so distracted by the question of children's innate potential (or otherwise) that they only judged it worth teaching those whose 'natures' were *conducive* to learning (ibid.). Clearly it would be a big step from such discussions to a point where most, or all, children were considered *capable* of being educated – let alone *worthy* of tuition. Ozment (1983, p. 177) interprets the moralizing of the 1500s as evidence that tuition, in tandem with parental discipline, was seen as a way of grooming children to become 'social beings' and put aside childish things: primarily 'selfish, antisocial behaviour'. This was an implicit positioning of the young as both unformed and prone to (innate) deviancy, yet pliant enough to be moulded into shape. As several historians note in relation to later centuries, 'schooling' children smacked of 'standardization' (Sommerville, 1990, p. 245) and reproduction of existing social norms, and was a world away from acknowledging that they had minds of their own – let alone *rights* to the brain-food best suited to liberating their individuality. Such a utilitarian philosophy can arguably be glimpsed in the watering-down of early adaptations of classic literature for children – Thomas and Harriet Bowdler's 1807 *The Family Shakespeare* removed 'everything that can raise a blush on the cheek of modesty' (ibid., p. 169) – and the use of conventional fairy-tales like those of the Brothers Grimm to indoctrinate them with contemporary moral codes. Again, children were being positioned as future ambassadors for existing cultural, political and socioeconomic order(s).

There was, of course, much to come from education that would not only benefit children, but engage them in ways that finally began to harness their individual inclinations and abilities. Britain's post-war settlement, which introduced comprehensive secondary education, may have in one sense continued the trend towards standardization through its social construction of children as 'pupils' rather than individual boys and girls (Hendrick, 1997, p. 47). But with the emergence of more humanistic teaching methods, under the influence of social reformers and educationalists like Kate Wiggin, Rudolf Steiner and Abraham Maslow, recent decades have seen an elevation of the concept of children's rights – and implicit recognition that not all boys and girls are the same, and moreover that childhood has a *purpose* other than to serve the interests of adulthood. Similar conceptions of children as potential model citizens (if schooled correctly) can be traced through Plato's disapproving fourth century BCE critique of Sparta's obsession with breeding only soldiers and heroes (Sommerville, 1990, p. 29) and Locke's influential *Some Thoughts Concerning Education*, published in 1693 and quickly translated into five other languages as a mark of its saliency and influence (Cunningham, 2006, p. 73). On the former point, one quirk of the way the nature–nurture debate – and wider questions about children's *value* – played out in certain civilizations was the unequal treatment meted out to girls and boys. The Spartans lionized 'the idea' of boys – despite systematically brutalizing them through 'dazing and ridicule' to instil 'unquestioning loyalty and physical and mental stamina' (Sommerville, 1990, p. 21) – while sacrificing many of their infant daughters, rather than investing the time and effort needed to rear them (ibid.). Similarly callous attitudes towards girls – as well as children otherwise 'disabled', and unfit for fighting – were exhibited by both Hellenistic Greeks (Sommerville, 1990, p. 52) and various Germanic tribes (Heywood, 2001, p. 74). In later centuries, gender divisions surfaced in other child-rearing practices, not least stark differences in the subjects girls and boys were taught (history, maths and outdoor pursuits versus literature and homemaking skills) with, once more, the differential *natures* of the sexes determining the manner and substance of their nurturing. Intriguingly, though, as we shall observe in the analysis of contemporary discourse on which coming chapters focus, gender divisions in the conception of children's natures have not always favoured boys: while there is little evidence for a 'positive or negative bias' towards either sex in today's media coverage of child 'victims', a stark emphasis on antisocial behaviour by male miscreants appears in narratives centred around juveniles as 'threats' (Valentine, 1996a and 1996b). This, in turn, reflects the disproportionate number of boys receiving ASBOs in contemporary Britain (Ministry of Justice, 2014).

What little we know about past *parenting* practices from documentary and archaeological sources appears to reflect how they were conceptualized by *society*. Though we can only go so far in interpreting artistic and literary sources as evidence of parents' actual treatment of children – and, even if we do accept representations at face value, it is a leap to infer from them anything profound about how people thought or felt about their offspring – one myth we can safely debunk is Aries' insistence that there is little evidence of parental affection before the later Middle Ages. If this were true, how should we interpret Philip of Novare's 13th century description of children as 'a source of joy' their parents 'would not exchange for all the treasures of the world' or 14th century diarist Giovanni Morelli's claim to have 'preserved the date, place and way' his son was conceived – and 'the joy he experienced in touching his wife's belly and feeling the movements of the foetus' (Shahar, 1990, p. 33)? Other Medieval sources allude to mundane but tender aspects of child-rearing like bathing, dressing and changing children – invariably described as 'especially beautiful' and with 'clear, white skin, pink cheeks like the rose or the lily' (ibid., p. 95). There are also scattered descriptions of parents at leisure that sound distinctly modern – including an entry in the biography of the 12th century French abbot Bernard of Clairvaux describing how peasant women attended fairs and festivals carrying their babies in neck-bands or ruck-sacks (ibid., pp. 96–7). Similarly, Aries' claim that children are either absent from – or depicted as 'miniature adults' in – early Medieval art is dispelled by numerous 'poignant' portrayals in 12th century works (Forsyth, 1976) and subsequent Gothic, Carolingian, Ottonian and Romanesque illuminations, paintings and sculptures (Shahar, 1990). As to the mini-adult claim, though some early images of the infant Christ portray him as outsized and/or with grown-up facial features, Aries' reading of the 'reasons' for this is arguably too literal and 'present-centred' (Heywood, 2001, p. 13). In the early wooden sculpture *Virgin and the Child in Majesty*, Heywood argues persuasively, the artist's deci-sion to give Jesus a 'mature' expression was meant to signify his 'divine wisdom' – at a time when adults, too, were typically depicted as sym-bols of their rank, social status and inner qualities, rather than with any attempt to capture their actual physical characteristics (Heywood, 2001, p. 13). Moreover, while Martindale (1994, p. 197) rightly identi-fies the 'more lively, more human, and more probable' turn that paint-ings of children took around 1300, the naturalism of these images perhaps owes more to the rediscovery of classical painting techniques than any sudden awakening among adults to the charms of the young (Sommerville, 1990). That said, in later eras a more sentimentalized 'myth of child goodness' (ibid., p. 204) would undoubtedly emerge – visible in everything from 17th century Dutch paintings depicting 'tender scenes' of fathers playing with and singing to their children (Heywood, 2001, p. 87) to Joshua Reynolds' portrait of an angelic girl in the *Age of Innocence* (1788) and Mendelssohn's 'six children's pieces', *Kinderstucke* (Sommerville, 1990, p. 209). That children were increas-ingly seen as *worthy* of close parental attention – and, by extension, of inherent *value* – seems beyond dispute then. But what consensus existed, if any, about the correct 'balance' between affection and disci-pline, and what does historical 'parenting literature' tell us about other aspects of how societies conceptualized children?

A semi-constant feature of child-rearing advice from both Church and lay authors is their emphasis on the importance of instilling obedience and decorum. The implication is that, left unchecked, children would revert to their innate savagery (Heywood, 2001, p. 92). So, while a clear recognition emerged in early advisory texts that children had *potential* to be groomed into worthy heirs or gentlefolk (or economically useful contributors), a firm hand was judged necessary to make sure this happened. As with many aspects of the evolving conception of children, it is impossible to chart a linear historical continuum in attitudes towards nurturing. Shahar (1990, p. 2) emphasizes that, although the 'dominant view of Medieval authors' was that under seven-year-olds should be 'treated with tenderness and not burdened with excessive demands for discipline and self-restraint', many 18th century authors 'advocated rigid discipline from the very earliest age and relentless battle even against infants to force them to obey parental commands'. Significantly, 'switches' (bundles of twigs used as makeshift canes) were all but ubiquitous in Renaissance pictures of children in school (ibid., p. 94), while the fledgling *British Medical Journal*'s exhortation to mothers to 'promote the future of the race' by forcing their children to respect 'the gospel of hygiene' (Cunningham, 2006, p. 151) typified newly medicalized advice literature of the late 19th and early 20th centuries.

But it is much more recent sources that present us with a more explicitly *child-centred* view of the way early-years rearing should be conducted. Reviving (and greatly expanding on) the late Medieval emphasis on the importance of nurturing and comforting younger children, the early pronouncements of the 'baby industry' fell back on a view that children's needs (if not wants) were paramount – with renewed emphasis on the importance of breast-feeding and, perhaps, a newer one on that of toilet and sleep training. While trends have oscillated since the early 20th century between the behaviourist approach to setting strict feeding and sleeping timetables favoured by F Truby King's Babycraft movement and latter-day authorities like Gina Ford and the *laissez-faire* humanism of Dr Benjamin Spock, these divergent approaches share a fervent belief that decisions should be taken in the child's best interests – and in accordance with his/her (declared or undeclared) needs and wishes. As corporal punishment has moved, in all but a handful of western societies, from being a centuries-old fact of life to socially unacceptable (even illegal), so, too, have calls for a return to a (romantic) recognition of the rights of the child to *be* a child and to *enjoy* childhood made by socially conscious 19th century campaigners like Kate Wiggin (Cunningham, 2005, p. 160), Elizabeth Barrett Browning (ibid., pp. 144–5) and Sir John Gorst (Hendrick, 1997, pp. 74–5) been normalized. That these perspectives have become progressively more ingrained at the same time as children's independence has been eroded by increased parental protectiveness arising from (disproportionate) concern about risk is a central paradox around which this book pivots.

As earlier centuries wound on, and the idea that children could be nurtured to mature into fully formed social beings entered ascendancy, recognition also emerged that they had *intellectual* needs (and rights), not just spiritual ones. Through early stories aimed directly at children, like *Little Red Riding Hood*, *Cinderella* and other fairy-tales by 17th century writer Charles Perrault (many featuring child heroes and, especially, heroines) and the revolutionary children's illustrated encyclopaedia *Orbis Pictus*, by Czech educator Commenius, we glimpse not only images of childhood innocence and vulnerability consistent with those drawn in earlier periods, but also a new understanding of the power of children's imaginations – and their capacity to read, learn, question and think for themselves. This marked a significant departure from the times when folk stories (invariably conveyed orally) were used primarily to terrify children into obeying their elders – intriguingly, often by invoking antecedents of today's stranger-danger concept, in the person of 'wandering beggars who steal children, disable them, and send them to beg' or 'the evil eye (*mal ochio*) of malicious old women' (Shahar, 1990, p. 139). By contrast, the new children's literature aimed to both entertain and educate the young, and the recognition by publishers (and, increasingly, parents) that this was a worthwhile endeavour indicates a paradigm shift in the *value* placed on children – and a triumph of the idea that they *could* be nurtured (whatever their inbuilt tendencies) over the narrow fatalism of original sin. Nonetheless, through the later writings of Darwin and Freud, and the resurgent religious fundamentalism represented by, for example, 20th century Christian evangelical movements, the idea of children's innate primitivism would repeatedly resurface – just as it permeates media discourse to this day, in response to the 'antisocial' and/or violent actions of 'feral youth' (Malthouse, 8 August 2011) or 'devil boys' (*Doncaster Free Press*, 2010). In the starkest examples of such popular narratives, Darwin's vision of the immature child as a microcosm of early stages in human evolution, and Freud's of the inborn sexuality informing the physical and emotional development of the young (Sommerville, 1990, p. 157), are perverted into images of native deviancy that no amount of attentive nurturing can overcome.

Younger-versus-older children

Flowing from the nature–nurture debate, a recurring discourse has sought to distinguish between the virtues and vices of *younger* children (especially infants) and *older* ones (notably adolescents/teenagers). Given the preoccupation in nature–nurture narratives with the question of whether children are born with any innate qualities – and how or whether such traits should be encouraged or eradicated – one might expect the young–old debate to be founded on the premise that the former state is more problematic than the latter. But the narratives about younger and older children that emerge from historical sources are in themselves contradictory. Every image or document portraying young juveniles as a 'drain' (Sommerville, 1990, p. 186), economic or otherwise, in contrast to their more self-reliant and/or productive elders, is matched by another favouring innocent, malleable infants or toddlers over wilful, corruptible (or already corrupted) adolescents. For any discussion about the view that historical societies took of younger-versus-older children to have merit, we first need to establish that they distinguished between these two age groups at all – and, if so, how. Fortunately, there is considerable evidence to suggest that distinct 'stages' of childhood have been recognized for centuries. As recent histories have demonstrated (Sommerville, 1990; Cunningham, 2006), words denoting 'child' and 'children' can be located in manuscripts dating back to antiquity, with some societies – notably those of ancient Greece and Rome (Cunningham, 2006, p. 2) – using several different terms to signify the same concept (an indication, perhaps, that they were already alive to the existence of separate developmental phases). Evidence of what Aries (1973, p. 6) termed the 'first sentiment of childhood', namely '*mignotage*' (coddling), can also be glimpsed in material from ancient Rome (Neraudau, 1984). While very young children might be viewed as stained with original sin, it is in the (deviant) actions of errant *older* children, and the punitive reprisals for which they increasingly became liable as they 'matured', that we glimpse a division between those too young to be held responsible for their actions and the morally 'culpable'. It is an analogous distinction between younger and older children today, of course, which underpins contemporary discourse about the age of 'criminal responsibility' (Gillen, 2006; Gumham, 2006; Cipriani, 2009) – and the point at which juveniles cross the boundary between unwitting misbehaviour and nefarious intent.

The Hippocratic tradition that juveniles progressed through a series of 'rites of passage' *en route* to maturity – and, in many societies, fuller personhood/citizenship – was widely embraced in the Middle Ages, where various Latin texts tell us that classical ideas were refashioned into a perceived journey from *infantia* (birth to age seven) through *pueritia* (seven to 12 and 14 for girls and boys respectively) and *adolescentia* (12 or 14 to 21) (Heywood, 2001, p. 14). Although there were some variations in perceptions of the number of childhood stages – with prolific Persian scholar Avicenna identifying five, leading up to the age of 30 (ibid.) – there emerged a widespread consensus that very young children were fundamentally different in nature/capabilities to those a few years older and, in turn, teenagers. Interestingly, there also appears to have been an early recognition among thinkers of the distinct period of adolescence – hundreds of years before the fabled 'invention' of that concept in the late 19th/early 20th centuries (Aries, 1962). In addition, the idea that 'childhood' – and, by implication, the potential delay in individuals' take-up of roles and duties associated with adulthood – might last until 21 (or even 30) raises the intriguing possibility that some early thinkers inclined towards a more gradual (even liberal) approach to ushering children into the grown-up world, with its attendant rights and responsibilities, than that prevailing in Britain today.

Several distinct debates emerge from a study of the historical sources on conceptions of younger and older children. As the previous section noted, sharp disagreement existed for long periods over the innate qualities of children, particularly (new-born) babies. But alongside familiar sin-versus-innocence arguments, more nuanced and intriguing shades of opinion can be glimpsed. To the Cambridge Platonists, Rousseau and the Romantics, young children were gifted with innate spiritual and aesthetic sensibilities that risked being lost or drummed out of them by too rigid and rapid an induction into adulthood (Sommerville, 1990, pp. 149–53). Conversely, while adopting a less one-size-fits-all view of the nature of children than early Christian moralists, some saw children as little more than unexposed photographic negatives who, while in need of nurturing to fulfil their potential, could only ever be expected to do so within certain pre-determined parameters inscribed (genetically) at birth. Schultz's appraisal of Middle High German texts concludes that adults in that society did not so much believe the way children were treated would *affect* how they turned out as grown-ups as that 'the discerning eye could pick out from childish traits what the future adult would be like' – regardless of how well they were raised (as cited in Cunningham, 1998, pp. 1197–8).

The one area of agreement that does appear to have emerged from early on, though, was the *need* to address children's spiritual and (in the broadest sense) pedagogic development – whether one saw the primary role of parenting and education as stifling children's inborn *animal* tendencies or liberating their innate *human* ones. However, setting aside questions about the socioeconomic barriers preventing some children from accessing education, there was disagreement among privileged classes about how early in life formal tuition should commence. By the 16th century, clear divisions were opening up between those who saw children aged seven and under as ripe for little more than petting and pampering, and early educationalists, like Erasmus, who declared 'the first years of life' of 'utmost importance for the future life of the child' (ibid.). Debate raged for centuries across Europe about the capacity of young children to learn, and in the event it wasn't until 17th century Weimar that the first elementary schools emerged, with Britain waiting a further 200 years to offer even the most basic formal education to the children of its poor (Heywood, 2001, p. 155).

A further debate that emerges from historical portrayals of/discussions about younger-versus-older children concerned the age at which it was acceptable for households (particularly poorer ones) to send juveniles out to work – and the related question of what implications economic usefulness had for the *value* that family (and wider society) placed on its offspring. To sickly, underpaid 18th century farmhands, any additional mouth to feed presented a severe burden to their already impoverished households – but should children survive to ages when it was socially acceptable to conscript them into the job market they might become an overnight 'economic asset' (Cunningham, 2006, p. 80). Just as poorer households today might struggle to fund their children's university education, when elementary schooling first became compulsory parents suddenly confronted the harsh truth that their sons and daughters – until recently working in mills or shinning up chimneys for a living – had reverted to being an 'economic drain' (Sommerville, 1990, p. 186). Each of these developments was a *reflection* of how perceptions of children had changed over time, as premature adulthood (born often of economic necessity) made way for a new emphasis on the 'rights' of the young to enjoy both 'natural' childhood freedoms (Cunningham, 2005, p. 73) and improved prospects as 'social beings' (Ozment, 1983, p. 177) when they came of age. Nevertheless, in transforming the ways industry and family worked, these changing practices would also *influence* how children were perceived in ensuing periods – as both present dependent and future keeper (Heywood, 2001, p. 73) or 'sacralized' innocent (Zelizer, 1985, pp. 184–5) and unruly free spirit (Cunningham, 1991, p. 145). And if infants – and, from the introduction of elementary education, those in the pueritia phase – were judged *economically* burdensome, so too were they considered *spiritual* millstones. A thread running through this chapter is the preeminent role played by the Church and its emissaries in constructing ideas about childhood. Religious writers were influential in (often contradictorily) framing children as innately sinful in infancy (Cunningham, 2005, p. 29; Sommerville, 1990, p. 55) yet prone to greater temptation (sin) from seven upwards (Shahar, 1990, p. 16) and liable to descend into 'frivolous and arrogant' behaviour from 14 (ibid.). Medieval children were also portrayed as a 'drain' on their parents' spiritual lives (Shahar, 1990, p. 11). *The History of Kyng Bocchus and Sydracke*, published in 1530, lamented how Man had become obsessed with the love of his children – investing 'all his energy and his money in their support and advancement', instead of devoting himself to 'the salvation of his own soul' (as cited in Shahar, 1990, p. 11). This theme was revisited by ecclesiastical writers in later centuries, with numerous of the 350 catechisms and 'question-and-answer' advice documents issued by Church authorities between 1549 and 1646 entreating fathers to discipline youngsters harshly, because their 'unstable and fanciful' mothers were too lenient (Cunningham, 2006, pp. 49–50). A similar sentiment informed 19th century evangelist Hannah More's portrayal of young children as 'sinful polluted creatures', even as she founded the Sunday School movement to 'save' them (Robertson, 1976, p. 421).

Not all evidence used to support the view that adults adopted callous, self-serving attitudes towards younger children is entirely convincing, however. Several authors have drawn attention to the longstanding prevalence of 'wet-nursing' or 'out-nursing' – the practice (even among wealthier families) of mothers avoiding breast-feeding by handing their babies to hired nurses – as support for Aries' view that infants and toddlers were deprived of affection in certain periods. Yet, while it may be harder to explain why more affluent households used wet-nurses, this book favours more prosaic explanations than Aries' fanciful notion that affection was 'discovered' at some indeterminate point in the Middle Ages. As Hendrick (1997), Anderson (1980) and others have argued, widespread wet-nursing among the lower classes – and the abandonment of many infants by poorer families – can best be understood as a reflection of harsh economic circumstances, with the former a 'product of family economic strategies that compelled mothers to be wage-earners in order to supplement the low wages of the male breadwinner' (Hendrick, 1997, p. 17). In this respect, it foreshadowed the widespread practice of entrusting children to childcare providers today – an arrangement which (as we shall see in coming chapters) has fuelled maternal anxieties about their safety. For the better-off, meanwhile, wet-nursing may have been viewed as a healthier/safer substitute for breast-feeding than alternatives, such as using unclean bottles, when the child's natural mother was unable to breast-feed or social etiquette prohibited this (ibid.).

As for the periodic rises in abandonment and infanticide through-out history, it is argued that economic considerations (or, in the case of illegitimate children, social taboos) largely account for these, too. Cunningham (2006, p. 93) notes 'a close correlation' between the num-bers of babies abandoned to foundling hospitals and years of 'economic crisis' in 16th and 17th century northern Italy. A tripling of abandon-ment rates in Limoges, France, between the 1740s and 1780s, meanwhile, coincided with a sharp rise in the price of grain (ibid.). More revealingly, he cites ample documentary evidence to suggest that disposing of even bastard infants was consistently regarded as unconscionable: in 16th century France, unmarried women who fell pregnant had to make dec-larations to magistrates vowing not to kill their offspring, and mothers of illegitimate children who died were presumed guilty of murder unless they could prove them stillborn under a law passed in 1532 by the Holy Roman Empire (ibid., p. 116). Whatever inequities such judgments might disguise about the relative social status of poorer-versus-richer (or legitimate-versus-illegitimate) children, they suggest that, by the late Medieval period, a value of sorts was being placed on even the young-est juveniles. Moreover, while in one sense older children might have been favoured over the young for their economic worth and (learned) maturity, a parallel discourse has slowly emerged in recent centuries to challenge the notion that older necessarily means wiser. According to Shahar's (1990, p. 25) analysis of secular Medieval legislation, for girls and boys respectively the ages of 12 and 14 were those from which they were generally entitled to certain 'rights' (principally marriage) – and, conversely, judged capable of bearing 'criminal responsibility'. The Medieval era saw familiar modern arguments about criminal intent rehearsed in relation to young people, with 13th century English jurist Henry de Bracton arguing 'lack of intention protects the child' (ibid.). Centuries later, documents relating to prosecutions of children for slan-der in colonial Massachusetts and Plymouth Colony suggest that, by the time pioneers were settling in North America, the perceived age of cul-pability for most crimes had risen to between 14 and 16 (Beales, 1975, p. 384). By contrast, in England and Wales today – partly in response to successive situated panics about juvenile crime of the late 1980s and early 1990s – children are deemed criminally responsible from as young as 10. While several countries (including Scotland, Ireland, Canada, Israel and Japan) match the lower Medieval threshold of 12, and others (China, Germany, Austria and Italy) end the defence of infancy at 14, only a handful (Argentina, Brazil, Belgium, Columbia, Peru and the Democratic Republic of Congo) extend it to 18 – still widely seen as the age at which adulthood commences.

This is not to deny that children's *rights* have been progressively extended in other ways – with, in Britain, the Children Act 1908 ushering in a century of reform engendering a 'more comprehensive and child-oriented legal system' and 'more generous and liberal provisions for children in all walks of life' (Hendrick, 1997, p. 49). Nonetheless, in important respects, our conceptions of children seem to have become *less* tolerant – and more contradictory – over time. Child welfare legislation in Britain offers levels of protection and redress for abused and neglected children undreamt of in the 16th or 17th centuries and, by way of preserving their childhoods, it is no longer lawful for anyone under 16 to marry. Yet the irony is that, in an age when the concept of childhood has never been more enshrined in law – and, with it, children's rights to *enjoy* that childhood, free from cruelty and exploitation – the opprobrium meted out to juveniles who stray from the path of 'innocence' can be so severe (Squires & Stephen, 2005). The dark flipside of children's (and teenagers') natures is a theme that has repeatedly been addressed in literature and the arts in recent decades – in stark contrast to the images of virtuous/victimized juveniles that prevailed in 19th century fiction (Sommerville, 1990, p. 204). In 20th century novels, such as William Golding's *Lord of the Flies* (1959) and Anthony Burgess's *A Clockwork Orange* (1962), concepts like original sin were revisited in the context of post-war debates about civilization versus barbarism and the medicalization of deviancy respectively (Conrad & Schneider, 1992). Each title explores concerns played out (by liberals and conservatives alike) in latter-day moral panics about juvenile delinquency and disorder – and, fittingly, each repeatedly resurfaces to this day in public/media discourse as shorthand for extremes of both (Scraton, 1997).

The economic versus affective child

Debates about the economic usefulness or otherwise of younger-versus-older children open up deeper questions about whether parental (and societal) affection towards juveniles has generally been reserved for those seen as immediate or potential assets, rather than burdens – and, by extension, whether early demonstrations of emotional attachment should be viewed as genuine, let alone unconditional, rather than intrinsically self-interested. The overwhelming documentary evidence relating to the economic position of children, from at least the

Renaissance, points towards seven or 12 being the ages from which it was deemed socially acceptable (even usual) for lower orders to send their children out to work and middle classes into apprenticeships (Shahar, 1990; Heywood, 2001). Is it not possible then, as some have argued (Thompson, 1977; Hendrick, 1997), that perceived economic usefulness was a *precondition* for being loved to many children – or, to put it differently, that affection shown to younger juveniles stemmed from their value to their families as future breadwinners and/or 'status symbols' (Cunningham, 2006, p. 72)?

The extent to which children were seen as fulfilling a primarily economic role in the shadow of the Industrial Revolution can be inferred from the way British imperialists fretted about the need to use a combination of school and 'mothercraft' to ensure the strength of future armies (Hendrick, 1997, p. 42) and German medical expert Arthur Schlossmann unashamedly preached to Rhineland notables that unacceptably high rates of infant mortality must be reduced not out of compassion for the poor but because 'the unrelenting [industrial and military] drive of our times demands a resistant, healthy population' (Heywood, 2005, p. 154). Even as they gradually gained more rights – and recognition that they were sentient beings entitled to realize their individual potentials – as late as the early 20th century the overriding establishment view of children was as economic units whose primary purpose was to help strengthen the prevailing social order (Gaskins, Miller, & Corsaro, 1992). As the 1900s wound on, begetting two world wars, this imperative became ever more urgent for industrial, military and governmental elites (Heywood, 2005, p. 154).

In 21st century Britain, economic factors arguably continue to influence the level of social value ascribed to (particular) children. As illustrated by the panic discourse(s) reflected in the coming empirical chapters, a key subtext to the narrative of the child as 'prey' versus the child as 'predator' is the underlying distinction repeatedly made by politicians, news media and individual members of the public between the types of households with which 'good' and 'bad' children respectively are associated. Arguably, pitting the parents of respectable, well-behaved children against those of truants, vandals and 'feral youth' (Malthouse, 2011) acts as a proxy for broader, more divisive, narratives used by politicians and press alike to discriminate between the economically useful and the burdensome (*www.bbc.co.uk*, 2010a; Porter, 2011). In dividing children and, by implication, their parents into these twin camps, society implicitly distinguishes between 'worthy' and 'unworthy', even 'deserving' and 'undeserving', families – a key opposition to which this chapter returns in its final section.

While it is important to recognize the economic (as opposed to *emotional*) value placed on children in history, though, it would be unjust to dismiss motives for parental affection as wholly selfish and materialistic. Documentary and archaeological evidence for the culture(s) of lived childhood (though scant) demonstrates the existence of toys such as marbles, spinning-tops, dolls and rattles – and, through them, a recognition of children's rights to play and entertainment – dating back to antiquity. Stick and wheeled toy horses have been recovered from ancient Persian archaeological sites, while pictures of dog-carts and hoops emerge from excavations of ancient Greek settlements. But perhaps the most compelling evidence to support the argument that children's 'rights' to childhood freedoms were recognized in earlier societies comes from Gordon's (1991, p. 148) analysis of records of miracles performed to heal injured juveniles by six English saints and martyrs between 1170 and 1500. Of the 358 miraculous recoveries recorded during this period, 135 related to accidental injuries suffered by children (predominantly boys) while playing at home, on roads and in streams, ponds and pastures. Equally illuminating are the recorded devotions made by the children's parents, which demonstrate that, far from being heedless of the dangers to which they exposed their offspring, they were distraught at the thought of losing them. What emerges from this, in fact, is a conception of childhood arguably more rational than that prevailing in Britain today: one recognizing that it is in children's *natures* to want to enjoy outdoor freedoms, free from constant parental monitoring, while also regarding the young with responsibility and affection. This is an impression compounded by a handful of documentary nuggets which call into question Aries' contention that it took Medieval children until seven to gain recognition as human beings – and that even then this only occurred because they were deemed old enough to work. Heywood (2001, p. 116) cites a 1422 census from Reims showing that, far from routinely moving into domestic servitude aged seven, girls did so between the ages of 12 and 22, while boys continued in this field from 12 to 30. Similarly, Kussmaul's (1981, p. 70) study of servants in early modern England quotes several mid-19th century documents, including worker registration schemes, confirming that the 'ordinary age of entry' was 13 or 14.

Richer versus poorer (civilized versus feral) children

Any discussion of the economic value placed on children inevitably leads to consideration of the relative status of those from poorer and richer backgrounds. History tells us that, while normative perceptions of childhood prevailed across given societies during particular historical periods, they were not always respected by – or seen as applicable to – all *sections* of those societies. Class and other socioeconomic barriers often fostered contradictory attitudes towards children, even at times when there was widespread agreement about their (conceptual) position in relation to adults. Even as Victorian social reformers and educationalists pushed for the introduction of universal schooling and others promoted an idealized view of children celebrating their beauty and innocence, the governing classes were turning blind eyes to the betrayal of these high-minded ideals in the interests of industrial expansion. As Sommerville notes:

> One of the puzzles of our history is the fact that the greatest exploitation of children coincided with the greatest glorification of childhood. (Sommerville, 1990, p. 188)

This book argues that these inherent contradictions in the conceptualization of children and childhood – encompassing conflicting ideas about everything from their innate qualities to their immediate and longer-term socioeconomic value – have clear parallels in the way(s) we perceive and portray juveniles today. The suggestion that class and economic inequality alone foster different perceptions of the role/ position of children in disparate parts of the same societies can be glimpsed in everything from alarmist 19th century newspaper reports about London's 'wild and incorrigible' street children and the 'dangerous classes in Paris' (Cunningham, 1991, p. 105) to the 'jarring' fact that, in the same era, children of the poor were routinely hired to hand-tint engravings in books aimed at the privileged offspring of the rich (Sommerville, 1990, p. 161). These patterns recur time and again through history – with clear modern-day parallels, arguably, in the dual positioning of threatened/civilized (middle-class or aspirational working-class) and threatening/feral (dysfunctional working-class or underclass) children in public discourse in Britain today (Valentine, 1996a), not to mention the use of developing world child labour to produce toys and trinkets for the young of the affluent West.

The clearest evidence for disparities in the treatment (and conception) of poorer-versus-richer children is to be found in distinctions made from early history between those *destined* for great things – even fame and fortune – and those doomed to lives of drudgery and/or servitude. Shorn of patronage from Church, charity or philanthropist, the children of the poor were deprived of education and/or training – and powerless to improve their lot, in the face of deeply socially embedded concepts of class and inherited wealth. As stated earlier, it took until the mid-19th century for compulsory elementary education to be introduced across Europe, with Britain among the last countries to embrace it. Rudolph (1994) and Cunningham (1998) have emphasized clear class distinctions between the treatment of children by Medieval and later European peasant families (and those exploiting them) and the middle and upper classes of their day. The former were forced to view their sons and daughters as economic resources to increase their meagre household incomes, while scattered documentary evidence from the latter suggests they were already using education to groom gentlemen heirs/ virtuous future brides and homemakers, whose marriages might buy them into yet higher status and influence. The poor languished firmly outside this closed circle. Class-related conceptions of the young can also be glimpsed in the arts – most poignantly, through the emergence of dedicated children's literature from the early 19th century onwards. Early children's stories reflect significant societal continuities through time that take the shine off more progressive attitudinal changes forged during the post-Enlightenment period. Through tales as diverse as Hans Christian Anderson's *The Little Match Girl* (1845), Charles Kingsley's *The Water Babies* (1863), Prosper Merimee's (1845) *Carmen* (and the Bizet opera adapted from it) and Robert Louis Stevenson's *Treasure Island* (1881–82), we glimpse the gruelling labour regimes still endured by impoverished children and the tragedies to which these could lead. The irony was that at the same time as children of the emerging 'educated classes' were gaining their own literature, reflecting their newly recognized status as social beings, the juvenile protagonists of those stories often hailed from parallel (uneducated) worlds of factories, mills, shipyards and street stalls. However, this did at least offer wealthier children a window into how 'the other half' lived. Though guilty of sentimentalizing poor children through *A Christmas Carol's* Tiny Tim and *The Old Curiosity Shop's* Little Nell (Sommerville, 1990, p. 204), in *Oliver Twist* (1838) Dickens not only elicited pity for abused children and orphans but humanized the juvenile folk-devils of his day: delinquent street urchins (May, 1973; Pearson, 1983; King, 1998). Through their portrayals of impoverished children, and those who used and abused them, these stories tell us (and told others at the time) much about how poor children were both treated and, by extension, *conceptualized*. This raises the possibility that the early to mid-19th century saw the consolidation of an underlying (largely class-related) discourse about 'worthy' and 'unworthy' children, and that juveniles from lower orders were still widely viewed (perhaps even by their own families) as being of a different, lowlier, breed to their wealthier peers. We glimpse this frame in the dramatic device at the heart of Captain Marryat's Civil War adventure yarn *The Children of the New Forest* (1847), in which four orphaned children from a landed Royalist family disguise themselves as the (by implication, antithetical) grandchildren of a poor forester. Throughout the 19th and early 20th centuries the arts appear to be telling us, often disapprovingly, that a dual conception of children prevailed: one that idealized *childhood* as a hallowed state, while distinguishing between 'good' and 'bad' (for which read, usually, 'rich' and 'poor') children, and reserving most of its idolatry for the former. The dual construction of 'worthy' and 'unworthy' children – by society at large, rather than writers and reformers who challenged it – paved the way for today's contradictory positioning of juveniles as 'angels and devils' (Valentine, 1996a).

Worthy versus unworthy children: positioning the young today

What all of these conflicts amount to can ultimately be boiled down to one central underpinning idea: that conceptualizations of children and childhood have for many centuries been characterized by a multifaceted ambivalence. Contrary to earlier theories (Aries, 1962), the *existence* of childhood and the distinction between children and adults has long been recognized. In so far as there was ever any transformation in how the *nature* of juveniles was conceived, this occurred during the 17th and 18th centuries, when awareness of their spiritual and intellectual needs appears to have sharpened – but beyond this the concept of childhood was neither invented nor discovered at any particular point in history. Instead, what *has* happened is that the status and position of children has been successively socially (re)constructed in different contexts to reflect (and buffer) dominant socioeconomic, political and cultural norms of the day. If any consistent pattern emerges from these constructions, it is one of ongoing ambivalence towards the universal *condition* of childhood – in other words, whether children's characteristics are inscribed at birth or can be crafted in later life – and repeated discrimination between the value of particular *types* of children (younger or older, economically useful or burdensome, richer or poorer).

This book argues that these discourses implicitly enshrine, now as in the past, deeper, more invidious, forms of moral ambivalence: ones that attempt to (legitimately) distinguish between younger and older, male and female, responsible and irresponsible, disciplined and unruly, civilized and feral – in short, 'worthy' and 'unworthy' – children (and, by extension, parents, families and communities). As we shall see in Chapter 3, there is often a clear correlation between our judgment about a child's degree of 'worthiness' (or 'unworthiness') and how well we know them – or how closely *related* we are to them. In other words, we have a tendency to value our own children – or those *like* them – more highly than other people's, or other *types* of people's. And, as Chapter 4 demonstrates, this 'people like us' worldview is systematically encouraged by the way children are contradictorily portrayed in the news media. But, while history tells us that such distinctions are nothing new, *today's* discourse around the place of juveniles in society has come about (like those before it) for reasons particular to this moment in time. Moreover, while the ambivalent gaze with which we regard children in present-day Britain shares many characteristics with the paradoxical positioning of juveniles in certain historical contexts, it also has aspects that are distinct, if not unique. It is the task of the rest of this book first to identify these qualities and then to try to explain them.

3
Our Children and Other People's: Childhood in the Age of Distrust

A unifying theme to emerge from all the audience research carried out for this book – from focus groups to textual analysis of newspaper discussion threads – was the creeping sense that Britain has become a less secure, more intimidating place than in times past. The consensus among both sets of focus group participants – the first drawn from Whitehawk, a working-class suburb of Brighton in one of the 5 per cent most deprived wards in England (Department for Communities and Local Government, 2012); the second from Hanover and Queen's Park, a middle-class neighbourhood a mile to its west – was that today's children are being reared in a more menacing, stressful environment than previous generations. By contrast, adults' memories of *their own* childhoods – and grandmothers' of parenthood – reflected a widespread view that the risks and threats faced by the children of yesteryear were less omnipresent than those of today. And it was not just adults who appeared sensitive to this uneasy atmosphere: a perception common to all focus groups, including those involving children themselves, was that the experience of *being a child* had become more pressurized and anxiety-inducing than ever.

The perceived threats parents identified were encyclopaedic. Everything from sudden and dramatic illnesses to violent films and video games to bullying text messages and emails from classmates to banal household objects like kitchen knives and razors were reeled off as hazards their children navigated on a daily basis. But, as in previous studies (Hillman et al., 1990; Shaw et al., 2013), two menaces consistently dominated their discussions: worries about children being run over by speeding vehicles and (above all else) abduction, abuse and/ or murder by predatory paedophiles. As we shall see, the peculiar potency of this latter fear owed much to the *source* from which it arose.

While parents' concerns about school bullies, mundane objects and hit-and-run accidents were often rooted in some degree of direct or vicarious experience, time and again they attributed their fears about children falling prey to sexual abuse and exploitation to stories they had read, heard or seen in the news – whether first-hand or (more often) second-hand, via playground gossip or social media. Moreover, the clear agenda-setting influence they ascribed to the news manifested itself in the ubiquitous guises in which they claimed to perceive potential malign intent, with references to highly publicized cautionary tales involving familiar strangers dominating lengthy exchanges between both parents and grandparents. Everyone from duplicitous doctors and teachers to the 'man in the park' where the working-class nursery worker's son played to hazily known acquaintances whose inner motives it was impossible to discern surfaced in the context of wide-ranging discussions shaped, in large part, by media narratives. As Jenkins (1992, p. 99) observed in relation to a highly publicized 1990 scare about 'bogus social workers', the underlying consensus appeared to be that 'no amount of streetproofing could safeguard children from abduction, assault, or murder'. The heightened anxiety detectable in this discourse echoes the simmering sense of parental panic underpinning previously cited studies by Hillman et al. (1990), Valentine (1996a, 1996b), Meyer (2007) and others – all of which identified widespread fears among parents about children falling prey to extra-familial threats if allowed too much unsupervised freedom. No sooner were they asked how much independence they habitually allowed their children than working-class participants alluded to sweeping, unspecified fears about 'the risks out there' and 'what could happen in life'.[1] And even relatively *laissez-faire* members of both groups – those claiming to be relaxed about letting their children walk to school, play outside or run errands alone – demonstrated acute awareness of the potential risks they took by granting such liberties. Despite claiming to have been relaxed about allowing her four children to walk to the corner shop alone from as young as seven, a 42-year-old middle-class nurse summed up the general feeling when she observed that 'anxiety ... really influences our behaviour'. The *extent* of this behavioural influence, moreover, was reflected in discussions held with two groups of nine- and ten-year-old children from the same areas, who testified to both the nature of their parents' fears and the constraints placed on their freedoms as a consequence.

The air of barely suppressed panic revolving around issues of child *jeopardy* was, though, only one element of the focus group discourse. In discussing the subject of children and their rights, participants repeatedly gave vent to a secondary framing of young people – upending the dominant positioning of children as (actual or potential) 'victims' by problematizing them as 'threats'. Again, discussion about this aspect of the juvenile problem was underpinned by what appeared to be a widely shared belief, particularly among working-class mothers, that today's children were harder to control than previous generations. That these two sides of the coin repeatedly recurred – often juxtaposed in overlapping or successive strands of conversation – is testament to the enduring legacy of the deep-seated moral ambivalence about children identified in the last chapter. Adults – and, to some extent, children themselves – still appear to be wrestling with conflicted feelings about the place of juveniles in society and, more particularly, their ability to look after themselves and act responsibly towards others. Perhaps more intriguingly, while some focus group participants openly aired concerns about their own children's behaviour in the context of the secondary discourse about child 'threats', more often than not a distinction emerged (however subtle) between conceptions of *their* children and *other people's*. The extent to which this discrimination appeared conscious, and its underlying significance, are two issues explored in coming sections. However, even at this stage, we can say one thing for certain: what most negative conceptualizations of childhood had in common was an implicit preoccupation with questions of *trust*. This manifested itself in concerns that *their* children could not be trusted to look after themselves (or each other) and, above all else, in a pathological fear that almost nobody else could be trusted with *them*.

This sensitization to the multifarious dangers apparently faced by children, and the significant menace they could pose to others – backed by a strong conviction that today's juveniles are both more susceptible to harm and more incorrigible than their forebears – was not confined to the focus groups. It also infiltrated discussion threads published beneath the online versions of newspaper articles analysed for this study – and (more or less explicitly) through many of the press narratives themselves. 'We are living in dangerous times', warned one woman from Manchester, in response to a *Daily Mail* story about a man fined £1,000 for alerting other parents to the fact that his ex-wife's new partner was a convicted sex offender (Dolan, 2011, p. 25), while a male poster from Birmingham lamented 'things 'aint [*sic*] what they used to be',[2] as he decried the 'abuse' of the benefits system exposed by a double-page article in the same paper focusing on the pregnant daughter of a welfare-dependent 'mother of 14' (Sears, 2011a, p. 11) – a tale categorized as 'hybrid'[3] for presenting children as both *victims of* and *threats to* Britain's (deteriorating) moral order. A common refrain in comments on stories about child misbehaviour was that 'liberal' or 'progressive' educational policies and/or 'political correctness' were undermining morality by letting children run riot – with one angry poster commenting on a *Daily Mail* story about the government's decision to allow teachers to smack 'unruly' children by lifting a '"no touching" ban' (Loveys, 2011), ranting that 'lilly [*sic*] livered nonsense' spouted by 'annoying left-wing busy bodies' had 'ruined classroom discipline', with the result that 'brats' were 'running aroun' [*sic*] whilst parents do ziltch!'.

During the month-long period of newspaper textual analysis – the focus of Chapter 4 – 23 discussion threads pertaining to articles framing children as 'victims' and/or 'threats' were analysed. While they represented just over 7 per cent of the 325 pieces bracketed in the above categories and barely 5 per cent of the overall sample (462), they provided a rich pool of data with telling characteristics. In total, 2,809 responses were posted – the overwhelming majority (2,244, or eight out of ten) taking the form of straightforward *reactive opinions*, with only 565 responses bringing any additional information and/or testimony to the table. And the clear overall consensus was acceptance of the dominant discourse promoted by these risk-based articles: namely that, when they are not posing a menace in (or to) themselves, children are constantly bombarded by external threats. In total, 2,372 out of 2,809 posts (84 per cent) amounted to unquestioning endorsements of the underlying narratives of articles on which they commented: either simple echo-chamber *reactions* parroting the newspapers' agendas or (in a minority of cases) *evidence-based testimonies* that supported and consolidated their portrayals. Only a small (if significant) minority – 437, or 16 per cent of the total – noticeably contested any aspects of texts to which they responded. In the case of all but a single article, posts endorsing the narratives on which they commented could be classified as supporting the (hegemonic) 'victim/threat' framing of children. The only problematic piece was a 21 July *Daily Mail* story about a proposal from then government 'education czar' Simon Hughes that ten-year-old schoolchildren should be given careers advice. This was an unusually nuanced article for the tabloid because while, in one respect, it framed children as victims (of both expensive university fees and a tough job market), its choice of sources – lecturers and students who branded the initiative a 'waste of time' (Peev, 2011) – seemed designed to steer readers towards dismissing it as an example of unnecessary mollycoddling by an interfering nanny state (a longstanding *Daily Mail bête-noire*). The 18 *negotiated/oppositional* posts that this story attracted, then – all supporting Hughes's proposals, to a greater or lesser degree – were arguably more in line with a straightforward 'victim' framing of juveniles than the article itself (or comments *endorsing* it). The other exceptional article – coincidentally, also published in the *Daily Mail* on the same day – was framed as a critique of the *laissez-faire* philosophy of an 'alternative' Steiner school, where a teacher had gone undisciplined for allegedly assaulting a pupil (Sears, 2011b). Again, there was a twist to the oppositional posts beneath this tale (all three of them), as each adopted a framing of children as unruly menaces: in other words, *upholding* the hegemonic positioning of juveniles, but as 'threats', rather than 'victims'. On the whole, then, the dominant discourse to emerge from discussion threads across the board affirmed the problematic dual framing of children as 'victims' and/or 'threats'. A breakdown of posts by type is given in Figure 3.1, while Figure 3.2 displays the balance of different reactive opinions. The minority of evidence-based posts are explored in Chapter 4.

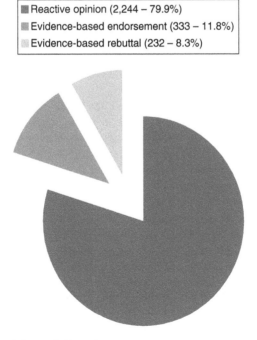

Figure 3.1 Breakdown of discussion posts

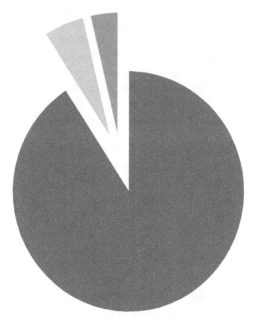

■ Affirming - 2,038 (90.8%)   ▨ Negotiated - 124 (5.5%)   ■ Oppositional - 82 (3.7%)

Figure 3.2   Breakdown of reactive opinions

We can be confident that these published posts were representative of the views of all those minded to contribute to discussion threads – and, by extension, that they offer as representative a snapshot of reader responses to these articles as any – on the basis of testimony from journalists responsible for moderating such forums. Contrary to concerns raised in earlier studies about the danger of web moderators acting as 'censors' of controversial views expressed by contributors (Noveck, 2004; Janssen & Kies, 2005), both the community manager of a national broadsheet and web editor of a local daily tabloid confirmed that the practical impossibility of individually filtering every post prior to publication forced them to moderate in a largely 'reactive' and/or *post facto* way. The local paper's default position was to publish *every* comment initially, however contentious – only removing posts if other readers complained about them and their grievances were upheld. As its web editor put it, 'case law has created a situation where you either actively moderate or you reactively moderate', whereas 'if you do *any* active moderation then you are deemed to be actively moderating, and you are therefore responsible for any content on the website'. Conversely, 'if you say, "our comments are reactively moderated", then it means you can't do *any* active moderating' (a reason she gave for her generally non-interventionist policy). Moreover, while there were a handful of exceptions to this rule – local community tensions discouraged her from running threads beneath stories about travellers – she had only ever 'banned' around 20 individuals from contributing to discussions, and only then for severe 'trolling' (Binns, 2012) or remarks bordering on incitement. Significantly, given the subject of this thesis, the incident she recalled most vividly concerned a poster who taunted other readers by quoting 'Chris Morris, particularly the paedophile stuff'. This referred to a much-criticized 2001 episode of spoof television talk-show *Brass Eye* (Conlan, 2001), which lampooned the moral panic arising from a succession of high-profile child murders, including those of Sarah Payne and the Soham girls, and a contemporaneous debate about Internet child pornography sparked by the prosecution of pop star Gary Glitter. Though the national paper took a slightly different approach – requiring web staff to systematically check threads for inflammatory comments after their initial appearance, rather than only after receiving complaints – limited resources necessitated its use of 'a combination of post-moderation and reactive moderation', explained its community manager. 'If you pre-moderate you are effectively publishing, if you post-moderate you are "hosting"', she said, adding the paper was legally 'okay' if it removed troubling posts 'in a reasonable amount of time' after noticing them.

As we shall see, questions of trust – or, more accurately, *distrust* – underpin most, if not all, of the threats (real and imagined) examined in the next two chapters. But if one of these threats trumps the rest it is the singular spectre of the familiar stranger: the half-known individual (usually an adult, but occasionally a child) whom we recognize by sight, perhaps even by name, but about whose inner nature we cannot be certain. It is the concept of familiar strangers – and the overarching atmosphere of 'threatening familiarity' they symbolize – that forms the locus for the central thesis of this book. This is the argument that the collective, and increasingly endemic, societal panic(s) about children in contemporary Britain are a projection of and, in some respects, *displacement for* a deeper social malaise: a long-term and potentially irreversible breakdown in interpersonal trust.

Defining the discourse: dominant popular narratives about children

Before we can explore the *meanings* of the (at times paradoxical) positioning of children that characterize today's juvenile panic, it is necessary to define the *parameters* of this discourse: that is, to categorize the threats that children are perceived to face (and, in some cases, pose). As we shall see, contributors to both focus groups and discussion threads identified a montage of threats – ranging from age-old anxieties about prowling bogeymen, busy roads and 'the dark'[4] to newer menaces like cyber-bullying, intrusive electronic gadgets and rampant consumerism. The main aspects of the 'scarier world' paradigm to emerge from this audience research can be broken down as follows:

- Abduction/molestation/grooming/murder by strangers
- Abuse/murder by adults known to the child – including family, friends, trusted professionals in *loco parentis*, neighbours or other familiar strangers
- Traffic accidents caused by dangerous drivers/careless children
- Violent assault or bullying by older children/teenagers
- Over-exposure to adult film and TV content, video games and electronic gadgets
- Corrupting effects of rampant consumerism and advertising

Abduction/molestation/grooming/murder by strangers

The first focus group participant to allude to stranger-danger was a 39-year-old working-class single mother-of-two, who described how neither of her daughters dared venture alone to the local park because she had 'drummed it into them' about 'the people'. Asked for clarification, this part-time volunteer in a community cafe nodded gravely as a married mother-of-four working as a trainee teaching assistant referred to 'paedos and stuff like that'. This, in turn, prompted a busy 25-year-old mum juggling single parenthood with a course in nursery care to interject that her son (aged six) was forbidden from straying beyond a patch of grass sandwiched between two roads immediately outside her ground-floor flat, because 'it's so close either way and someone can grab 'em so easily in a car'. Fears about unsupervised outdoor play were echoed by a second single mother, 32, with three primary school-aged children, who fretted that if she 'saw something about to happen' to her seven-year-old daughter she would be unable to reach her in time because two flights of stairs separated her second-floor flat from the pavement below. Similar concerns were raised by another tower-block tenant, living with a partner and two children (four and six), who had barred her eldest from playing in her close for fear of 'the alleys'. She once 'went to pieces' after finding her six-year-old son missing from the backseat of her car minutes after leaving him to drop her daughter at nursery, when 'all he had done was followed me in, but the first thing that come into my head was, "what if someone has opened that car and got him?"' These mothers' rationales for imposing such restrictions bore striking similarities to accounts given by both sets of children. The middle-class nurse's nine-year-old daughter described being allowed to play in her front garden solely on condition she kept the gate closed – adding that she would not be permitted to walk her dog to the nearby park until she was ten, because her mother worried about 'the park, the actual park'. When she was asked to expand on this point, a friend interrupted with words strikingly similar to those uttered by the working-class mothers: 'those people, those strangers there'. This almost phantasmagoric idea of unspecified predators lurking just out of sight, ready to pounce the moment parents' backs were turned, was also raised by a nine-year-old working-class boy, who said he was only allowed to play out until early evening 'in case people try to take you'.

Not all concerns expressed by children about dangers posed by unspecified 'people' can be dismissed as irrational or based purely on hearsay. One working-class girl who said her father considered most things 'dangerous', and only let her walk alone to school because this did not involve crossing roads, revealed she had recently moved in with him after being withdrawn from the care of her abusive mother. However, a common thread of working-class mothers' remarks was a sense that they needed to restrict their children's independence out of *self-evidently* justified concerns about 'the people', 'paedos' and the prospect that 'someone might get' their children – an ingrained fear of abduction that, when unpicked, appeared to have little basis in their own experiences. Fears of abduction and/or murder by strangers also surfaced early in middle-class discussions. For these mothers, the concept of child-snatching arose in the context of a generalized exchange about fears of the dark. Responding to a remark from the nurse that she let her children walk to the local swimming pool from the age of eight, a 46-year-old writer framed her concerns using a mix of vicarious experience and literary allusion:

> It's just the dark. I don't know what I think is going to happen in the dark that wouldn't happen in the day ... And even now with my youngest, ten, I'll go, 'yeah, can you send him home now cos ... it's on the brink of dusk, you know, before it gets dark'. It's like this mythical ... *cut-off*.

It was in the context of the ensuing discussion that mention first arose of a source of mothers' concerns beyond their own direct purviews: the media. The writer's remark about 'the dark' prompted a 51-year-old worker in a homelessness hostel – who confessed that the nature of her job inclined her towards viewing the world as 'slightly more dangerous' than 'other people would think' – to mention the news. In justifying her fears, the single parent of two sons (nine and 13) observed that 'more ... stories that you read in the newspaper of people being abducted in alleyways ... do happen in the dark'. This notion of the news as a *trigger* for pre-existing parental concerns – priming mothers (and fathers) already sensitized to the prospect of their children being harmed by malevolent others to project alarming news narratives onto their own circumstances – resurfaced time and again in both sets of focus groups. Significantly, the middle-class mothers' extensive deliberations about 'the dark' were reflected in a shorter debate among the working-class mums about the wisdom of letting children play outside on winter evenings, because of fears about 'losing sight' of them. A shy 22-year-old mother-of-four became unusually animated on this subject, recalling tussles with her 12-year-old son over her edict that 'he will not disappear from the street when it gets dark' if he wanted to avoid being 'grounded'. Interestingly, though, while middle-class mothers were generally more self-critical than working-class ones about the irrationality of fretting about stranger-danger, at times their discussion became contradictory – and the reasoning they used to *question* the true scale of this threat was replayed as *justification* for their concerns. A point repeatedly made was that there were almost certainly no more paedophiles at large than in the past – and it was *awareness* of risk, rather than risk itself, that had increased over time, due to public information campaigns, Criminal Records Bureau checks for adults working with children, heightened media coverage and registration of child sex offenders under 'Sarah's Law' (Blacker & Griffin, 2010). Yet greater awareness was itself conceived as a *cause* of potential worry. A married 46-year-old working with parents of children with special educational needs raised concern that closer monitoring of paedophiles might send them 'underground' – making them *more* threatening. And the hostel worker mused that, though abductions had occurred just as often when she was young (even if they were not so well publicized), parents today were cursed with the fact 'we *know* loads of children go missing'.

This suggestion that British society had become over-sensitized to risks that have always existed but were less widely recognized previously was endorsed by both sets of grandmothers – most of whom recalled enjoying far more carefree childhoods than their own grandchildren. A 55-year-old working-class teaching assistant, originally from Glasgow, was one of several who had walked to school alone by the age of seven, and could not remember '*any* limitations' to the independence she was allowed. But, while she vividly described the 45-minute walk that took her 'down past a canal' to her secondary school, she confessed to having been much stricter on her own children and, in due course, grandchildren – largely (and counter-intuitively) due to the heightened *public profile*, rather than incidence, of child abuse and abduction cases. Although she conceded that society had become 'more aware' of 'paedophilia', rather than the problem itself becoming any more pervasive, she said that (unlike her own parents) she would always walk her children to school, while she habitually followed her granddaughter to a nearby park to keep an eye on her, because 'at the back of my mind I'm thinking, "oh please God, don't let anything happen before I get there"'. Others remembered enjoying even greater liberty as children. Another working-class grandmother, who had lived in the same area her whole life, recalled making 'camps in the bushes', going 'over the [rubbish] tip' and beneath a coastal 'under-cliff, where the water used to come up' – leaving her and her friends 'absolutely drenched'. Yet, despite having tried to adopt a similarly relaxed attitude towards her own children's outdoor activities, she conceded she was 'just so worried for the kids these days' because 'you hear more about paedophiles'.

Middle-class grandmothers appeared to have experienced childhoods that were freer still, reflecting the comparatively low-crime areas in which most recalled growing up. A 65-year-old retired teacher remembered being allowed to travel to France alone aged 13 – an experience which informed similar levels of freedom she allowed her own children, whom she permitted to go to London by train on their own to visit their father from as young as eight. And, while there was a general consensus that it was acceptable for children in the 1970s and 1980s to play out alone and walk themselves to school by the time they reached seven or eight, one retired women's refuge worker said she had let hers walk to the local shop unsupervised from as young as three. Asked why they felt today's parents had become so much more protective, invariably the finger was pointed at the media. A widowed former health visitor earned nods of agreement when she recounted how, despite the fact it 'had been going on for ages', around '30 years ago' newspapers had 'all of a sudden' been flooded with allegations of child 'sexual abuse'. An 82-year-old divorcee concurred that 'being worried about children being abducted' did not 'enter into it' when she was bringing up her daughter (the middle-class nurse).

The mothers' frequent (usually unprompted) references to the media in these discussions often took the form of recollections about specific high-profile news stories. A notorious missing child case raised by both groups was that of Madeleine McCann: the three-year-old British girl who vanished from the Portuguese holiday apartment where she had been left sleeping beside her siblings while her parents dined at a nearby restaurant in May 2007. Despite the fact that this heavily publicized incident happened on foreign soil, all the women identified with the scenario – an indicator, perhaps, that the notion of children being snatched while asleep in a supposedly safe location (whether at home or overseas) makes this as yet unsolved media *cause célèbre* a singular embodiment of the disquieting idea of 'threatening familiarity'. This theme arose repeatedly, and was crystallized by the writer, who proactively raised another story symbolizing the dangers that might lurk in innocuous-seeming locales: the 1996 slaying of mother and daughter Lin and Megan Russell in a country lane in Kent:

> ... if I'm feeling anxious ... I always think of that woman ... the Michael Stone case, in broad daylight in a beautiful village that they'd moved to because it was so idyllic and safe ...

Similarly, one working-class mother translated a newspaper story about two (then recent) murders of people in their homes – drawn from her local paper, the *Argus* – into a source of worry about dangers that could potentially befall her children *outside* the home. As she put it:

> If they're going to come into your house and do it, what're they going to do if children are *out*?

Another intriguing extension of paedophile fears was the working-class mums' concern that, unlike in days gone by, children could no longer be wholly insulated from stranger-danger even at home. The nursery worker feared that personal images and details innocently posted on social networking websites like Facebook could act as magnets for online stalkers, as 'all they need' is for 'someone' to 'put a picture up of the kids playing outside your house and it's got the street name'. Despite professing a laid-back attitude towards her children's independence, the teaching assistant admitted being so worried about her younger daughter being groomed by paedophiles posing as children on Facebook that she had censored her profile to avoid 'some man' exploiting it by thinking, 'hang on, I've got a vulnerable little girl who ... likes this, that and the other'. This story prompted the single mother-of-three living in a high-rise to recall intercepting a message to her seven-year-old from someone she had 'added ... on Facebook' who 'she ... thought was [singer] Peter Andre' and was suggesting, '"come and meet me"'.

Though relatively few press articles about abduction/abuse were accompanied by discussion threads – presumably because most concerned cases that were subject to criminal prosecution, making the publication of comments legally problematic – concerns about the supposedly high risk of abduction and/or molestation peppered the handful of threads that did relate to such matters. The earlier mentioned *Daily Mail* report about a man fined for warning other parents that his ex-wife's partner was a convicted paedophile provoked several such responses – including colourful tirades epitomizing the strain of opinion that the (supposed) increasing prevalence of child abuse over time was symptomatic of the fact Britain had 'gone to the dogs'[5] (a favourite narrative of the *Mail* and *Telegraph* titles, to which we will return in more detail in Chapter 4). One poster dismissed today's UK as 'a haven for paedophiles, the work shy, uneconomic migrants and rather unpleasant for ordinary decent people'. And, though less often than in focus groups, when readers indicated the *sources* of their perception that society had changed for the worse – with paedophilia becoming more widespread – media coverage was often explicitly identified as an influence on this belief. One Manchester-based poster responding to this *Daily Mail* story alluded to a report 'some time back' in the same paper that there were now '160,000 hits a day on child porn websites' – adding that 'this article' was the 'closest we get to see what is happening'.

Abuse/murder by familiar strangers

At least as prevalent as fears about predatory strangers among focus group participants were repeated declarations of concern about children being abused/killed by trusted familiars. And, as with their worries about more conventional forms of stranger-danger, this issue was consistently viewed through a media prism. Scenarios symbolizing a sense of threatening familiarity surfaced powerfully among working-class parents when, during a highly self-reflective discussion about the distrust with which parents sometimes (unjustifiably) regarded men they met in parks and playgrounds, the single mother-of-three recalled a high-profile news story that had disturbed her precisely because it *confounded* conventional stereotypes about child-abusers. 'That woman ... she was ... abusing the children', she said, referring to Plymouth nursery worker Vanessa George – convicted of molesting pre-school children in December 2009. The case had 'horrified' her because 'as a mother ... you would think it was a natural thing that women wouldn't'. She also raised the more immediate case of school-teacher Nigel Leat, from Weston-super-Mare, who had been jailed for serial sex offences in the same week her focus group first met. 'I would have thought you could trust teachers', she said, returning to the recurring issue of misplaced confidence, and adding that Leat's case was all the more alarming because he had gone unpunished for so long, with 30 people complaining over 15 years but only 11 being 'taken any ... further'. A more infamous story illustrating the threatening familiarity paradigm raised by middle-class mothers was the Soham killings: the abduction and murder of ten-year-old Holly Wells and Jessica Chapman by Ian Huntley, partner of their teaching assistant, Maxine Carr, in August 2002. In an apparent admission of a form of (limited) media effect on her behaviour, the special needs worker, who had three children, aged eight, 11 and 12, relayed to a chorus of 'mms' from other mothers how such stories left her suspicious about men that she and her children encountered locally:

> I kind of get anxious, you know, when you hear about ... the Soham murders. For a period ... I remember ... even looking suspiciously at ... men ... odd-looking men.

A common thread of such exchanges – as with others prompted by recollections of infamous media stories – was for parents to *project* them onto themselves and their neighbourhoods. For example, the nursery worker recalled her loss of innocence some years earlier, when her former German teacher was convicted of storing child pornography on his computer. She remembered 'a fantastic teacher' her mother had 'trusted ... 100 per cent'. Again, the term 'trust' recurred time and again in these discussions – in relation to horror stories about everyone from predatory professionals to sadistic friends and family members. Both sets of mothers raised the haunting prospect of parents/carers sexually and physically abusing their children in private while presenting doting facades in public. Prompted by another mother's recollection of the case of eight-year-old Victoria Climbie – who died after two years of torture and neglect by her great aunt and uncle in their London bed-sit in 2000 – the aspiring teaching assistant raised the spectre of abusive parents who presented 'the happiest-go-lucky' facades while subjecting their children to 'absolute hell ... behind closed doors'. The middle-class hostel worker raised similar concerns about the deceptive facades presented by 'plausible' adults.

As with the broader notion of threatening familiarity, such underlying worries about the possibility of trusted individuals betraying that trust recurred consistently, not only in parents' discussions but children's – with a middle-class boy sparking a lengthy exchange about the possible duplicity of benign-seeming adults by cautioning that 'sometimes they're vaguely friends of your grown-ups', in response to mention of 'strangers'. He also raised the subject of 'what happened in Wales' (a reference to the abduction and murder of five-year-old April Jones, explored in Chapter 5) – prompting the nurse's daughter to comment that she had been 'surprised' by this story 'because it was just a friend's dad and apparently they were really nice before'. Explicitly projecting this concept onto her own life, she added she would normally 'trust' the dad of the girl sitting beside her 'to drive me home'. Again, the salience of the threatening familiarity concept was illustrated by the fact that, of all 'child victim' discussion threads analysed, by far the one with the most reader posts (290) was that focusing on the familiar stranger figure of the paedophile stepfather discussed earlier. One particularly sweeping evocation of familiar stranger concerns was the following stream of invective from a London-based poster:

> This will come as NO SURPRISE to many individuals who have had to report the seen abuse [of] children, only to have to stand by and watch as the children are left in danger and who are indeed, in many cases 'seen' to be further mind and body twisted, or killed, by their IDENTIFIED abusers. There is something seriously wrong with the whole child protection in practice situation, in England on A National Level, which is putting children at risk.

As stated earlier, it is an argument of this book that heightened sensitization to the prospect of deception by trusted familiars reflects a more fundamental crisis in interpersonal trust in contemporary Britain. The coming chapters will demonstrate that the particular salience of tales about children being abused, exploited and betrayed by familiar strangers is not just a recurrent feature of discourse among members of the public (especially parents), but also a common aspect of many of the most widely publicized news stories about child victims. For this reason, it forms not only a focal point for discussion in coming chapters, but a core pointer towards the book's conclusions.

Dangerous drivers and careless children

Fears about speeding cars and children's heedlessness in crossing busy roads were marked in both parent groups – with many mothers drawing on personal anecdotes or official data to illustrate the rational, evidence-based, nature of these concerns. The special needs worker was more worried about traffic than other threats because 'statistically' it 'supersedes all that'. Asked outright what their main concern was when they weighed up whether to allow their children out alone, middle-class mothers replied in unison: 'the roads'. Mothers in both groups mentioned fatal accidents involving children that had sharpened their anxieties about road safety. The teaching assistant recalled having to explain to her young children that a friend's son had died after being 'hit by a car'. And a 36-year-old single middle-class mother-of-three criticized drivers who 'flash' their headlights to indicate it is safe for children to cross – a practice she blamed for the death of a child at her son's secondary school, who started crossing after being flashed by one car, only to be run over by another.

For working-class mothers, 'dangerous driving' tended to be couched, like the predations of strangers (familiar and otherwise), as a form of deviancy: with the focus on the menace posed by teenage joy-riders, rather than motorists generally. Their concern about *antisocial* drivers – a corollary of broader worries about thuggish youths detailed in the follow-ing section – arguably reflected the relatively high-crime neighbourhood in which they lived; a pattern familiar from earlier studies identifying ele-vated crime perceptions among communities blighted by comparatively higher levels of criminal activity (e.g. Hirsch, 1980, 1981). A concern about joy-riders was best expressed by the timid mother-of-four, who spoke excitedly about motorbikes careering along alleyways and 'up and down at God knows however long, up until 12, what, one o'clock, two o'clock in the morning'. And a further theme to emerge from discussions about traffic risks was the sense that road fatalities were often as much the fault of careless children running out in front of vehicles without looking as of drivers: in other words, kids were sometimes risks to *them-selves*. In this vein, a tower-block dweller recalled the day her 'little boy ... legged it out of school' and 'straight across the main road'. Yet, despite maintaining that their concerns about traffic were well-founded, middle-class mothers offered a self-reflective insight into how their worries about road safety might nonetheless be overblown. Just as they criticized society's (and, by extension, their own) irrational fixation with stranger-danger, so, too, they observed that previous generations had exhibited a healthier attitude towards traffic. The hostel worker crystallized this point by asking aloud why her mother – despite having been an 'anxious' person – had permitted her to roam so much more freely outdoors than she would dream of letting her own children, even though roads near her childhood home were as busy then as today. 'It *was* a busy road *then*, but we were allowed to go wherever really', she recalled, adding that her mother 'always imagined dreadful things happening', yet would 'allow us to do all that'. Directly posing the million-dollar question about rising parental insecurities, she asked: 'what's going on?' As we shall see later, the self-questioning, often contradictory, discourse around road safety and stranger-danger (particularly among middle-class mothers) appears to relate to a broader crisis of confidence in parenting, and maternal self-identity, linked to wider changes in British gender roles.

Though there was widespread agreement among these mothers that their concerns had a rational basis (not least because of the surge in car ownership since their childhoods), they struggled to reconcile memories of being allowed significantly greater freedoms, including the ability to cross busy streets, with the tight rein they exercised over their own children's movements. Echoing an admission made by working-class mothers that they routinely used mobile phones as a way of keeping tabs on their children's whereabouts (a behavioural response to heightened anxiety about juvenile vulnerability that we examine in detail later), the writer reflected that her own parents 'didn't need to know where we were, whereas now ... they [children] have mobiles and we can contact them ... and we need to know'. Her concerns about over-controlling parents were echoed by the nurse's memory that 'it never *occurred* to people then to hang on to children'. At 'six or seven' she had accompanied a friend 'to the countryside with her pony – just one pony and us – for *miles*'. It was, though, the single mother (a midwife) who best summed up this group's collective frustration with its own state of anxiety, by explicitly honing in on 'the mobile phone' as a *symbol* of parental neurosis and insecurity:

> If you text somebody and you haven't heard within, like, five minutes, you start thinking to yourself, 'oh ... I wonder what's going on there?'

Worries about road safety were echoed by children, with the main freedoms they listed – such as being allowed to walk alone to a corner shop or school – frequently qualified as short trips they could make without crossing busy streets. A shy middle-class girl said the only journey she was allowed to make independently was to a local dance studio she could reach without crossing a road, while a working-class boy who lived some distance from both his school and the nearest park complained of being deprived of liberties his peers enjoyed because of the number of roads he had to navigate to reach these locations. And, in an echo of the midwife's concern about drivers giving children mixed signals by flashing their headlights, one boy said his mother worried that 'if they give me a signal to cross the road and I cross' they might still 'squash' him. Once again, grandmothers offered a helpful *historical* perspective on the changing nature of road traffic risks – echoing their reflections on escalating sensitization to child abuse. While several criticized irrational public perceptions (and media portrayals) of the prevalence of paedophilia, they agreed that, by contrast, soaring levels of car ownership had introduced a *genuine* menace where none had previously existed. A 71-year-old middle-class grandmother recalled the lively 'street life' she experienced in the 1970s – a time when cars were far less widespread and, consequently, it was safer for children to play outside. Similarly, the retired women's refuge worker recalled that, when she grew up in Norwich, traffic was so minimal that 'playing out was something everyone did'. As a result, it was 'very rare to be totally on your own' – a fact she saw as reducing the likelihood of children coming to *other* kinds of harm. A 62-year-old working-class grandmother married to an ex-police officer reflected that, when she was young, only one household had a car on her Brighton estate – allowing her to roam freely along the middle of their road. But quieter, less busy, streets were only part of the picture: equally important was the 'genuine community spirit' she remembered from her youth, as characterized by memories of her 'neighbours' looking out for one another and her knowing the woman next door as 'Auntie Grace, not Mrs Watkins'. An office worker (56) recalled enjoying similar freedoms, first in south London, then Saltdean (a coastal suburb), where she would walk unaccompanied to her local lido and use a doll's pushchair as a makeshift go-kart.

Violent assault or bullying by older children/teenagers

A fourth category of threat mentioned frequently in discussions was that posed by other (predominantly older) juveniles. However, here there emerged significant differences between the two sets of parents, with working-class mothers relaying personal anecdotes based on their own experiences and middle-class mums largely relying on third-hand (principally media) accounts or sporadic incidents they had witnessed involving individuals unknown to them personally. Moreover, there was marked disagreement between the two groups about where the *blame* lay for aggressive juvenile behaviour – with working-class mothers inclined to criticize miscreants themselves (or their parents), while middle-class mums generally adopted the more liberal view that the root causes of delinquency lay in wider social problems. The working-class consensus was neatly encapsulated by the teaching assistant's vivid recollection of her son being beaten up – an assault he referred to himself, when he described being rounded on by 'five year sevens'. 'My little boy last year got beaten up by a 14-year-old person, and he come home covered in blood', she recalled, adding, 'there are so many parents that don't put rules and boundaries in place and let their kids do what they want'. Others made similar observations. The shy contributor said her son was afraid to visit the park 'because he's been bullied down there', while the nursery worker criticized the 'gang mentality' among 'older ones who group together and ... think they rule the roost'. She recalled a time when her brother had brought her son home minutes after taking him to the swings, complaining about 'big kids ... swearing, shouting' and 'drinking alcohol'. A further aspect of parents' concerns about bullying was the potential for modern technologies to be used as weapons. The nursery worker explicitly referred to the 'scarier world' paradigm by distinguishing between today's 'gangs' and 'the olden days', when 'if you had an argument with someone you'd have a little fight, and that was it'. 'My friend's daughter wouldn't go to school because they'd come to the school and ... beat her up and videoed it', she recalled, adding that footage was put 'on the Internet' and 'their friends got it ... texted to their phones'. As with her comments about online grooming, it was this mother who crystallized anxieties about children's access to new gadgets – stressing the sense that social media were breaking down (or making porous) once solid dividing lines between public and private spaces. 'That's the problem with the Internet now – they can be bullied ... sitting in your house', she said, adding, 'you *think* they're safe' but 'you can't even trust' that they are – yet another explicit allusion to a (this time generalized) sense that trust was becoming an ever more elusive commodity.

This sense among working-class mothers that bullying and intimidation by *other people's* children represented an increasingly ubiquitous threat was intimately bound up with an undercurrent of more general disapproval towards what politicians and some sections of the media might term 'feckless' or 'problem' parents or 'troubled families' (e.g. Phillips, 2011; Great Britain. Cabinet Office and Prime Minister's Office, 2011). When the subject of youth indiscipline recurred in the context of a newsgame exercise in which mums were asked to recount 'facts' about the August 2011 riots, both the nursery worker and another single mother aired vocal opinions about other local parents they regarded as irresponsible and workshy. That both were themselves benefit claimants lent their comments clear echoes of the heterogeneous views voiced by both low-paid 'blue-collar' workers and even other *unemployed* people towards jobless 'scroungers' in earlier studies (Golding & Middleton, 1982).

Moreover, their remarks supported this researcher's hypothesis that discourse about 'good' and 'bad' children often acts as a proxy for broader societal distinctions between worthy and unworthy – or, in this case, 'deserving' and 'undeserving' – families/parents. The strongest criticism of 'undeserving' families came from more aspirational mothers – the teaching assistant, married to a taxi driver, and the soon-to-be qualified nursery worker, who explicitly referred to her studies as a way of lifting herself off benefits. Her most outspoken comments were prompted by a cutting from the *Sun* that she was shown during an exercise designed to stimulate discussion about negative parental stereotypes. Responding to the headline 'No dole if you let kids bunk school: PM vows blitz on feckless families', she pointedly distinguished between herself as a 'single parent on benefits' and others who 'have children, get the money, and let the children do whatever they want'. When another mentioned a local family in which there were nine children but no working adult, she added, 'if you've got that many children and you cannot work to afford them ... it's not right'. Similarly disapproving attitudes towards 'undeserving' families emerged from these mothers' responses to another news-game exercise, requiring them to write newspaper-style captions to accompany black-and-white photographs of children and teenagers looting shops during the August 2011 English riots. Responding to one such image, depicting a group of hooded, masked youths clambering through a smashed shop window and removing items of clothing, the nursery worker wrote:

Free loading teenagers getting something for nothing.

In her second caption, accompanying a photo of a group of masked and hooded boys, one of whom appeared about to hurl a makeshift flamethrower, she wrote:

Youth of today! Our countrys[6] future.

Meanwhile, the married mother-of-four, who had earlier criticized other parents for failing to set 'rules and boundaries', was one of several to insinuate nefarious motives for the looting youngsters, beyond a desire to get 'something for nothing' (at the time, an all-too-familiar political catchphrase, particularly among Conservative ministers – e.g. Great Britain. Cabinet Office and Prime Minister's Office, 2011), with the following caption:

Joining in stealing to make money in taking cloths to pay for habits.

Therefore, though the parents had been asked to pen captions *in the style* of a newspaper, rather than ones reflecting *their own views* of the scenes portrayed, in several cases (including both of those quoted above) there were clear correlations between the written word and the opinions that the same mothers expressed in discussions. If nothing else, this demonstrated a clear meeting of minds between the feral youth discourse(s) promoted by newspapers and politicians and the perspectives honestly held by these mothers (and shaped, at least partly, by their own experiences). In so doing, it pointed to the existence of precisely the sort of 'consensus about reality' often seen as a crucial agent in the construction of successful moral panics (Cohen & Young, 1973, p. 431). However, not all aspects of these mothers' critique were universally shared by fellow focus group participants. Despite the widespread agreement among working-class mothers that parents should only have as many children as they could afford, not all concurred with clear-cut deserving/undeserving distinctions. The separated mother-of-three, who had previously worked at a local superstore, mentioned the 'poverty trap' – arguing that there was little incentive to take up a low-waged post when, by doing so, you could lose benefits and end up worse off. And even the most critical mothers interspersed their invective about irresponsible parents with complaints about the stigma attached to their own reliance on social security and popular myths about single parents. One mother who had been particularly critical of parents who had children irresponsibly without the means to support them summed up society's sweeping condemnation of poorer families reliant on benefits by invoking the stereotype, 'single mum, got kids, out of control'. Just as middle-class mothers sometimes offered contradictory readings of the extent of real danger presented by predatory paedophiles and traffic, then, working-class mums were similarly conflicted about the true scale of juvenile disorder and problem-parenting. More marked than this ambivalence about news narratives with which they were presented, though, was a firm conviction that – whatever society might think to the contrary – sweeping caricatures did not apply to *them*. In other words, it was *other people's* children (and *other* parents) who were guilty: further evidence of a 'them and us', worthy/ unworthy fault-line predicated primarily on the notion that lack of parental discipline, rather than welfare dependency, was to blame for youth disorder.

Unsurprisingly, given that they lived in a relatively low-crime area, middle-class parents seemed less concerned about threats from other children – with only one or two able to recall any instances of bullying or antisocial behaviour of the kind described by working-class mothers. Nonetheless, there was agreement even in this group that unruliness among (older) children in some neighbourhoods *did* exist, and presented a genuine menace to residents of those areas. One significant difference between the views expressed by this group and the other, however, was the former's dismissal of simplistic narratives about individual culpability and repeated reference to the complex causal factors that it held responsible for outbreaks of juvenile indiscipline – chiefly poverty, broken families and domestic abuse. The contrast between these liberal attitudes and more socially conservative ones expressed by the working-class mothers emerged both through dialogue and news-games. The hostel worker chuckled at the use of the word 'feckless' in the 'no dole' article, while the writer lampooned its wording in a faux-hysterical voice, mocking phrases like '*Shameless*-style families' (a reference to a Channel 4 comedy-drama about a dysfunctional family blighted by intergenerational unemployment) and 'mums and dads must make sure their kids obey the rules'. A 50-year-old single mother and ex-teacher went further, criticizing this story's underpinning anti-scrounger narrative and suggesting that governments should 'give them [families on benefits] *more* money so they've got some room to breathe and look after their kids!'. Before writing captions to accompany the riot pictures, the middle-class mothers repeatedly asked for clarification of the aim of this exercise. As a result, in contrast to working-class mothers, their contributions appeared more reflective of framing devices used by (tabloid) newspapers in such cases, rather than their own views on the subject. A wide range of well-worn news clichés emerged in these captions, among them several pejorative labels for the UK as a whole, including 'feral Britain', 'Great Britain?' and 'broken Britain' – a favourite term of then Conservative Work and Pensions Secretary Iain Duncan Smith (quoted in Thorp & Kennedy, 2010). Moreover, their preoccupation with mimicking familiar news-frames was reflected in a lengthy critique of the assumed *intention* of the reporter and headline writer responsible for a *Daily Star* article entitled 'Leave our kids alone: Cam's campaign on net porn' (Nicks, 2011) – focusing on a crackdown on everything from ease of access to Internet pornography to billboards advertising lap-dancing clubs.

The skilled professional and public/voluntary sector backgrounds of most of these mothers (all but one university-educated) was also reflected in a more general critique of popular discourses around working-class families. Explicit reference was made to the then recently published book *Chavs* (Jones, 2011) and the demonization of youth through terms like 'hoodie' – suggesting considerable scepticism about the reliability and objectivity of news narratives and, by extension, a willingness to adopt negotiated or oppositional responses to the media's output. That the same narratives provoked more acceptant reactions from working-class mothers appears to demonstrate that news can strongly *reinforce* existing perspectives among those whose own experiences chime with those they read or hear about in the media – a finding in keeping with previous studies of sensitization to the threat of criminal activity among residents of high-crime neighbourhoods (Doob & Macdonald, 1979; Hirsch, 1980 and 1981; Liska & Baccaglini, 1990). In this one area, then, there was some disparity between the instinctive endorsement of dominant news-frames displayed by most working-class mothers and the much more qualified middle-class responses – a fact that appears to question the existence of a simple, *society-wide* 'consensus about reality' (Cohen & Young, 1973, p. 431) in relation to diagnosing *causes* of juvenile indiscipline. Conversely – and equally significant – the fact that middle-class mothers did not dispute the *existence* of threats posed by other juveniles is arguably evidence that just such a consensus prevails when it comes to identifying the *nature* of the risks faced by their children. Indeed, the sense that delinquency (whatever its causes) represented a real and present menace, not only to other children but to society as a whole, peppered discussion threads across the spectrum, from tabloids to broadsheets. A 10 July 2011 *Daily Mail* story headlined 'Teachers will be allowed to use force on unruly pupils as ministers lift "no touching" ban' (Loveys, 2011) generated 260 comments – many using the detail of this particular story (relaxation of a 'ban' on the 'use of force' prompted by figures showing 1,000 assaults a day on teachers by pupils) as a springboard to launch into sweeping generalizations about the supposed collapse of respect and discipline among today's youth. A typical diagnosis was this from 'Christopher, Kent', who lamented the 'simple lack of discipline and poor parenting compounded by the nanny state which has left Britain devoid of any pride, common sense, work ethic and responsibility' – a conflation of all-too-familiar themes in this right-wing tabloid, which took implicit aim at everything from political correctness to welfare dependency. More extreme was a capitalized rant by 'GB, London' that saw the very existence of a 'no touching' rule as symptomatic of Britain's descent into a 'ONCE PROUD LAW ABIDING NOW TRASHED NATION'. Interestingly, a phrase that surfaced repeatedly in relation to the perceived need to introduce tougher discipline for children was 'rules and boundaries'. This phrase – echoing the exact wording of the working-class teaching assistant – appeared in responses not only to the 'no touching' article but also a story in the following day's *Daily Mail* about 'violent little emperors' assaulting their parents (Harris, 2011a). Again, as with many comments on stories about paedophilia and child abuse, a recurring notion was that juvenile delinquency not only *existed* as a social problem, but had grown *worse* over time – making it both a cause and symptom of a wider decline in morality. This sentiment – an echo of earlier studies that have identified successive generations' collective amnesia about problems faced by previous ones (notably Pearson, 1983) – was reflected in 'Dee, Middlesex's' despairing conclusion that the 'little emperors' story symbolized the fact that 'we have lost the ability to parent along with our morals on right and wrong' and 'Mrs B, Great Britain's' similarly nostalgic contention that an 'increase in over indulgence by parents', visible 'everywhere you go', stood in 'marked contrast to when I grew up in the 60's [*sic*]', when children 'knew that parents made the rules'. As a woman from Bridgnorth put it more bluntly:

> Would you like to know why children are getting like this? Because the discipline we were given by our parents was stopped by our nanny state, so now we have to deal with thugs.

Though fewer in number, and less hysterical overall, hand-wringing remarks about the decline of juvenile discipline – both at home and in school – could also be found in posts responding to a *Daily Telegraph* story about two pupils expelled from progressive private school Bedales for having 'sex in a sandpit' (Sanchez, 2011). 'UK education is totally redundant', opined one poster, adding that for 'spotty virgins' school was now 'a case of Game and Facebook studies', with a menu of 'drink, drugs, sex academy/virtual big brother in school hour' for 'the rest'.

As with all the other threats identified by audience members, the role played by newspapers in constructing and/or exploiting the widespread consensus on youth indiscipline detectable in both focus group responses and discussion threads – and their wider contribution to the discourse of juvenile panic of which this is but one manifestation – is explored in Chapter 4.

Exposure to adult films and TV, video games and electronic gadgets

One category of threat identified by both sets of parents offered a late-modern twist on decades-old fears about the potentially desensitizing effects of adult imagery on impressionable juveniles: the ubiquity, addictive properties and violent/sexualized nature of electronic media. While the media involved might be different from the 'horror comics' and 'video nasties' blamed for corrupting children in the past (Barker & Petley, 1997), many initial concerns raised by working-class mothers, in particular, focused on unsuitable content that their children stumbled across on mobile phones, the Internet and, especially, social media. A tower-block tenant recalled her four-year-old daughter screaming 'there's a man trying to kill me' after unwittingly accessing a Youtube video of her favourite TV character, Hannah Montana, that had been 'mashed-up' to create the impression someone was shooting out of the screen. Working-class mothers also expressed worries about their children's exposure to violent and/or sexual content through traditional media forms – notably TV dramas, news bulletins aimed at adults, and 'shooting games'. Programmes ranging from *The Simpsons* to *EastEnders* were name-checked, with the nursery worker singling out an episode of the soap focusing on a cot-death which 'really upset' her 'friends' kids' because 'they didn't realize it was not real'. At times, more candid mothers confessed to being directly responsible for their children's exposure to TV and film violence. The teaching assistant, who had previously voiced a *laissez-faire* attitude towards her children's outdoor activities, confessed she and her husband both 'love our horrors' and '*all* of my kids will watch them' – with the caveat that she first explains 'they're all made up, it's not real blood, they're not real guns' and 'it's *all* pretend'. Nonetheless, her admission to exposing her children to fictional violence – confirmed by her nine-year-old son, who enthused about watching '18 films' and playing adult-rated games like *Call of Duty* – marked a significant point in the working-class mothers' discussion. By flaunting her 'love' of 'horrors' in the context of a strand of debate that began with another mother recalling the real-life Bulger murder, she was both reflecting on a notorious crime in which media influence was implicated, however erroneously (Franklin & Petley, 1996), and conflating real-life horror stories with imaginary ones. This prompted the nursery worker to raise the risk of children being confused by this distinction – arguing that 'when you get stories on the news where it's very similar, a lot of them then sit there and say, "well mum, that happens … That's very similar to what happened in that film and you said was make-believe"'. Significantly, the horror-loving mother was also demonstrating the same interest in *true* horror stories she had mentioned in an earlier meeting, when recounting the compulsion she felt to read the diaries of Kate McCann, mother of

Madeleine, 'because I've got kids and I thought to myself, "I've got to read it"', and a recent decision to buy the *Sun* 'for the pure fact that I saw on the front-page some kiddie had died'. Such admissions add weight to the suggestion that attempts by newspapers to whip up panics about child vulnerability for commercial gain are, in part, *responses* to a genuine public fascination with grim real-life dramas – an idea to which we return in Chapter 4.

While concerns about violent games and Youtube videos surfaced principally in working-class discussions, an issue which drew more or less equal condemnation from parents in both groups was the ubiquity of sexually explicit imagery – even in programmes (and public locations) where children might see them. Responding to the *Daily Star* story about the Government's proposed crackdown on Internet porn, the middle-class midwife criticized 'things like Rihanna on the *XFactor* in a bikini dancing around at six o'clock at night' – arguing it had less 'to do with "special" websites' and more with 'all of that [pop] culture'. Her observation was echoed by the ex-teacher, who recounted how one of her eight-year-old son's friends had 'showed him how they'd put in the word "cock" – as in cockerel – to Google, and come up with some images ... of penises pierced'. Concerns were also raised by middle-class mothers about the *portability* of new technologies – and the difficulty of prising gadgets away from children. These frustrations tended to be linked to worries about children's physical (rather than mental) health – and a fear that, by spending too much time in front of screens, kids were missing out on valuable exercise and the chance to indulge in physical play and forge friendships. 'I remember being at a farm and seeing a kid ... on his game ... I just thought that was ... *wrong*', recalled the writer, while the hostel worker revived the 'scarier world' paradigm by describing her mother as 'judgmental' about the fact her grandchildren 'play too much on the computer and ... *don't* go out', despite recognizing 'that it's a different world' today. Most illuminating about this latter anecdote, however, was the intriguing disjunction it highlighted between the notion that today's outdoors represented 'a different world' from that of her mother's day and the same mother's earlier recognition that today's fears about road safety, specifically, were *disproportionate*. Similarly, she highlighted other contradictions in her own parenting behaviour, reflecting that while she generally followed the pattern of *increased* parental protectiveness she observed in peers, the one area in which her children were *less* controlled was in their use of technology. This sense of *abdicated* parental authority (echoed by others) has a flipside, though – in the *involuntary* loss of authority the nursery worker alluded to when fretting about cyber-bullying and the ex-teacher's concern that 'when my son goes to stay with the other ... partner ... I'm informed almost nothing about what goes on and ... I *am* concerned that he would set up a Facebook page for my son'.

Although none of the articles accompanied by discussion threads specifically focused on the negative effects of video games or violent/pornographic imagery, tellingly, these perceived threats were raised proactively in some posts. Responding to another poster's remark that he had managed to raise two children responsible enough not to indulge in under-aged sex, a commentator on the *Daily Telegraph's* Bedales expulsion story using the *nom-de-plume* 'dissavowed' (*sic*) argued that this would only have been possible if they were brought up before the age of 'extreme hardcore porn, in the school playground, that is freely accessible from just about every mobile phone these days'. Similarly, 'snidely, London' suggested that 'Sky tv and Hollywood constantly shoving violence porn in our childrens [*sic*] faces' might have something to do with the rise in classroom violence that had prompted the Government's rethink on the 'no touching' ban. A *Daily Mail* poster using the pseudonym 'm.e., wales' [*sic*] mused rhetorically that 'surely these video games contribute to fuelling the aggression shown by children', while even television shows specifically aimed at the young failed to escape criticism as potential inspirations for juvenile misbehaviour, with 'Rusty, Surrey' challenging fellow readers to 'have a look at children's TV – that'll show why the little brats behave so badly'.

Corrupting effects of rampant consumerism and advertising

Concern about the omnipresence of advertisements – and the materialistic values they project – emerged from both groups, albeit in different forms. The special needs worker couched her distaste in 'scarier world' terms by describing 'the whole consumerist culture' as a 'threat' that was 'pervasive and ... degenerate'. Nodding agreement, the midwife criticized her eldest son's 'frivolous' spending habits, predicting 'he's going to turn 18, get a load of credit cards, max them all out and be in debt quite quickly'. Whereas 'in my day you made a packed lunch for yourself and *then* you went out', her son would say, 'oh I'm going to get a Subway, I'm going to get a McDonald's' and spend 'more money, more money all the time for such throwaway things'. The working-class mothers were equally critical of shallow consumerism – though it took the stimulus of being asked to reflect on the riots for them to vent these feelings. For these financially straitened parents – all but one of whom were either unwaged single mothers or living in households where neither partner worked – criticisms were often personalized and couched in terms of peer pressure that they and their children felt to buy unaffordable designer labels. Yet it took the only mother from a waged household – the teaching assistant – to crystallize the consensus, by complaining, 'if they [the Government] still drop our money and put things on hold, how are we still going to afford … our kids', who 'aren't disappearing when they reach eight' but 'getting more expensive' and demanding 'Adidas trainers, tracksuits'. There was strong agreement that these pressures had intensified over time, with the ex-shop-worker observing that, in the six years separating her arrival at secondary school from her younger brother's, a 'strict school uniform' policy had been supplanted by a *laissez-faire* culture in which 'you were allowed to wear your Adidas jacket or your Reebok coat and … Nike trainers'. It was perhaps unsurprising that acquisitive aspects of the rioting surfaced more visibly in captions written by these mothers than those from the middle-class group. In a lengthy description of the photo of looters plundering a shop, the volunteer café worker wrote:

> 2 young kids under the age of 18 entering through a shop window to get their label items to either keep for themselves or to sale [sic] on to other people.

But the punchiest response came from the shy contributor, who explained that her caption reflected the bullying her son endured for being unable to afford 'one of those new tracky jackets':

> Labels cause chaos as theifs [*sic*] steal.

A further criticism of advertising was sparked by the caption-writing exercise focusing on the article about the government initiative to protect juveniles from explicit images – which also referred to concerns around the promotion of sexualized children's clothing. Harking back to both the discussion of adult media content and her own criticism of irresponsible parents, the teaching assistant complained of 'porn everywhere … porn on buses', before returning to her familiar refrain that 'a lot of it is down to parents' and arguing, 'you don't take your little girl shopping and go, "you get what you want": you *choose* what your daughter wears'. Again, similar sentiments emerged from several discussion posts, with a teacher using the pen name 'Me, Here' responding to the '"no touching" ban' story with a complaint about the difficulty of 'controlling unruly kids who have been either never told no or spoilt with material posessions [sic] that they are unable to handle classroom rules without a present of an xbox at the end of the day'. Meanwhile, the aforementioned 'Mrs B, Great Britain' explicitly related her other bugbears – including 'volatile households', 'babies easy to have on welfare', 'TV and computer games used as babysitters' and 'immature parenting' – to our worsening 'materialistic society'.

Working-class versus middle-class: differences of opinion

While there was overall agreement between working-class and middle-class groups about the nature of perceived threats to children and the potentially deleterious effects of certain changes in society (notably runaway consumerism and technological advances), certain concerns were peculiar to each cohort. Working-class worries were generally more grounded in the hard reality of personal experience than those of middle-class participants – which might account for the different *emphases* already highlighted, such as their greater concern about bullying and antisocial behaviour. Another example was the stress placed by working-class parents on the peer pressure that they and their children faced in relation to advertising. While middle-class mothers raised consumerism as a general issue – albeit a socially corrosive one – for working-class mums it was a source of day-to-day material anxieties. When one mentioned the fact that school uniform offered a relief from her children's demands for designer labels, a lengthy exchange ensued about the punitive cost of blazers. The nearest middle-class mums got to replicating this point was a brief exchange about parents who insisted on 'two holidays a year' (writer) or paying for independent schooling (special needs worker). As the latter put it, 'there's pressure on parents to work even … if they don't need to – to consume', when they should be 'spending time with the children'. By contrast, working-class mothers projected consumerist pressures onto themselves (and their lean circumstances) – complaining about the difficulties of fending off requests for the latest MP3 player or mobile phone. 'I think all kids have got a phone – all three of my older ones have got phones', reflected the teaching assistant, in a typical illustration of the peer pressures their children faced.

While mobile phone ownership *per se* was viewed as a positive thing by these mums – principally in enabling them to track their children's movements – for middle-class parents it was a cause of stress. A particular concern raised by these mothers – all juggling parenthood with demanding jobs – was what the nurse and special needs worker both described as the 'incessant' barrage of text messages and emails, and the intrusive impact these had on family life. '*Why* are we more busy?' asked the latter rhetorically, musing, 'I think it comes back to technology', as 'in the past you would have spoken to your friend on the phone ... but now you send emails [and] get texts'. The nurse expressed frustration that there was always 'something else to do' – prompting the writer to ridicule a fellow scribe who had installed a computer program which asked her each morning 'how much freedom' she wanted to write unimpeded, before blocking incoming emails for the duration of her writing session. 'It's so pathetic', she reflected, 'the ... *language*: "I want four hours of freedom. Freedom from *myself*: freedom from my own desire to go and check my emails"'. For these *time-poor* women, then, interruptions from the outside world during precious family time were sources of stress – unwelcome reminders of the occupational commitments other studies have identified as causes of guilt and anxiety among working mothers (Social Issues Research Centre, 2011). By contrast, more *money-poor* working-class mums viewed mobiles and (as we will see) social networking tools like Facebook as liberating: vital sources of *interaction* with the same outside world.

In terms of other perceived threats, a marked contrast between the two groups was the emphasis that some working-class mothers placed on dangers inherent in mundane domestic objects. Again, given the relatively long hours spent by these (largely unemployed) mums at home, this is perhaps unsurprising. One lengthy exchange between the nursery worker and another parent was sparked by the former's recollection of a news story about a girl stabbing herself with a butter knife while making sandwiches. This anecdote was one of several which pointed towards some level of media effect, as the former explicitly attributed the fact 'my boy ... knows he does not touch anything in that kitchen' to 'this story in the paper' – adding that she 'would never have thought of a kid of that age trying to make himself a sandwich' otherwise. The other mother recalled a report about a child getting trapped in some blinds, and admitted to reinstalling a baby gate across the doorway to her kitchen – which she had labelled 'the dangerous area' – after finding her four-year-old daughter standing over her cooker with the gas switched on. Other parents expressed fears about hazards ranging from safety razors and toasters to cleaning fluids – the nursery worker recounting how her friend's son once drank a cup of white spirit after his uncle handed it to him, mistaking it for milk. These wildly varying concerns about household safety – significantly, all *inanimate* threats present *within*, rather than outside, the family home – are redolent of the 'bads' identified by Beck (1986) as increasing causes of late-modern risk anxieties or the (often humdrum) sites of parental policing grouped by Critcher (2003) and Hier (2008) under the heading 'moral regulation' issues. Taken together, these concerns hinted at a generalized, ill-defined unease that one might easily equate with the permanent latter-day 'amoral' panics envisaged by Waiton (2008) and the increasingly diffuse categories of danger highlighted in Beck's (1986) concept of the 'risk society' and Bauman's (2000) of 'liquid modernity' – all redolent of the 'scarier world' paradigm that emerged consistently from all strands of the audience research.

One other concern raised specifically in middle-class discussions was the danger of children being introduced to illegal drugs and alcohol. As with the plentiful anecdotes from working-class mums about bullying and teenage violence, the source of this fear was personal experience – with the midwife fretting about the fact her son 'dabbles in smoking pot and stuff with his friends and I'm sure that ... plenty of them go further than that'. Revealingly, mention of drugs sparked a lively discussion about the 'downside' of moves towards greater social 'inclusivity' in state schools (something all participants agreed was a good thing), as it prompted the hostel worker to suggest threats like 'drugs, girls getting pregnant, violence, violence in the home' now felt 'closer' to middle-class families than they would have done in previous generations – a further expression of the dominant 'scarier world' paradigm:

Inclusivity ... changes the way we view ourselves and ... risk. In the past, I think, it was 'us and them'. *Them* were the ones who ... fucked up, basically. *We* were okay ... I think if you were of a certain class you didn't worry as much because you thought that happens to 'them' – not me. Whereas now ... we're all kind of in the same boat, so we're far more likely to ... get exposed.

Agenda-setting, personal influence and Chinese whispers in the social media age

As we have seen, in voicing their concerns about risk and threats both sets of focus group participants alluded to a melange of influences on their perceptions – from first-hand/vicarious experiences to news reports. When, early in their first meetings, they were explicitly asked where their anxieties stemmed from (*besides* their own experiences), the working-class and middle-class parents respectively gave the following one-word answers: 'news' and 'media'. Each reply was greeted with murmurs of agreement and nodding heads from fellow participants – making it difficult to dismiss as a 'default' response (Hartmann, 1979). Of all fears attributed (directly or indirectly) to the news media, none was raised more frequently than child molestation/abduction. And the impromptu mentions of cases ranging from the Moors murders to the McCann disappearance testify to high levels of sensitization to stories that (from these adults' perspectives) had originated in the news. More significantly, some mothers insisted that particular reports had had a tangible effect on both their anxieties and *parenting practices* – a clear testament to the idea that, even if we are living through an age of 'selective exposure', as some recent studies suggest (e.g. Bennett & Iyengar, 2008; Iyengar & Hahn, 2009), in the minds of audience members themselves media discourse still has the power to exert a strong agenda-setting influence. Indeed, it is hard to overstate this point: people might well have an increasing tendency to expose themselves to a limited range of news media (BBC TV news, the *Argus*, the *Sun* and *Daily Mirror* being the favoured outlets of the working-class mothers; Radio 4 and the *Guardian* of the middle-class ones), and much of their news consumption might be *indirect*, having first been mediated and passed on via social networking sites. Nevertheless, to deny that these reports, and the dialogues they generate, are in some small way telling them 'what to think about' (McCombs & Shaw, 1972, p. 13) would be to ignore the overwhelming impression to emerge from both focus group discussions and the results of the news-game exercises.

Of course, it is a significant step beyond this to suggest that media effects not only have the power to shape agendas – in this case, maternal (and grandmotherly) concerns about extra-familial threats to juveniles – but to influence *behaviours*. Nonetheless, if the anecdotal evidence emerging from these focus groups can be treated as honest and accurate, then news narratives (however heavily processed *after the event*) do, indeed, appear to be affecting parenting practices – and not solely by reinforcing *existing* ones. Besides the scattered claims by working-class mums that stories had moderated their domestic safety routines around breadknives and suchlike, some of the (generally less risk-averse) middle-class mothers said the McCann case had moved them to change their behaviour more profoundly (even if only temporarily). While working-class mums united in condemning Madeleine's parents for leaving their children alone in bed the night she vanished, middle-class parents had a more live-and-let-live attitude – with the writer admitting that, prior to reading about this story, she and her partner also 'used to leave our kids when they were sleeping ... to go next door to a restaurant'. However, she claimed she 'did notice my behaviour changing in direct relation to that story ... I think our practice did change', though 'probably only ... for a certain amount of time'. The ex-teacher felt her behaviour had been similarly influenced – albeit more by parenting literature than conventional media, to which she claimed to give herself 'limited exposure'. Further evidence of strong (short-term) emotional and behavioural reactions emerged when these mothers were reassembled to discuss the abduction of April Jones, the subject of Chapter 5.

Undeniably, though, the most oft-cited influence on both groups of mothers was not so much direct media exposure but what might be described as news-generated rumour or (to quote the nursery worker) 'Chinese whispers': the main conduit being Facebook. Significantly, when parents were asked to complete questionnaires detailing the media outlets they most frequently accessed (as listed above), the social networking site was cited by several mothers, across both groups, as their main source of stories. While most said they received some news from television (primarily BBC1), and several that they/their partners regularly bought national newspapers, the most commonly cited outlets were the (free) online version of their local paper, the *Argus*, and Facebook. That the latter is not in itself a news site – but a forum within which media reports are, at best, disseminated by sharing hyperlinks and clips and, at worst, distorted and/or exaggerated via the virtual rumour-mill – adds ballast to previous suggestions that many people are not so much *directly* influenced by news narratives as indirectly, via *other people's representations* (and interpretations) of those stories. It is hard to see this as anything other than a latter-day manifestation of the 'two-step' or (given the viral nature of so much of today's social mediation) 'multistep flow' of communication identified more than 70 years ago by Paul Lazarsfeld and colleagues (Lazarsfeld, Berelson, & Gaudet, 1944; Roper, Katz, & Lazarsfeld, 1955). What emerged consistently from both sets of focus groups was that, whether they first encountered a story in the media *themselves* or by picking it up *vicariously* through gossip spread by trusted 'opinion leaders' in their social networks (ibid.), both mothers' and grandmothers' consumption of news was significant. Crucially, however, this consumption was subject to an awful lot of processing – perhaps more so, given its multifarious forms, than in the pre-digital age that formed the locus for Lazarsfeld et al.'s ground-breaking insights into the power of 'personal influence' (ibid.). It was through this system of processing – mediated today as much by Facebook and other social networking sites as the classic watercooler/school-gate conversations of old – that these adults arrived at both their *understandings* of news narratives and their *responses* to them. If these narratives could be said to have influenced their attitudes towards the perils of parenthood and childhood, then – as they surely could – these effects owed as much, if not more, to the processing as the processed.

The most powerful demonstration of the influence of Chinese whispers related to a news story originating in the *Argus* – which provoked a lengthy, often critically reflective, discussion among working-class mothers about the heightened concern they felt when stranger-danger reports occurred in their area, compared to geographically distant ones like Praia da Luz (scene of the McCann disappearance). The first reference to the *Argus* story arose when the parent who initially raised concerns about 'the people' said she had seen a 'black car' parked outside her home a few days earlier. Intriguingly, the previous summer had witnessed a flurry of local media publicity about sightings of a mysterious black car in the vicinity of schools across Sussex, including in Brighton and Hove, and head teachers throughout the city had sent letters to parents alerting them, as well as verbally reminding their pupils about stranger-danger. The *Argus* had devoted several news items, at least one lengthy background feature and considerable space on its letters page and discussion threads to these sightings, and several instances in which children had reportedly been approached by a man driving a black car along their routes to school. These reports – analysed in Chapter 4, in the context of testimony from one journalist involved in writing them – were also vividly recalled by middle-class children, with the nurse's daughter remembering this clear instruction from her mother:

My mummy said, 'never get into a black car with a stranger'.

Interestingly, the parental instruction alluded to here – an indicator, if only anecdotally, of a level of *behavioural* response from families to the perceived abduction threat – was mirrored by some comments to be found on the *Argus* discussion threads. In one flappy, sparsely punctuated post, 'monique56' lamented that the 'scary' situation was 'only gonna get worse now its school holidays, so now i cant let my kids play out which means the KIDS suffer cos of some sick pervert', while 'Brightondad' echoed her sentiments, stating he would now 'have to tell' his daughter she could no longer 'go round the shops for me … unless shes with a adult'. Yet, despite clearly being unnerved by these tales, focus group members demonstrated a keen sense of self-reflexivity about their tendency to be easily panicked by exaggerated peer-to-peer retellings of unproven incidents. While working-class mothers, in particular, projected blame for fostering panics onto *other* adults (an echo of their recurring criticisms of more irresponsible parents), the irritation they displayed towards this panicking was framed, paradoxically, as further justification for protecting their own children – in this case, from being unnecessarily frightened. A lengthy exchange between nursery worker and teaching assistant began with the former condemning 'these parents' and their children for 'mouthing off' about 'this man … taking them' and the latter describing the viral nature of rumour-mongering in precisely those terms: as being 'like a bug'. The nursery worker recalled 'about three different dads that drive black cars', who would pick up their kids and 'because it's a bloke pulling up in a black car' it was 'all going round, "oh, it's a black car, it's a black car, it's *that* car" … like Chinese whispers … Every time a black car parked outside the school, everyone panicked'. This sense that children are often needlessly spooked by tales of prowling bogeymen was echoed by one middle-class schoolgirl. The eldest daughter of separated parents, she described how, two years earlier, she had been scared by classmates telling her 'there's a kidnapper at Queen's Park' where 'we all go down' to 'have a play'. Her fear about lurking menaces in familiar places was stoked, she said, by a mobile phone text message her mother had received from the school warning parents to 'please be aware we've had a notice about a guy in black hanging around the toilets'. Tellingly, the nurse's daughter had separately mentioned 'a kidnapper in black' at a previous point in the meeting. And what was the primary locus for such alarmist gossip-mongering besides playground and school-gates? When asked, the mothers once again united in singling out social media: specifically, Facebook.

One clear behavioural response to fears about abduction or abuse while playing out or walking to or from school was the rudimentary mobile phone tagging system several working-class mothers admitted using to monitor their movements outside the home. Most of these mums said they issued their children with phones so they could easily contact them, and set up reciprocal ring-round systems with other parents designed to keep tabs on each other's kids, rather like a makeshift Neighbourhood Watch cascade scheme. Even when older children were allowed ostensibly unsupervised outdoor activity, arm's-length supervision was still routinely used to ensure they did not stray too far – with youngsters ordered to take their phones everywhere, and vigilant neighbours exchanging text messages if they spied one another's kids where they were not meant to be. Evidence of this rudimentary tagging system also emerged from children, with all but one working-class pupil confirming that a condition of being permitted to play out was that they took mobiles with them. The middle-class nurse's daughter, meanwhile, revealed she would be 'allowed to go to town on my own' only 'when I get a phone' in 'year six' (aged 11). Typical justification for this approach came from the married working-class mother-of-four, who, despite allowing her children to walk to and from school alone from seven, confessed to phoning friends if her 11-year-old daughter was late home, as she liked 'to know where they are and who they're with'. 'If the other child has got home and she hasn't, then what's happened from their house to mine?' she added.

However powerful the circumstantial evidence for (direct or indirect) media agenda-setting effects that emerged from these discussions, though, of overriding significance was the sense that the tales that affected individuals' risk perceptions were those chiming with their own *experiences*. Whether it was the writer speaking of her (temporary) change of habits in relation to leaving her children at home unsupervised following the McCann case or the lone parent bringing up three young children in a tower block, who confessed that news 'frightens the life out of me' – name-checking recent reports about predatory nursery workers and people being murdered in their beds – clear evidence emerged that, when alarming news narratives tapped into their personal 'schema' (Graber, 1984), framing effects could be significant. That the dominant schema shaping these mothers' processing of stories about children should be so negative – i.e. clouded by a belief that their offspring were inhabiting a scarier world than the one they recalled from their own childhoods – raises the inescapable question of how and why such an ominous view of their social environment had come about.

The *roots* of 'scarier world' thinking: some working hypotheses

As the above analysis demonstrates, the issues raised during discussions were not only shaped by interpersonal processing, Chinese whispers and news discourse, but also individuals' socioeconomic circumstances and wider cultural, and neighbourhood, environment(s). More specifically, the parental responses demonstrated evidence of a decline in social trust, particularly among single mothers and/or those living in the relatively high-crime working-class area. They also testified to the increasing pressures these mothers felt to multitask, by juggling school runs and mealtimes with job-hunting, training and/or working life – trends noted in several studies mentioned previously (for example, Hall, 1999; OECD, 2001; Harper, 2001; Li, Pickles, & Savage, 2005; *European Values Study Group and World Values Survey Association*, 2006; Llakes, 2011; Social Issues Research Centre, 2011). It appeared to be the cumulative effect of these pressures, combined with the creeping sense that it had become harder than ever to trust one's peers, which best explained why *certain* news stories/rumours sparked greater concern than others. In essence, these narratives tapped into deep-seated anxieties related to the very position of parents (especially mothers) in late-modern Britain.

The suggestion that fears revolving around juvenile vulnerability should provide such a peculiarly salient locus for wider (parental) anxieties *at this time* – for *both* sets of parents – reflects the findings of previous studies that have identified the currency of this issue in the context of similarly pressurized socioeconomic drivers. As we saw in Chapter 1, Best located his 1990 analysis of America's 1980s 'missing children' panic against a backdrop of growing financial insecurity spawned by economic instability in the 1970s and toughening welfare regimes in the USA – an issue fundamental to the personal circumstances of all working-class mothers interviewed for this study at a time when Britain's government was introducing swingeing cuts and stricter qualifying conditions for working-age benefits. Meanwhile, De Young (1998) identified the sea change in mothers going out to work in the early 1980s as a stimulus for the 'Satanic day-care' panic that took hold in America at around the same time – another driver that can be seen as highly pertinent to the multitasking pressures faced by those interviewed for this study. In the next chapter, we will develop our analysis of the juvenile panic discourse that emerged from focus groups and discussion threads to examine the question of how the sinister and disquieting narratives that fuel it come to be constructed in the first place.

4
Commercializing Distrust: Framing Juveniles in the News

As the previous chapter demonstrates, popular perceptions of (and attitudes towards) children are intrinsically related to their portrayals in the news. Time and again, baleful media stories about abuse, abduction, youth antisocial behaviour, fatal road crashes and even accidents in domestic settings were raised by focus group participants as reference-points for their decisions about how to safeguard their children – including from other people's. Meanwhile, the minority of audience members who took time to post direct responses to online newspaper articles projecting these twin frames of juvenile 'victim' and 'threat' overwhelmingly echoed this simmering sense of parental panic. Like focus group parents writing their captions, they often directly aped tropes and phraseology routinely reproduced in the press. But identifying an apparent correlation – if not quite a causal connection – between how juveniles are conceived by the public on the one hand and newspapers on the other only gets us so far in our mission to explain how contemporary childhood has come to be constructed as a social problem. Just *how* 'dominant' (Hall, 1980) is the media's day-to-day problematization of juveniles as objects (and, occasionally, agents) of peril, when measured against the many and varied other ways in which they are represented on the page? Moreover, assuming these distorted narratives *do* prevail, how – and, crucially, why – have newspapers come to portray children so negatively? And, in an age of user-generated content and social media, to what extent are citizens themselves responsible for contributing to and perpetuating these constructions – rather than simply consuming and/or reacting to them? This chapter argues that the key to disentangling how and why a juvenile panic discourse asserts such a grip on both press and public lies in the *interplay between the two*. In crude terms, there has come to be a meeting of minds between the uses and gratifications (Katz et al., 1973) of a public increasingly ill at ease with itself – namely an interest (perhaps morbid) in stories that tap into personal anxieties about misplaced trust and insecurity – and those of a late-modern news media motivated less by any genuine public-interest ethos than an overriding preoccupation with generating profit, in this case by pursuing alarmist editorial to gain readers (and sell advertising). In setting out this case, we begin by examining the extent to which a juvenile panic discourse dominates the way children are represented in the British press, before attempting to unravel the complexities of how – and why – the frames used to project it are (repeatedly) constructed.

Defining the juvenile narrative(s): how texts were analysed

Before presenting the findings of our textual analysis, it is important to explain how the method was applied. Given this study's emphasis on investigating the *framing* of newspaper (and public) discourse, a hybrid analytical approach was judged most suitable: one that was quantitative in that it involved counting the number of articles portraying juveniles in particular ways, but qualitative in allowing scope to make inferences about the *underlying agendas* of individual pieces, based on close interpretation of the language, images and other packaging devices used to frame them. Inspiration was drawn from Curran's appeal for an end to the 'academic apartheid' (1976, p. 12) which applies doctrinaire distinctions between quantitative and qualitative methods for analysing texts when the two approaches might be more constructively applied together. In the end, the study drew heavily on frame analysis: in particular, Gitlin's (1980, p. 6) focus on discerning the 'principles of selection, emphasis and presentation' underpinning a text's construction and Entman's (1993, p. 53) application of the verb 'frame' to describe the tendency to 'select some aspect of a perceived reality and make them more salient in a communicating text, in such a way as to *promote* a particular problem definition, causal interpretation, moral evaluation, and/or treatment for the item described'. This latter definition is especially relevant to the business of drawing out meaning from news articles that problematize children.

But which *elements* of each article should be analysed – and in print or electronically, using a labour-saving search tool like LexisNexis? To begin with the latter point, as Deacon recently argued (2007, p. 10), relying exclusively on electronic databases skews researchers' focus solely towards the 'linguistic' framing of articles, to the exclusion of the 'visual dimension of news'. While aspects of framing, like the presence/

nature of accompanying photographs, the relative size of articles and their positioning on the printed page are difficult to quantify scientifically (Bell & Garrett, 1998), they act as 'key mechanisms by which news-makers dramatize reports, assist readers' comprehension, corroborate the "truth" of a reported event and, sometimes, qualify, or even subvert, the linguistic substance of a related news item' (Deacon, 2007, p. 10). Indeed, the ability of pictures to *consolidate* agendas reflected in accompanying texts is well documented – not least by Kitzinger, who was told by focus group participants that an image she showed them of an anonymous crowd symbolizing the 'invisibility' of AIDS carriers to help them write reports about this subject was '*determining* the script' (Kitzinger, 1993, p. 281). Unlike, say, the subscription-based Guardian and Observer Digital Archive, LexisNexis also offers no way of reading entire editions of newspapers from cover to cover – making it difficult to gain a tangible sense of how children may have been represented *in the round* in a single paper on a given date. For these reasons, physical newspapers were analysed – if only to facilitate impressionistic observations about the ways in which, beyond the *overall wording* of texts, elements like 'headlines, story structures' and 'graphical arrangements' (van Dijk, 1998, p. 31) were mobilized in framing. Another factor that counted against the use of electronic tools was the danger of throwing up 'false positives' (e.g. confusing the *act* of rape with the *plant*) and 'false negatives' (Soothill & Grover, 1997), with over-specific search terms misleadingly excluding relevant articles.

In the end, the core framing devices analysed were as follows: type of article/section of paper; page number (and whether an article appeared on a facing or non-facing page); headline wording; phrasing of opening sentence/paragraph (intro); use of subjective language in the body of the article; and the journalist's choice of sources. Perhaps the hardest of these to evaluate through textual analysis alone was source selection. The importance of analysing the role that claims-makers (particularly elite sources) play in framing news narratives is well documented (Tuchman, 1972; Chibnall, 1977 and 1981; Gans, 1979; Fishman, 1980; Bantz, 1985; Schlesinger, 1987), but to make judgments about such matters one first has to wrestle with the difficulty of *identifying* which sources have been used and which omitted. It is easy enough to note the occurrence of quotes explicitly attributed to named individuals or organizations – the council announcing a crackdown on antisocial behaviour or the judge condemning a 'sex pest' as he sends him to prison – and the relative prominence of one claims-maker's view over another's. But the occurrence of anonymous comments which could easily have emanated from any number of sources muddies the waters, and there is also the question of where incidental material presented as factual in articles has originated – though no source is explicitly credited. While it proved possible to ask some reporters interviewed where they had obtained their information, and how they *habitually* sourced material, it was impractical to ask the same of every journalist whose writing was analysed. As a result, this aspect of analysis remained unavoidably inferential.

The decision to place a heavy emphasis on intro wording was based the importance attached to this narrative element by journalists and their trainers as a device to 'draw the reader into' an article (Keeble, 2006, p. 111), communicate its overall news-line (frame) and outline its 'who, what, where, when, why, how' elements. Headlines, meanwhile, were analysed because of abundant research evidence suggesting that they can be highly influential in shaping audiences' responses to news discourse (e.g. Philo, 1996; McCombs, 2004). But, while it was relatively easy to quantify the lexical components of headlines and intros, given their comparative brevity, doing so for entire articles was problematic. For this reason, we focused on particular terminology and turns of phrase indicative of attempts to frame them in emotive or otherwise subjective ways (Bednarek, 2006; Richardson, 2008), and other obvious 'semantic relations' or 'collocations, assumptions' and 'grammatical features' (Fairclough, 2003, p. 133) apparently used to promote a particular 'vision' of the world (ibid., p. 130). Inspiration was drawn from earlier (moral) panic researchers, notably Cohen (1972), Hall et al. (1978) and Golding and Middleton (1982), and the 'discourse analytical approach to content analysis' favoured by van Dijk (2000, p. 14) to infer latent as well as manifest textual meanings. The heaviest debt, though, was to the multidimensional mode of textual analysis advocated by Philo, in arguing for 'a method which analyses processes of production, content, reception and circulation of social meaning simultaneously' (2007, p. 175). His critique of the limitations of 'text-based' methods used by van Dijk, Fairclough and others (ibid., p. 191) for explaining the 'origins of competing discourses', the impact on articles 'of external factors such as professional media practice', let alone 'what the text actually means to different parts of the audience' (ibid., p. 175), are concerns central to the triangulated methodology applied here.

Having determined which *elements* of articles to analyse, the next task was to identify a set of *categories* into which they could be divided. To elicit as objective an impression as possible of how children are portrayed in British newspapers, the decision was taken to analyse not only 'victim' and 'threat' stories but *all* articles about juveniles, irrespective of their angles/focus. Moreover, to categorize this coverage in a way that reflected the actual range of frames used to portray children – as opposed to forcing the sample to fit 'predetermined categories' (Beardsworth, 1980, p. 375) – a 'data-driven' approach was adopted (Pfeil & Zaphiris, 2010, p. 8), requiring the author first to immerse himself in the texts to develop the most suitable headings, based on patterns that emerged from them. Having begun with this method of 'inductive category development' (Mayring, 2000, p. 3), he used 'deductive category application' (ibid., p. 4) to allocate each article to one of six categories: 'child victim', 'child threat', 'child survivor', 'celebrity children', 'child hero/achiever' and 'other articles about children'. The 'child hero/achiever' category was chosen to reflect various articles encountered about, for example, children winning prizes and passing exams, while pieces about overcoming illness or other forms of bravery were bracketed under 'child survivor'. A more diverse (though less numerous) collection of pieces about everything from cute babies to breakthroughs in paediatric medical care was analysed under the 'other' heading. Although the divisions between these categories may seem self-evident, allotting articles to them sometimes proved problematic. For example, a story about children being physically assaulted by other juveniles arguably slots into two categories – 'victim' and 'threat' – and the occurrence of such pieces meant that, to avoid double-counting, a seventh category had to be introduced: 'hybrid'. However, some stories remained stubbornly hard to pigeonhole: should a report about new medical research into cot death prevention be listed as an 'other' article about children or one problematizing (young) juveniles as vulnerable, and therefore as 'victims'? Such dilemmas were addressed on a case-by-case basis, with the balance of emphasis in each individual article weighed up before they were categorized. Final categories, then, and the precise wording of titles applied to each, could only be refined once the author had spent an initial period 'immersing' himself in his sample material, to 'get a general "feel" for its content and structure' (Hansen et al., 1998, p. 107). Even then, it was necessary to carry out a limited recoding exercise to ensure that the initial categorizations had been accurate. Just over one in ten articles were reanalysed for this purpose – producing a match of nearly 94 per cent. Significantly, in most categories the match was 100 per cent: the only reason for the slight disparity in coding the second time round was that a handful of pieces (three out of 47) were placed under the 'victim' heading, rather than the 'survivor' one (as they had been originally). As we shall see, the distinction between some stories listed under these two headings is moot, given that, by their nature, 'survivor' stories position juveniles as having either *survived* victimhood or narrowly *escaped* it. This was the case for these particular articles (all focusing on a girl coming to terms with her father's death in Iraq).

The decision to analyse *every* child-related article, rather than just those slotting neatly into 'victim' and 'threat' categories, can only take us so far in our quest to establish how dominant the juvenile panic discourse is in contemporary newspaper representations of children. The other question is how prevalent such narrative concerns are across the *spectrum* of the press: in broadsheets as well as tabloids; both liberal and conservative papers. To guard against the risk of choosing papers arbitrarily, or with some form of (unintentional) in-built bias (e.g. 'left wing' or 'right wing'), the decision was taken to sample every national title on the chosen dates, with four exceptions: the *Financial Times* (*FT*), *i*, *Metro* and *Morning Star*. The *FT* was excluded on the basis that it is a more specialist title whose primary focus is economic news, meaning that its breadth of coverage of other issues, including ones concerning children, was likely to be unrepresentative of general mainstream discourse. The *i* was omitted because it was, at the time, a simplified version of the *Independent* and most of its content appeared simultaneously in that title. The *Metro* and *Morning Star* were both left out principally on grounds of their limited geographical distributions: the first could only be accessed in and around metropolitan centres; the second was only sold in a limited number of retail outlets, predominantly in urban centres. One other title that can lay some claim to national status, on the basis of its widely recognized agenda-setting influence, was also excluded. This was London's *Evening Standard* – which, however influential, is only distributed in and around the capital. In the end, the national dailies analysed were as follows: the *Guardian, Independent, Daily Telegraph, Times, Daily Mail, Daily Express, Sun, Daily Mirror* and *Daily Star*. On the single Sunday on which newspapers were sampled (31 July), all nine nationals then published were read: the *Observer, Independent on Sunday, Sunday Telegraph, Sunday Times, Mail on Sunday, Sunday Express, Sunday Mirror, Daily Star Sunday* and *People*. In addition, to go some small way towards testing the idea that the posited discourse around children was not confined solely to *national* papers, the decision was taken to include a single local title: the Brighton *Argus*. A daily paper with a print circulation below 14,000 (Gilley, 2015), this was chosen partly because of its status as a typical local – its owner being Britain's biggest local newspaper group, Newsquest – but also on the grounds that it was the main press presence in the city where focus groups were held, and, as a result, its coverage frequently surfaced in discussions. There was one additional consideration: given the nature of the narratives examined, it was felt that selecting this paper might offer the possibility of an illuminating comparison with its earlier incarnation as a paper of record during the clashes between Mods and Rockers that provided raw material for Cohen's seminal 1972 study of a youth panic.

Having determined one aspect of the overall sample – which publications to examine – the next dilemma involved deciding which dates to sample. As the aim was to investigate whether panicky narratives dominated *consistently*, rather than being subject to fluctuations depending on, say, which day of the week/time of the month a paper was published, the decision was taken to sample issues every fifth day throughout July 2011, beginning on the first. In following this tried-and-tested approach (Troyna, 1982), the author settled on five-day intervals, as this was felt to provide a substantial quantity of data without being overwhelming, which it might have been had he sampled daily or every other day. The length of month chosen (31 days) had the added virtue of enabling him to sample issues published on each day of the week, including a Sunday, while avoiding the pitfalls of, say, an 'every seventh day' method, which would have left him with only four editions of each paper, all from the same day of the week – presenting an intrinsically distorted picture (Hansen et al., 1998, p. 104). Although July might be an atypical month in some respects – the summer is conventionally labelled the 'silly season (ibid., p. 103), due to the absence of parliamentary proceedings/major political events and the customary press focus on lighter topics like the weather – it was judged suitable for several reasons. Firstly, the object of the analysis was not to investigate whether panicky narratives about children – or, indeed, narratives about children *generally* – outnumbered those about any other subject (or subjects), but whether, out of all editorial relating to juveniles, articles positioning them as either or both 'victims' or 'threats' predominated. In this respect, *any* month would arguably have produced an appropriate pool from which to sample articles, as it was the comparative emphases of one juvenile-related story versus another – as opposed to the balance of stories about children and those about everything else – that were of primary interest. In the event, July 2011 turned out to be far from a typical 'silly' month anyway, with several major national and international stories competing to provide a more-than-usually dramatic backdrop to the summer news agenda. These included the rapidly escalating (legal, political and commercial) fallout from allegations of phone hacking at the *News of the World*; the mass shooting of Norwegian Labour Party supporters (including children) by right-wing extremist Anders Breivik; and an unfolding famine in Somalia. If panicky narratives focusing on juveniles succeeded in gaining prominent day-to-day airings against such an atypically eventful summer news backdrop, this would arguably further underscore the sense that they assert a disproportionate hold on UK press discourse.

The victim–threat paradox: deconstructing the juvenile discourse

The overwhelming impression to emerge from the 462 juvenile-related articles sampled – and the 23 discussion threads accompanying pieces framing them as 'victims' and/or 'threats' – is that today's children are beset by challenges and hazards at every turn, from conception to coming-of-age. From health stories warning about the dangers of this diet or that behaviour for pregnant women and unborn babies to cautionary tales about suicides induced by exam stress, cyber-bullying and online grooming, the world that kids inhabit is consistently portrayed as one of intense day-to-day pressure flecked with moments of darker foreboding – echoing the montage of risk anxieties characterizing focus group discussions about late-modern parenting practices. And, significantly, while it might once have been possible to argue that media narratives were primarily constructed by journalists and their sources, the analysis of online newspaper discussion threads conducted alongside that of news texts demonstrated a strong degree of active complicity between 'news-makers' and 'audience members' in not only affirming but *collaboratively constructing* these menacing images of reality. While articles positioning children as vulnerable to external threats proved the most prevalent category, the next most typical underlying narrative, predictably, was that conceiving of juveniles themselves (especially teenage boys) as threatening. Again, the discussion threads accompanying online newspaper reports of this kind were not only littered with condemnatory comments from readers *endorsing* the worldviews presented: often the collusion between journalists and audience members went deeper than this, with contributors posting a mix of straightforward *reactive* responses to stories and personal and vicarious anecdotes supporting, if not strengthening, the newspapers' frames. One key trend to emerge, then, from this analysis of *complete* newspaper narratives – that is, articles penned by journalists *taken together with* discussion threads flowing from them – was that of 'active' audience members (Hall, 1980) as citizen 'claims-makers' (Cohen, 1972). Rather than simply receiving and reacting to news narratives constructed by in-the-know professionals, more engaged readers contributed their own *evidence* to fortify those constructions. This collaborative form of news-making blurred the lines not only between audience member and journalist but also audience member and *source*, as the former offered direct and informed inputs to substantiate and/or build on those of primary claims-makers or 'knowers' (Fishman, 1980) – namely the officials, press officers, eyewitnesses and/or victims quoted in the stories – and the 'secondary definers' (journalists) responsible for writing them (Hall et al., 1978).

None of this is to say that agreement about the nature and emphasis of news narratives among those commenting on them was universal: more intriguing than evidence-based responses *affirming* an article's dominant discourse were the small but significant minority *contesting* the frames that the journalists adopted. Though 206 of these (just over 47 per cent) took the form of straightforward reactive opinions – remarks disputing at least some aspects of the perspectives implicit in articles – the remaining 231 (53 per cent) *backed up* their counter-narratives by alluding to direct or vicarious experiences/expertise enabling them to question authoritatively, or reject outright, the dominant discourse. While 333 evidence-based responses, then, *endorsed* the narratives on which they were commenting (or to which they were contributing) four out of ten (232) offered viewpoints that were at least 'negotiated' (Hall, 1980) – if not downright 'oppositional' (see Figure 4.8). Though few in number, these *counter* claims-makers are important, in that – as with the occasional points of disagreement between fellow focus group participants – they demonstrate the existence of a body of vocal citizens willing to contest otherwise largely hegemonic narratives (in this case, about the vulnerability and/or unruliness of today's children and wider issues of personal trust these social concerns signify). This suggests that newspaper discussion threads – though peopled predominantly by individuals whose views chimed with those of the publications concerned (Iyengar & Hahn, 2009) – still have *potential* to become sites of debate and contest comparable to those that others have identified on social media outlets like Facebook (Gustafsson, 2012), issue-specific forums (Witschge, 2005, 2006) and the wider blogosphere (Macgilchrist, 2012).

Despite these intriguing exceptions, the dominant underlying conceptualization of children to emerge from textual analysis was one positioning them as either or both of 'victim' and 'threat' – or, to quote Valentine (1996a), 'angels and devils'. Altogether, 63 national newspaper editions and six issues of the *Argus* published during July

2011 were sampled. All articles focusing on children (defined as under 18-year-olds) were isolated, before being divided into the seven categories outlined above: 'victims'; 'threats'; 'hybrid' (victim and threat); 'survivors'; 'achievers/heroes'; 'celebrity children'; and 'other articles about children'. A substantial majority (262, or 57 per cent) presented juveniles as vulnerable to external dangers and, though significantly smaller, the next biggest category (46, or one in 10) positioned them as dangerous in themselves. Intriguingly, in addition to 17 hybrid stories straddling *both* these categories – invariably focusing on one child victimizing another – the third biggest group were the 27 (6 per cent) listed under the 'survivor' heading, of which several related to children narrowly escaping serious injury, illness or death through everything from birth defects ('Jigsaw op saves lad', the *Sun*, 16 July; 'iPad baby is the apple of my eye: Tot born at 23 weeks home with mum', *Daily Mirror*, 26 July) to accidents ('Pilot saved our lives', the *Argus*, 1 July). Had these articles been included in the 'victim' category, its dominance of the prevailing discourse would have been even more pronounced. The overall breakdown of articles analysed is detailed in Figure 4.1.

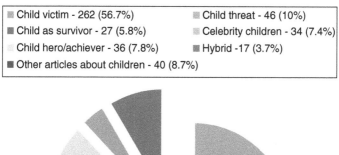

Figure 4.1 Breakdown of articles about children for July 2011

On the biggest 'news day' (6 July) 73 'victim' articles appeared (seven out of ten of the total) with eight (just under 8 per cent) positioning children as threats (see Figure 4.2). Breakdowns of articles for the newspapers featuring the most and fewest stories about juveniles – the *Sun* and the *Guardian* respectively – as well as the *Argus* can be found in Figures 4.3 to 4.5.

Victim and threat articles were divided into sub-categories, as seen in Figures 4.6 and 4.7.

As illustrated in Figure 4.6, nearly a third of articles positioning children as victims (86 out of 279) focused on paedophile crimes, with a quarter (70) concerning serious/fatal emergencies and/or illnesses. Other forms of attack/abuse, besides those of a sexual nature, accounted for another 8 per cent (22 articles). Of those positioning children as threats, the highest proportion (42.9 per cent, or 27 out of 63) portrayed them as attackers or killers, with nearly one in three (20) focusing on more general issues relating to juvenile aggression or antisocial behaviour (see Figure 4.7). Inclusion of a hybrid category in the overall breakdown of articles made it necessary to incorporate the small minority of

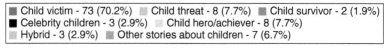

Child victim - 73 (70.2%)   Child threat - 8 (7.7%)   Child survivor - 2 (1.9%)
Celebrity children - 3 (2.9%)   Child hero/achiever - 8 (7.7%)
Hybrid - 3 (2.9%)   Other stories about children - 7 (6.7%)

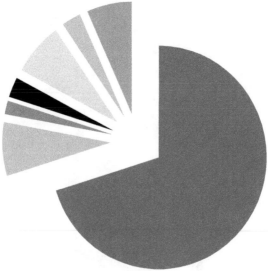

Figure 4.2 Breakdown of articles for 6 July 2011

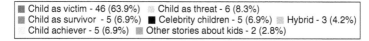

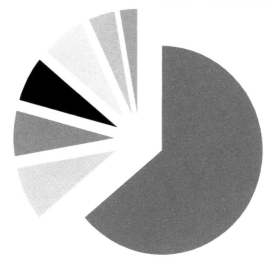

Figure 4.3 Breakdown of articles in the *Sun*

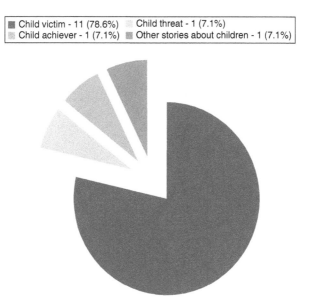

Figure 4.4 Breakdown of articles in the *Guardian*

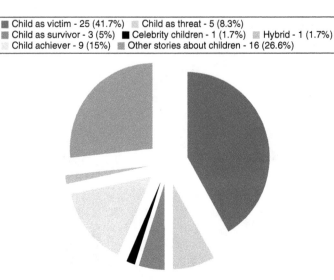

Figure 4.5 Breakdown of articles in the *Argus*

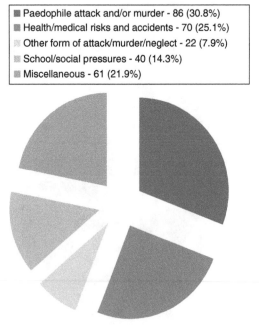

Figure 4.6 Breakdown of threats faced by children

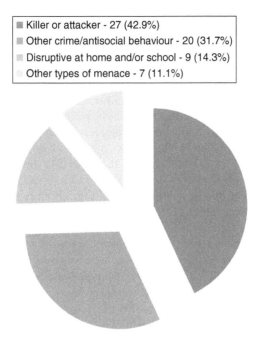

■ Killer or attacker - 27 (42.9%)
▨ Other crime/antisocial behaviour - 20 (31.7%)
▧ Disruptive at home and/or school - 9 (14.3%)
Other types of menace - 7 (11.1%)

Figure 4.7   Breakdown of threats posed by children

pieces in which children were positioned as both victim and threat in Figures 4.6 *and* 4.7.

Framing 'juvenile panic' narratives: some examples

Just as adult focus group participants identified a melange of disparate threats to children's wellbeing, then, textual analysis also spotlighted a bewildering array of risks and dangers. 'Victim' articles covered everything from familiar menaces like paedophiles and errant drivers to a multitude of other horrors spanning the spectrum from banal to bizarre. During the month readers learnt of attackers stabbing children to death ('Mum of stab lad begs: no revenge', the *Sun*, 11 July); hanging them ('Afghan insurgents hang boy, 8', the *Independent*, 26 July); clubbing them with gym equipment ('Dumbbell teacher ban', *Sunday Mirror*, 31 July); sawing the tops of their ears off ('Teen's ear hell', the *Sun*, 11 July); and, through saturation coverage of the Norwegian killings, massacring them ('The victims' stories: young lives cut short by a merciless killer', the *Independent*, 26 July). Safety risks reported included various terrors rooted in nature – ranging from peanut allergies ('Allergic reaction', *Daily Telegraph*, 11 July) to falling branches ('Strike day girl killed by branch: Off school 13-yr-old hit in park', *Daily Mirror*, 1 July); wild animals ('Teenagers mauled in bear attack', the *Independent*, 26 July); and starvation ('First Africa famine in 27 years: Brits help dying kids ... why can't rest of Europe do it too?', the *Sun*, 21 July). But these were nothing compared to the multifarious manmade perils, embracing computers ('Too much internet use "can damage teenagers' brains"', *Daily Mail*, 16 July); goalposts ('Boy "killed" by goalpost', the *People*, 31 July); 'sugary food' ('Blast for toy ploy', *Daily Star*, 1 July); Chinese-style 'floating fireworks' ('Warning over sky lantern craze as family flees roof fire', *Daily Telegraph*, 11 July); and a supposed new craze for 'bling' babies' dummies encrusted with beads and precious stones ('Bling baby dummy risk', *Daily Mirror*, 11 July). On one day alone (6 July), a single paper (the *Sun*) alarmed readers with tales of a nine-day-old infant who died of the common cold-sore virus ('Coldsore baby dies'); pupils left 'terrified' after a 'screaming illegal immigrant ... clung to the bottom of their school coach' ('Asylum shriekers'); a mother prosecuted for abandoning her children in a boiling vehicle ('Car kids' 104 degree F hell'); and a 16-year-old youth who died of electrocution – albeit while stealing copper from a disused power station ('Wire theft boy killed'). This is to say nothing of three paedophile-related stories it reported that day – including the revelation that glamour model Katie Price's great uncle had been unmasked as a convicted child abuser ('Jordan uncle is molester').

Of course, not all threats identified in these articles related directly to British children. Equally, it would be a push to suggest that all, or most, were cases of journalists whipping up hysteria over minor or non-existent risks, or disproportionately exaggerating the seriousness of genuine crimes/terrors (a subject to which we return in Chapter 6). Charges of sensationalism can hardly be levelled at coverage of the Breivik case or Somalian famine. Nonetheless, the fact remains that the overwhelming emphasis of narratives about juveniles selected from the 'news net' (Tuchman, 1978) by UK papers in July 2011 positioned them in victim roles. The sheer dominance of articles framed around fear and foreboding, rather than positive aspects of childhood, was a clear corollary of the discourse of distrust and insecurity articulated so vocally by focus groups – adding weight to the case that today's public sphere conceives of children as vulnerable, helpless and/or unruly, rather than capable, self-reliant and responsible.

Familiar strangers and declining trust in juvenile discourse

A common trope that newspapers consistently used to dramatize their framing of children as susceptible to all-pervading dangers was the menace posed by familiar strangers. The haunting idea that the avuncular façade of a family friend or neighbour might mask malign intentions repeatedly surfaced in sampled papers, personifying the potent concept of threatening familiarity which arose as a key concern of focus group parents. By way of illustration, a 1 July story widely reported in both red-tops and broadsheets – the twin ends of the newspaper spectrum – concerned the life imprisonment of 39-year-old Italian citizen Danilo Restivo for bludgeoning a mother-of-two to death, placing clumps of hair in her hands, and leaving her mutilated body to be found by her teenaged son and daughter. The tone and phrasing of these reports' headlines and intros gave a flavour of the lurid (at times vengeful) wording they would adopt throughout. Under the screaming heading 'Teen's horror', the *Sun*'s intro focused on claims that the murdered woman's daughter, now 19, remained 'haunted' by the image of her mother's corpse. Restivo was described in the intro as a 'hair fetish fiend' and similarly extreme language littered the story (Nash, 2011, p. 11). He was not jailed but 'caged', while the only source quoted besides the daughter was the judge, who in sentencing him decried his 'inhuman depravity'.

Restivo's positioning as demonic and sub-human recurred in several reports – in common with many other articles focusing on violent/ sexual crimes involving children (Meyer, 2007). Though the *Mirror*'s version was more measured in tone, confining itself largely to describing the grisly details of his crimes, rather than inserting its own value-judgments, it used a similarly alarmist approach for the rhetorical headline 'Life for fetish psycho: why was hair fiend free to kill?'. The *Times*, meanwhile, carried a lengthy quote from the judge, condemning the 'cold, depraved, calculated killer' with a 'sadistic, sexual appetite' for leaving two children to find their mother 'butchered on the bathroom floor' (de Bruxelles, 2011, p. 21). Building on the portrayal of this murder as devilish in nature, the *Guardian* – normally more measured, if only marginally, in reporting such matters (Meyer, 2007) – incorporated the judge's 'depraved' and 'inhuman depravity' quotes in its headline and intro respectively, before describing the deed as a 'ritualistic killing' (Morris, 2011, p. 9). Its story, run along the top of a prominent facing page, omitted little emotion – using the words 'fetish' and 'mutilating' in the second paragraph, and telling readers in the fourth that some jury members 'wept' on hearing the daughter's testimony. Again, the phrases 'sadistic, sexual appetite' and 'cold, depraved, calculated killer' were included, as was a quote absent from other accounts, in which the judge emphasized the 'callous and calculating' way Restivo had targeted the mother, whose children 'knew him as a neighbour' – a trope recognizable from numerous high-profile stories positioning juveniles as victims of trusted extra-familial adults (e.g. the Soham murders), and the focus groups' concerns about familiar strangers. Of the four papers carrying the story, the *Guardian* also stressed the daughter's heart-wrenching statement most heavily – placing a long extract in a separate box, headlined 'Why my mother?', and opening with a quote describing how she 'felt as if my heart had been ripped out'. Significantly, all four titles placed the story in highly visible positions on facing pages – used by editors to draw readers towards articles they expect to be of greatest interest. All but the *Guardian* carried a police mug shot-style photo of Restivo, looking unshaven and wild-eyed behind his glasses, with both News International titles (*Sun* and *Times*) juxtaposing this with photos of the traumatized daughter and her murdered mother.

The other key element of othering underpinning Restivo's story besides his portrayal as a devilish killer – his foreignness – recurred prominently in equally widespread coverage of a nefarious predator on 6 July. The *Daily Star* (2011, p. 21) set the tone for the tale (covered by every tabloid) of Iranian national Homayon Narouzzad, who had been jailed a day earlier for sexually abusing 18 under-aged girls. Describing him in its headline as a 'foot fetish paedo', it told how the 'Iranian-born asylum-seeker' with 'a paedophile foot fetish' befriended and then 'preyed on' girls aged 12 to 15 while working at a fast-food takeaway – another example of threatening familiarity, enhanced on this occasion by the revelation that his business went under the chilling name 'Family Guy'. The paper's pithy seven-paragraph report told readers how Narouzzad 'persuaded' a 13-year-old girl to 'pimp' her friends, whom he 'bribed' with food, cigarettes and £50 a time to 'touch and kiss their feet while he masturbated'. As with Restivo, the perpetrator was pictured in a police mug shot, looking unshaven and impassive. The *Mirror*'s report was equally sensational – though far longer, running to a page-lead. Like other papers, alongside the head-shot familiar from the *Star* it also included a waist-length photo of Narouzzad posing bare-chested, with muscles flexed, tattooed torso and manic ear-to-ear grin. Beneath the headline 'Foot fetish abuser paid for perving: he's jailed for preying on youngsters' (White, 2011, p. 22), it again led on the image of a 'fast-food shop worker with a foot fetish' being jailed for having 'sexually abused' girls. Once more, the adjective 'Iranian' was prominent – arguably an irrelevant fact, inappropriately emphasized and in danger of breaching the then Press Complaints Commission editors' code of practice (Press Complaints Commission, 2014) – as was his having exploited one girl to procure others. In common with tabloid reports of other sexual crimes, the paper tactfully avoided the word 'masturbate' – referring only to Narrouzad's 'carrying out a sexual act'. It went on to stress the long-term damage done to his victims, describing how they had been 'left psychologically scarred' and quoting two sources emphasizing this point: Detective Inspector Jane Little, who condemned the 'abuse', and Judge Maureen Roddy, who told him 'the innocence of those victims was destroyed by your actions'. While the *Sun*'s version was significantly shorter, it, too, carried the photo of Narouzzad posing (albeit truncated to his head and shoulders) – under the headline '4 yrs for "asylum" sex fiend' (Moriarty, 2011, p. 4) and an intro dubbing him 'a perverted Iranian asylum-seeker'. Describing the girls he abused as 'sex slaves', it was peppered with value-laden verbs and adjectives, bestializing Narouzzad as a predator who 'lured' them to his 'sordid lair' before persuading them to perform 'sex acts' and sate his 'fetish for SOCKS'.[2] It also teased out another disturbing detail that enhanced his portrayal as a malign bogeyman masquerading as an avuncular familiar: the fact that his victims had previously known him as 'Smiley'. Both mid-market tabloids (*Daily Mail* and *Daily Express*) gave the story page-lead treatment – reproducing the full-length shot of Narouzzad the bodybuilder. As in the *Sun*, these versions were liberally scattered with references to the twin aspects of his deviancy: his perverse sexual predilections and asylum-seeker status. The *Mail*'s story – headlined 'Foot fetishist who abused 18 girls in flat over takeaway' – emphasized his familiar stranger qualities, relating how 'the tattooed body-builder was a popular figure in the area, known by the teenagers who flocked to the cafe as "Smiley" for his happy demeanour' (Tozer, 2011, p. 27). As in all other reports, mention was again made of his takeaway's name. But this story dwelt on Narouzzad's kinky sexual tastes and his victims' resulting loss of innocence, by relaying how many girls were 'still dressed in their school uniforms' as he persuaded them to 'let him kiss their feet or perform sex acts upon him'. As well as drawing attention to Narouzzad's asylum-seeker status, the *Mail* went further than any other title in othering him on the basis of his foreignness – explicitly conflating his case with other, then recent, grooming crimes involving predatory Asian men and white schoolgirls. It cited statistics from a respected claims-maker – the Child Exploitation and Online Protection Centre – revealing that 28 per cent of the 2,379 offenders suspected of using drugs and alcohol to lure children over the preceding three years had been Asian. To many readers, the repeated allusions to Asian pimps might have been taken as references to the high-profile near-contemporaneous prosecutions of nine men of Pakistani and Afghani origin for raping and sexually exploiting girls as young as 13 under the cover of two takeaways in Rochdale (Carter, 2011). Reflecting an apparent anti-immigration agenda, the *Express* angled its account more directly on Narouzzad's asylum-seeker status – and, by implication, the fact he had abused not only under-aged girls but also his host country's hospitality. Headlined 'Iranian paedophile is jailed, but WON'T be sent back home' (Riches, 2011, p. 7), it highlighted demands from 'campaign groups' for him to be 'kicked out of Britain when he has finished his sentence'. As well as dwelling on his 'vile foot fetish' and repeating the detail that many victims wore school uniforms while being abused, it blamed 'European Human Rights legislation' for obstructing his deportation – attributing this claim to an unnamed 'legal expert' (despite assurances from the UK Border Agency, also quoted, that he would be sent home). Several other sources were claimed to support the paper's zero-tolerance line – including 'locals' and right-wing pressure group MigrationWatch UK. The paper even ran a phone-in poll alongside the article – asking readers the loaded question 'should all foreign crooks be deported?' – and cross-referenced to an opinion piece on this subject on another page.

The child as familiar stranger

As with the numerous articles focusing on juvenile victims, those positioning them as threats evoked all manner of scenarios to demonstrate the scale and variety of menaces posed by unrulier children. Kids were portrayed as victimizing other children ('Are our parks safe for children or are they a haven for drug dealers?' (the *Argus*, 21 July); parents ('Mum run down by daughter', the *Sun*, 21 July); cute animals ('Sick yob blows up possums', the *Sun*, 16 July); the mentally and/or physically disabled ('Why was Gemma abandoned to be murdered for fun by a gang of savages who she thought were her friends?' *Mail on Sunday*, 31 July); the elderly ('Shocked mugger routed by ex-bouncer granny, 63', *Daily Express*, 1 July); public safety ('12-year-old boy warned for hoax yacht emergency', the *Argus*, 6 July) – and even global security ('British boy of 16 held over CIA and PayPal hacking', *Daily Mail*, 21 July). In some cases, children were depicted as risks to themselves. On 6 July both the *Sun* and the *Daily Mirror* – under the respective headlines 'Lad thick as plank' (the *Sun*, 2011d) and 'You utter plank: Boy, 14, risks life on rail line in web craze' (Thornton, 2011a) – ridiculed a teenage boy for endangering both himself and others by lying down on a railway track to have a photo taken for his Facebook page (a 'craze' known as 'planking'). One widely covered 'survivor' story even boiled down to a case of a (careless and unsupervised) child narrowly avoiding injuring *himself*. This was 17-year-old Lewis Tavernier, who boasted to several tabloids he 'didn't feel a thing' when a bolt fired from his hunting crossbow lodged itself in his face (the *Sun*, 2011a).

Common tropes in the various articles focusing on children as *victimizers* were the pejorative framing of (invariably older) juveniles as faceless 'thugs' or 'yobs' often characterized by unsavoury dress codes: a delinquent variant of the familiar stranger trope. The most frequently mentioned item of clothing was the 'hoodie' (hooded top) – a term which, at the time, was often used interchangeably as shorthand for both this attire and a youthful malefactor him or herself (Lett, 2010). A textbook example of this could be found in a 'good news' story (Ettema & Peer, 1996) about an ageing have-a-go heroine who tackled a teenage mugger, reported in two newspapers (*Daily Mirror* and *Daily Express*) on 1 July. The *Daily Mirror*'s account – headlined 'Hand to handbag combat: Liz gets better of mugger' (Armstrong, 2011, p. 19) – began as follows:

> A TEENAGE thug who tried to nick a 63-year-old woman's handbag got more than he bargained for – his apparently vulnerable victim used to be a nightclub bouncer.

The story relayed how 'plucky' Elizabeth Bonson chased the 'yob', still clutching a handbag containing 'cherished family photos' – despite having suffered a 'bloody nose, cut chin and fat lip' when he 'punched her twice in the face'. The only source referred to besides the victim (Cumbria Police) was indirectly quoted as disclosing that 'the mugger, who wore an oversized grey hoodie, is believed to be a teenager'. The *Daily Express*'s account (topped by the headline 'Shocked mugger routed by ex-bouncer granny, 63') went so far as to describe him as a 'teenage hoodie' in its second paragraph, before reverting to 'yob'. Its first sentence also played up the image of a heartless, opportunistic attack on a vulnerable pensioner, describing her as a 'lone, grey-haired grandmother' – despite the fact that (as in the *Daily Mirror*) the story was accompanied by a portrait of a spry and youthful-looking Elizabeth. Another common framing of children as threats was that focusing on deviant school pupils, and the impact of their behaviour on classmates and teachers. A widely reported 26 July story concerned a 45-year-old primary school head teacher, who resigned after being suspended for pinning a boy against a wall. All three tabloid reports were angled around the fact that he was so respected by parents that many had withdrawn their children from lessons in protest. The *Sun's* pithy three-paragraph account opened with an intro describing how parents 'rushed to back' him after he quit over 'being accused' of assaulting the 'disruptive pupil' (the *Sun*, 2011i, p. 30). The paper emphasized that the autistic child had since been excluded for biting another teacher – a detail apparently calculated to persuade undecided readers that the head's actions were justified – while a protesting parent was quoted as branding the teacher's dismissal 'a disgrace'. A lengthy *Daily Mail* story adopted an even heavier-handed approach to underlining the injustice of his reluctant resignation. Beneath the headline 'Parents' revolt as headmaster is forced out for pinning violent boy against wall' (Narain & Eccles, 2011, p. 23), it told of a 'dedicated head' who had been 'forced to resign, despite a parents' protest and the staunch support of even the "victim's" mother and father'. Again the boy was described as 'disruptive', but this time the sense of unfairness was compounded by quotes attributed to the boy's parents, who reportedly condemned the school's governors for 'carrying out a "vindictive" witch-hunt against a well-respected head'. Another parent condemned the head's treatment as 'diabolical', while choice biographical details were included to back up assertions about his respectability – including the fact that he served on the finance board of the Diocese of Shrewsbury and (according to one dad) spent 'numerous extra hours' looking after socially deprived children. Like the *Daily Express*, the *Daily Mail* framed its print coverage with portraits of a smiling, open-faced head juxtaposed with that of the smirking, spiky-haired schoolboy. The latter's report was all-but identical in length, structure and emphasis to the *Daily Mail's* – again stating in its headline that the head was 'forced out', and describing the pupil as 'disruptive' and 'unruly'. The quotes branding the head's treatment 'a disgrace' and 'appalling' were also reused. Significantly, the online version of this story was even more heavily framed as a condemnation of juvenile indiscipline, bearing the loaded headline 'Headmaster resigns after being suspended for "manhandling" 8-year-old – despite pupil's family saying he did nothing wrong'. Hardly surprising, perhaps, that it was one of several stories about *threatening* children that tapped into a rich vein of punitive public sentiment by provoking 124 discussion posts, most highly supportive of its pessimistic and authoritarian outlook. Several posters viewed the tale as a parable symbolizing a deeper decline in standards of morality – a view which, as we shall see, mid-market journalists openly ascribed to their readers.[3] One typical observation, from a poster in Bradwell, lamented it was 'because of cases like this that this nation is producing so many scumbags and thugs, who think that they can get away with anything!'

'Hybrid' victim/threat stories – when categories blur

Some stories were harder to categorize – not least those focusing on victimization of one child by another. The story that proved most problematic also happened to reported more than any other during the month. This was a court case surrounding the macabre tale of a teenage boy who, for a bet, bashed his girlfriend to death with a rock. In various articles about this unfolding story – most carried by papers from the *Mirror* stable – no opportunity was lost to emphasize the severity of the crime and the psychotic-cum-demonic nature of its perpetrator. In the most extensive single article on the case – published in the *People* on 31 July, under the uncompromising headline 'Let him rot in hell: heartbroken family of murdered girl speak out on killer' (Jeffs, 2011, pp. 16–17) – readers learnt that murderous Joshua Davies 'had a fixation with horror films', 'used the internet, texting and social network sites' to plot 15-year-old Rebecca Aylward's death, and, after leaving 'her bloodied body face down' in woodland, 'chilled out with friends' by 'calmly' watching [BBC1 entertainment show] *Strictly Come Dancing*. Worst of all, he had been 'smirking' as, days earlier, he was convicted. And alongside details portraying Davies as unhinged (he had been detained in 'a secure unit' and 'revelled in the nickname Psycho') there were numerous quotes from the victim's family alluding to the idea of malevolence hiding behind a benign façade – an aspect of the familiar stranger paradigm that repeatedly surfaced in both newspaper and audience discourse. The murdered schoolgirl's uncle (described, in pointed contrast to Davies, as 'a carer') recalled her family's mistaken impression of him as 'an ideal teenager' who would 'help set up the dinner table, was polite and would do anything to help'. He was even 'from a church-going family, academically gifted – everything you could want for your own daughter'. Until Davies's conviction, Rebecca had been the only protagonist whose name or image had appeared in articles about this story. The tragedy of her murder had been further underscored by the repeated use of head-and-shoulders snapshots depicting the pretty 15-year-old smiling on a beach. Headline wording had also reflected the bias towards focusing on Rebecca, rather than Davies: on 1 July, the *Sun* headed its story 'Pal: I saw girl victim' (the *Sun*, 2011b, p. 7) and the *Mirror* wrote '"Killer mate showed me Becca body"' (Smith, 2011a,

p. 24), while five days later the latter used the headline 'Becca ex in "fake river rescue" plot' (Smith, 2011b, p. 27). However, in an echo of the convictions of Jon Venables and Robert Thompson for the James Bulger murder two decades previously, on sentencing Davies the judge determined that the gravity of his crime meant that his anonymity should be removed – and from this point on the story's emphasis was as much on the *murderous* child as the murdered. In the end, to avoid distorting the overall total of articles by double-counting, the decision was taken to classify it as 'hybrid', alongside a handful of other (less widely reported) tales.

Journalism in the online era: the professional–participatory interface

As Chapter 3 revealed, 84 per cent of the 2,809 discussion posts published beneath the online versions of 'victim' and 'threat' articles took the form of reactive opinions. However, before we dismiss these reactions as little more than passive endorsements and (occasional) challenges to the dominant newspaper discourse, let us pause to consider their significance in the context of the wider, post-Internet, public sphere. Much has been written about the process of active 'meaning-making' (Hall, 1980; Deacon et al., 1999) in which audience members engage while processing news, individually and collectively. In many respects, the patterns of meaning-making discernible in discussion threads analysed here display similar characteristics to those observed in numerous pre-Internet (let alone pre-social media) reception studies involving focus groups (for example Kitzinger, 1993, 1999; Boyce, 2007) and/or ethnography (Morley, 1980). There is nothing new about the idea that it is audiences' *processing* of journalistic texts that leads to the *manifestation* of narratives latent in them – nor that, by actively engaging with news discourse, its 'recipients' are themselves helping to construct (and, at times, contest) hegemonic notions about social reality (Corner, 1983). What *is* new about the ways that meaning-making is negotiated in the virtual (rather than physical) public sphere is that, unlike the water-cooler/school-gate conversations of old, these new sites of processing are *visible* to everyone else – including those *not* contributing themselves. The ability of audiences to post responses to news does not necessarily add extra complexity to the meaning-making process itself – but, in that they are *publishing* their thoughts, leaving records of them for others to read, at least they are adding extra layers of (reactive) material for more 'passive' readers to digest (and accept/reject).

It is in this guise – as social *actors*, rather than mere *reactors* (the role we ascribed to them in the last chapter) – that we should consider the significance of audience members who posted various classes of reactive opinion here. Of the 2,038 affirmative reactions, most served as mere 'echo-chambers' (e.g. Albrecht, 2006; Treviranus & Hockema, 2009; Edwards, 2013) or 'positive feedback loops' (Bimber, 2012, p. 118) for the sentiments of articles beneath which they appeared: straightforward, opinionated comments that gave explicit expression to meanings implicit in what journalists had written. However, other responses went further – extending the process of meaning-making in the reception of particular stories to vindicate wider (apparently pre-formed) worldviews. By way of example, the most common response to articles about unruly children and, conversely, those who mistreated or abused the young was, predictably, outrage. The single comment posted beneath a 6 July *Sun* story about a woman who learnt of the premature prison release of her abusive stepfather – headlined 'Shy weeps as paedo stepdad freed early: abuse campaigner's fury' (France, 2011, p. 12) – was typical in tone and content of most reactions to paedophilia-related stories. 'Buffy71' wrote that 'this man should rot in jail, until the space reserved in Hell for him is ready for him to rot there', before condemning 'the "justice" system in the UK' as 'far from its title'. Indeed, it was the recurring suggestion in stories about both predatory adults and feral children that 'the law' was 'on the side' of criminals (rather than victims) that provoked the fiercest, most persistent gut reactions. 'That about sums up the British legal system', moaned 'Rob, Lincs', responding to the *Daily Mail* report, discussed extensively in Chapter 3, about a father prosecuted for warning fellow parents that his ex-wife's husband was a child abuser (Dolan, 2011, p. 25). Several others explicitly endorsed the father's actions, with 'Michele, France' and 'Karen, Stoke, England' both branding him a 'hero'; 'skyguy, Wallasey, UK' describing himself as 'speechless and beyond despair' at the injustice of his treatment; and 'Dave, Surrey' urging everyone to ignore the magistrates who punished the whistle-blower and 'inform neighbours, friends and others with whom they have contact, to pass on information of any disgusting paedophile', in the knowledge that 'the courts won't. ENGLAND 2011'. It fell, though, to 'Paula, working hard for a charity in Stoke on Trent' to crystallize the consensus, remarking that such incidents could occur 'only in england'. Injustice was also a running theme of reactions to the story about the 'dedicated head' forced to resign for disciplining a 'disruptive' pupil. 'Maximus, Wakefield' spoke for fellow *Daily Mail* posters in decrying his treatment by school governors as 'shameful', while 'the History Man, France' lamented 'another talented teacher lost to the profession'.

Another *Daily Mail* article that provoked a string of kneejerk reactions manifesting its latent feral youth narrative focused on allegations that a 'gang' of travellers or Gypsies (specified as boys and men) had drowned a pony in a lake (*Daily Mail*, 2011a). The tabloid's lurid version of this widely reported tale of juvenile deviancy – headlined online 'Gang "deliberately drowned" pony in lake in front of horrified families' – provoked much sentimentalizing about 'helpless' ('Shocked, London') and 'defenseless' ('Emma, West Yorkshire') animals, juxtaposed with cries of 'monsters' (ibid.), 'scum' ('Chaz, Rainham, Essex') and 'murderers' ('Furious and Frustrated, Richmond, Surrey'). 'Ray, Leeds, UK' summed up the consensus, with the despairing question, 'why do we have so much trash living in this country?'

Superficially, such responses – for all their sound and fury – can be classed as impulsive reactions that do little more than parrot received (or perceived) narratives. However, in explicitly endorsing the thrust of articles on which they comment, and their underlying 'broken Britain' discourse (Thorp & Kennedy, 2010), they arguably *reinforce* the social constructions favoured by the press. Some such reactions, moreover, might even be described as *extensions* of the discourses to which they respond – in that they appeared to read into them deeper levels of signification. As discussed previously, the article attracting the most comments was an 11 July double-page spread in the *Daily Mail* about the pregnant teenage daughter of a welfare-dependent 'mother-of-14' – hyperbolically headlined 'Pregnant at 15, daughter of Britain's most prolific single mother (And, of course, she's on benefits – just like mum)' (Sears, 2011a, p. 11) – which generated 745 posts. While readers amassed to condemn the mother's 'breeding' habits ('Charlotte, Cape Town'; 'J Thompson, Bangor'; 'Cathy, West Yorkshire'), others launched into wider invectives about the 'underclass' ('deji, London'), using lurid language like 'vermin' (ibid.) and 'scroungers' ('Jane von M, the Netherlands') to describe both the family itself and others like it. A stark example of an attempt to elide deeper meanings from the 'worthy/unworthy' (or, in this case, 'deserving/undeserving') discourse underpinning this tale of feckless parenting was a lengthy rant from 'Steve, London', which read into it evidence of a deliberately engineered dependency culture arising from 'the goal of Labour and indeed Socialism' to 'get as many people reliant on the government as possible to ensure a permanent grip on power' (despite the fact that, by this point, the Labour Party had been *out of* government for more than a year). Similarly extreme tirades against the supposedly corrosive effects of liberal thinking surfaced in responses to several stories focusing on juvenile indiscipline. Another *Daily Mail* story, published online on 10 July under the headline 'Teachers will be allowed to use force on unruly pupils as ministers lift "no touching" ban' (Loveys, 2011), prompted the prolific 'Rob, Lincs' to condemn 'progressive enlightenment from the sixties' for undermining the 'simple concept' of 'herding' children 'into a big building' and teaching them 'stuff they need to know'. And another variant of the affirmative comment was that disputing the *particulars* of a given article – and/or fellow posters' reactions to it – while still endorsing its underlying *discourse*. For example, 'Sofia, Berlin, Germany', argued in response to the 11 July story single mother story that, while 'not a supporter of people havind [*sic*] so many children and then receiving benefits', these particular offspring 'look pretty happy, healthy and okay'. Intriguingly, the 5.5 per cent of reactive opinions that adopted a *negotiated* stance (124 out of 2,244) tended to be lengthier, as their authors visibly wrestled with ambivalent feelings about a narrative. Though implicitly endorsing the hegemonic *Mail* 'worthy/unworthy' discourse around families, a London-based poster disputed its portrayal of the *scale* of this problem in society. In an extensive post responding to news of the pregnant daughter of 'Britain's most prolific single mother', she argued that 'families like this are uncommon' but 'given maximum coverage in the DM'.

As one might expect from audiences choosing to visit particular news outlets in preference to others (Iyengar & Hahn, 2009), overtly *oppositional* posts were rarer – accounting for fewer than 4 per cent (or 82) of all reactive opinions. For this reason, though, they were more pronounced when they occurred. Among the boldest challenger to the collective character assassination mounted against the single mother – and the anti-welfare discourse underpinning it – was 'Jessica, the beautiful south', who criticized fellow readers' 'nasty comments', challenging them to admit whether they were suggesting 'this lady and her children' should 'starve'. 'The benefits system was set up to help those who cannot help themselves, i.e. people just like her', she added. A similarly counter-hegemonic perspective adopted by 'luke, london' led to the following testy exchange with a more typical poster:

Luke, London:	Can we stop attacking the poor please?
Fool on the Hill, Costa del East Anglia:	Can the poor stop having children they can't afford please.

Yet even oppositional readings of a narrative can come with a twist. While 'Brenda M, UK' contested the single parent-baiting aspects of other comments – pointing out that this mother was 'married to their [the children's] father' until this 'didnt work out' and 'couldn't exactly go out and find a job with the children at home' – other aspects of her defence took an orthodox *Daily Mail* line. Picking out a theme running through several oppositional comments – the idea that, as 'Richard, Bedford' put it, 'lots of babies' were needed to 'fund the pension and healthcare costs' of Britain's ageing population – she described the 14 children as 'clean, well behaved' and 'white' (qualities needed 'in a country with a falling indigenous English birth rate'). More intriguing still were the minority of posts that might best be characterized as pro-hegemonic readings of the *details* of a story which were simultaneously oppositional, in that they questioned how they were *presented* by reporters. For example, a Facebook-style 'like' and 'share' device informed readers browsing the thread under an 11 July *Independent* story about poor children's academic under-achievement (headed 'Three in five of the poorest 11-year-olds lack basic literacy') that 'seven people like[d]' a post by 'Thrasos' that would have been more at home on a less liberal website. In it, he dismissed the article's 'typical lefty logic' that 'the problem is poverty', when 'the truth' was 'those with the least ability become the poorest' and their offspring 'inherit their genes'. The spectrum of reactive responses may have been wide-ranging, then, but on balance it was overwhelmingly dominated by a discourse endorsing and consolidating social constructions latent in articles on which readers commented. More crucially, what the necessarily selective cross-section quoted here shows is that even purely reactive posts have more to offer us than a virtual (and self-selecting) focus group – or an ability to eavesdrop on the instant *reactions* news discourse generates. Rather, by *publishing* their opinions for everyone else to read, these respondents contribute to both news narratives themselves and (by extension) the construction of wider meaning in the public sphere.

News as collaboration: audience members as news-makers and claims-makers

For all the contribution that reactive posts make to the construction of news (and wider public) discourse, however, their value is arguably vastly outstripped by comments that go beyond *responding* to professionally produced articles, by providing additional/alternative *evidence* with a bearing on the facts of articles, as reported, and/or their (implied) signification. In these instances, audience members do not simply contribute to the construction of meaning in the *traditional* sense, namely by actively negotiating interpretation with a text and validating or challenging the version of social reality it presents. By contrast, active posters are effectively collaborating with journalists on the wording of *texts themselves* or (on occasions when they think they know better – and are willing to say so) authoritatively contesting, reshaping or even *writing their own versions* of it. In this respect, they are bringing additional knowledge/information to the table which can have the effect of making articles more (or less) persuasive than they might otherwise have been – a highly empowered form of 'produser' (Bruns, 2009) behaviour illustrative of the democratized news-making practices that other researchers have recently noted (e.g. McCoy, 2001; Tremayne, 2007; Muthukumaraswamy, 2010; Lewis, 2012). Significantly, a substantial minority of discussion posts analysed – 565, or one in five – went beyond simply reacting to the representations conveyed by journalists, to contribute additional information and/or informed insights to the narratives concerned. In adding evidence-based testimony, posters were directly participating in the process of social construction in which papers were engaged – in some cases, acting as both *news*-makers (citizen journalists) and *claims*-makers (citizen sources) simultaneously. Perhaps more intriguingly, while the overwhelming mass of purely reactive posts (2,372 out of 2,809) wholly or largely echoed agendas latent in articles on which they commented, as discussed previously, two-fifths of *evidence-based* responses drawing on posters' own information and insights adopted standpoints that were negotiated – or downright oppositional. A breakdown of all evidence-based responses is presented in Figure 4.8.

Of the *affirming* evidence-based responses, a large number consisted of posts endorsing the (implicitly) critical framing of articles – for example, value-laden language and strongly worded intros/headlines used in stories about menacing children or those who menace them – by explicitly referring to posters' own experiences. 'Aussiemaverick' responded to a 26 July *Independent* story about the withdrawal of the Vatican's ambassador to Ireland following Irish Taoiseach Enda Kenny's condemnation of its handling of a long-running controversy over paedophile priests (Day, 2011, p. 22) with a comment drawing on the personal trauma of being 'physically and psychologically' abused by nuns at a Melbourne school. In so doing, he/she not only endorsed the underpinning (hegemonic) panic narrative – the familiar stranger/abuse

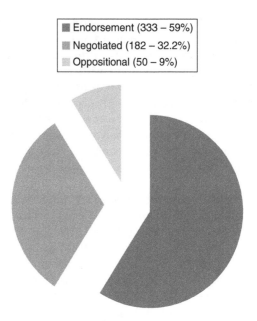

■ Endorsement (333 – 59%)
■ Negotiated (182 – 32.2%)
▨ Oppositional (50 – 9%)

Figure 4.8 Breakdown of evidence-based responses

of trust paradigm repeatedly raised in focus groups – but *reinforced* it by supplying independent evidence of its legitimacy. Similarly, 'Ruth, Essex' affirmed the feral youth narrative signified by the principal claims-makers (the Department for Education and an outspoken former deputy head teacher) quoted in a 10 July *Daily Mail* story about ministers' decision to lift a ban on 'touching' disruptive schoolchildren – claiming she had given up teaching herself after 34 years following a 'breakdown' caused by parents' failure to discipline their children. A common characteristic of oppositional or negotiated responses, by contrast, was their presentation of additional and/or contradictory factual claims (e.g. references to data or other acquired knowledge) casting *doubt* on the validity of a story's details and manifest/latent meanings, as framed by a newspaper. Some posters attempted to undermine or debunk key aspects of certain articles. On 26 July, 'Christine, Newport' posted a comment on the *Daily Mail* website countering a central claim of its story about the headmaster 'forced to resign' after 'manhandling' an autistic boy – namely that teachers were barred (by nonsensical laws) from using physical force to protect themselves or (good) children against (bad) classmates – by drawing on her own teaching background to cite rules permitting use of 'appropriate restraint methods'. A jittery

21 July *Daily Mail* story headlined 'Mothers using nicotine gum to avoid smoking in pregnancy "put unborn babies at risk"' (Borland, 2011, p. 13) provoked 'Elizabeth, Cardiff' to defend moderation over total abstinence by mocking those who preached a mantra of 'don't drink, don't eat certain foods, don't smoke (but don't get stressed) or you'll KILL YOUR CHILD'. Another form of oppositional evidence-based response was the post which *re*-presented facts contained (but buried) in the original article – *emphasizing* these details over ones foregrounded by the journalist to contest the story's framing. 'Louise, Danby' drew fellow readers' attention to a key detail hidden near the bottom of the sacked head teacher story – arguing that the decision by governors to investigate him might have been far from the unjustified 'witch-hunt' portrayed in the article. His local council, she pointed out, had 'said he had been suspended after "other issues around his discipline methods"'.

Of all oppositional evidence-based responses noted, though, the most powerful were those contradicting the *Daily Mail's* version of the widely reported story alleging that a 'gang' of feral youths and men had callously drowned a pony in a lake. Stripping out the 204 (largely condemnatory) *comments* on the alleged crime – conveniently attributed to 'Gypsies' – 12 posts contained claims by people purporting to hold informed views on the subject. Eight were oppositional – outnumbering those affirming the details/framing of the *Daily Mail* article two to one. Oppositional posters drawing on unspecified background knowledge about travellers (or horses) to bolster their criticisms of the *Daily Mail's* line included 'Polly, Yorkshire', who disputed the likelihood of their abandoning the pony's trap and tackle (as the story stated), given the cost of this equipment, and 'horace4831, Gravesend, Kent', who contrasted the paper's account with the BBC's version of the same incident, which made 'no mention' of the culprits 'being Gypsies'. In a direct attack on the folk-devil positioning implicit in the story's headline, 'Ella, Newton Stewart, Scotland' breathlessly reminded other readers, 'not all folk with horses and traps are gypsies' and to suggest so was 'a slanderous statement' – tantamount to 'assuming that all asians are fundamentalist muslims and might bomb us'. Most noteworthy of all, though, was a post by 'John, Reading', which mounted a wholesale contradiction of key claims in the report, based on a claimed second-hand eyewitness account omitted from the *Daily Mail's* coverage. In an authoritative evidence-based post citing his 'friend' as a *direct* protagonist in the events, he condemned the 'awfully inaccurate and rather spiteful' report, 'bordering on racism'. The friend in question, 'who works at the lake, teaching sailing', had assured him 'the horses were taken into the water to cool off after a hot ride' and the 'member of public who went to hospital sustained his injuries from several kicks to the head from the HORSE he tried to rescue'. Indeed, not only had his friend witnessed this incident: he had himself 'jumped out of his boat and pulled him [the attempted rescuer] out of the water'. Describing the occurrence as 'a terrible accident, nothing sinister', he insisted that, though 'guilty of stupidity' for 'leaving the scene of an incident and not being compassionate', the ponies' owners were 'certainly not guilty of deliberately trying to drown' them. Those doubting his testimony could 'check this out', he added, by calling 'Hawley Lakes Sailing Club, who would confirm this story'. 'John, Reading' therefore went well beyond merely *contesting* the framing of the *Daily Mail's* story in the sense this term has conventionally been used: by effectively writing his own account of the incident, he persuasively *contradicted* it, to the extent that anyone bothering to read the discussion thread with an open mind might have emerged with an entirely altered impression of both the story's detail and signification. In this sense, his post was less a response than a *counter-narrative*: an entirely contrary version of the story drawn from an alternative (arguably better informed) claims-maker to reject its feral youth agenda. However significant such voices appear when they emerge, though, such confident, well-informed oppositional comments represent, for now, a tiny minority of all evidence-based responses – and an even tinier one of the total number of discussion posts. The fact that they leap out so vividly when they occur is precisely *because* the over-whelming mass of discussion thread commentary tends to endorse the framing imposed on events and issues by journalists. In so doing, these threads act not only as echo-chambers, but as cheerleaders – collectively *reinforcing* the narratives that newspapers construct and, more crucially, the discourse of insecurity and distrust underpinning them.

Constructing distrust: fear and loathing in the digital news age

It seems beyond dispute, then, that the dominant discourse about children found in today's newspapers conceives of them as objects (and, occasionally, subjects) of multifarious threats and risk anxieties. Equally indisputable is the fact that the narratives journalists use to popularize this discourse – particularly those revolving around menaces posed by familiar strangers – are increasingly *contributed to* by active audience members, reflecting a wider public consensus that the concerns they evince are rationally based and salient (as our focus group findings demonstrate). Yet, as we learnt in Chapter 1, empirical research into the frequency with which child abuse, abduction, teenage disorder, fatal road accidents and other dramatic juvenile scenarios routinely conjured up by journalists occur in *real life* unequivocally exposes these media-stoked fears as disproportionate (e.g. Best, 1990; La Fontaine, 1994; Grubin, 1998; Furedi, 2001). So, if this is the case, why do the papers – and the sources on which they depend – insist on sensitizing us to threats we are unlikely to ever encounter? As the testimony of most practitioners interviewed for this study indicates, the dominance of panicky narratives about children is no accident. In a 24/7 digital age in which time-poor, forever-on-the-go audience members have access to more news outlets (and distractions) than ever before, the commercial pressure on journalists to generate sellable stories that persuade people to read their newspapers, visit their websites and linger long enough to engage in discussions (providing a fertile market for advertisers) is hard-wired into every aspect of the news-making process. The imperatives of this unashamedly 'market-driven journalism' (McManus, 1994) are crystallized most blatantly in data circulated among news editors and reporters on a day-to-day basis – expressed as print sales graphs, online hit rates and complex analytics that break down their shifting audience demographics. In this way, journalists whose remit was once (ostensibly) to apply normative professional judgments about newsworthiness when researching and writing stories have been explicitly co-opted into the business of generating copy designed to maximize their publications' readerships and profitability – with incentives liberally deployed to ensure that they do so. So it is that staff on a Somerset-based weekly paper are 'incentivized with the promise of an iPad for the reporter with the most hits per quarter', according to one such reporter, and named and famed (or, implicitly, shamed) at weekly 'Fizzy Friday' sales meetings that involve 'gathering around a blackboard' to compete for recognition over their 'successes of the week'. In addition, newspapers' embrace of digital, as well as print, has further intensified the pressure on reporters, as they race to file bespoke versions of stories for each medium (sometimes simultaneously) and go beyond producing articles to actively *promote* them – by tweeting their top lines and interacting with readers. Today's reporters, according to a Devon-based crime specialist, are 'encouraged' to actively '"sell" our product – not just blithely write articles and bugger off home, not caring whether anyone reads it'.

Commercially motivated decisions are as instrumental as objective judgments about newsworthiness in almost everything today's journalists do, from identifying events and issues likely to appeal to their target readership(s) through justifying the time needed to research them – particularly if this involves lengthy (for which read unproductive) periods away from the office. Choices of wording, headlines and pictures used to frame articles are also viewed as crucial to maximizing papers' appeal to as wide and varied an audience as possible. And, against this intensely competitive backdrop, they have become more focused on telling highly charged and dramatic stories – including narratives playing on today's pervasive, deeply ingrained societal concerns about children. When asked about their news instincts, reporters and editors appeared highly attuned to the resonance that alarming/tragic stories involving juveniles had for readers – and, though most denied proactively *searching* for such narratives, almost all conceded that they instinctively recognized their commercial value whenever they came across them. A key argument of this book is that the disproportionate degree of newsworthiness attached to dramatic stories about children – especially those revolving around their abuse by malevolent adults or threats *deviant* juveniles pose to others – is related to the steady erosion, over time, of social trust. By focusing on the 'murder mystery' and/or 'horror movie' elements of such stories – unsupervised outdoor play, mysterious cars and the predatory behaviour of nefarious adults/youths – and *dramatizing* them in narratives that they construct online and in print, papers are actively tapping into, and cynically *playing up*, this atmosphere of unease and suspicion for commercial gain.

Of the competitive forces that journalists cited in describing their day-to-day duties, four in particular appeared most conducive to the emergence of news values favouring dramatic narratives about children. The first three (explored below) illuminate the commercial pressures, editorial routines and institutionalized news values that lead to papers placing disproportionate emphasis on covering (and dramatizing) such stories. The fourth offers an insight into how journalists *rationalize* the compulsive appeal of these narratives – and conceptualize their relationship with audiences in the context of this febrile popular discourse:

- Increasing pressure on journalists' time, including newsroom economies and demands for both print and web copy – resulting in greater dependency on official/elite sources
- Pressure to *generate* more dramatic, entertaining and 'interactive' stories, based on quantifiable measures of interest in a subject – including reader feedback and participation, print sales, online hit rates/page impressions and unique visitors

- Explicit and implicit pressure to *present* stories in dramatic and entertaining ways – and 'market' articles direct to readers, as well as write them
- Journalists' rationales for the popular appeal of dramatic stories about children, their relative newsworthiness over other stories – and the reporter's role as storyteller

Increasing pressure on journalists' time – and over-reliance on elite sources

The bewildering array of routine demands facing reporters since the introduction of digital publishing is widely documented – as are the coincidences of rising print costs, increasing commercial competition, falling advertising revenues and, inevitably, staff and budget cutbacks (Sweney, 2012). As a result, today's newspaper journalists are under more pressure than ever to be constantly productive. 'Time is money', explained one specialist on a mid-market Sunday tabloid, recalling how being seen in the office on a Tuesday (the first day of his working week) used to be 'frowned upon', but it was now 'frowned upon to be *out* of the office' [author's emphasis] – let alone 'wasting' the afternoon on 'a dead end'. A common tool that editors now used to keep tabs on reporters' whereabouts and productivity, a colleague added, was to demand memos proving they were 'actively engaged in something' and (to quote the specialist) already demonstrating '*massive* progress' by Tuesday afternoon. Such time pressures are felt even more intensely on newspapers with *daily* print runs, whose news desks rely on similarly obsessive memo-driven cultures to monitor reporters' output. Before leaving his house, one national broadsheet crime correspondent would 'start my day' at 8 a.m. by sending 'a note to the desk' with 'a story or two', while a weekend news editor on a national mid-market tabloid expected all his reporters to file memos before the paper's morning news conference to tell the desk 'this is what's around in my patch'. This ever-increasing pressure for journalists to both continually update their news desks on work-in-progress and deliver the goods with finished copy results in various treadmills: an experienced Sunday broadsheet specialist recalled her editors 'always pushing for "scoops"' for their one hit of the week – regardless of the 'limits of their paper', resource-wise – and a tabloid rival stressed his editor's demand for 'quality, not quantity'. By contrast, local reporters complained of pressure to produce daily 'quotas' of articles in a manner others have labelled 'churnalism' (Davies, 2008).

One *effect* of this 'sausage factory' approach to news-making (Nesbitt-Larking, 2007, p. 152) is to force journalists to rely heavily on pools of predictable and reliable contacts – in particular, elite/establishment sources equipped with the knowledge and communications infrastructures to provide continuous flows of oven-ready material to fill their infinite online space (and meet their perpetual deadlines) with eye-catching, advertiser-friendly content. Journalists' dependency on sources considered authoritative and credible – whom they can speak to on the record and contact easily from their desk-bound environments – contributes to a disproportionate reliance on officialdom. This leads, in turn, to over-emphasis on reporting subjects promoting those contacts' own agendas. Given the exhaustive demands placed on their time, it is unsurprising that today's multitasking, multimedia journalists rely more than ever on the classic 'primary definers' (Hall et al., 1978) or official 'knowers' (Fishman, 1980) – police, courts, councils and government departments – so instrumental in framing media-stoked 'crime-waves' of past decades (ibid.). By extension, it comes as little surprise that panic-fuelled narratives are influencing news agendas so heavily. That the 'first job in the morning' for a recently retired crime reporter on a daily paper in southern England was to pursue the 'kernel' of a story by calling the local 'police press line' – a recorded tape updated overnight by duty inspectors and press officers with incidents that journalists might consider newsworthy – was significant, as it biased the ideas he pitched to his editors towards narratives casting the police in a favourable light (successful arrests) and/or demonstrating the importance of their work (witness appeals). Though he would later visit 'the nick' to meet contacts directly in search of tip-offs, he remained reliant on what officers would (and would *not*) tell him, with the press tape representing an initial filter for redacting stories that the force did not want publicized – and emphasizing those it did. His memory of this routine was remarkably similar to the experiences of crime specialists working today. The Devon-based crime reporter listed 'cops and punters [the public]' as his principal sources, with those officially 'in-the-know' coming out top, 'because they rarely "fold" [withdraw quotes] after they've told you something on the record'. Similarly, time constraints were acutely related to judgments that the Somerset-based reporter made in habitually turning to official sources in the expectation that they would yield readily usable stories, with the fire service and ambulance press officers favoured because they 'put a lot of incidents on their website' and 'give us log numbers we can then bring to the police' respectively. This routinization of official information channels echoes numerous earlier studies, in which the prevalence of crime news was directly related to an over-reliance on (ideologically motivated) police forces and law enforcement agencies (e.g. Chibnall, 1977, 1981; Hall et al., 1978; Gans, 1979; Fishman, 1978, 1980; Bantz, 1985; Schlesinger, 1987).

Ease of access and willingness to offer on-the-record quotes, no matter how humdrum, are just two of many reasons why official sources are favoured over unofficial ones. Police and other statutory agencies are also routinely approached to verify claims made by non-official contacts, primarily for legal reasons (costly litigation being scrupulously avoided in today's tightly budgeted newsrooms). The Somerset reporter would 'always check everything out that comes from someone who calls us up', but 'would feel pretty safe' to quote a police or council press release 'as it is'. Similarly, an assistant news editor on a national mid-market tabloid said his paper favoured official sources when searching for 'something solid' – though it also liked to humanize stories to appeal to readers, by speaking directly to 'those involved' or their 'friends or family'. But, while journalists' normative news instincts might favour heartfelt quotes from grieving relatives or dramatic claims by anonymous whistle-blowers over witness appeals couched in police jargon or bland official denials, these impulses are consistently trumped by their (reluctant) acknowledgement that establishment sources are usually more 'reliable' – or less 'risky'. This combination of hard-nosed pragmatism and institutionalized common sense guided the Devon-based crime reporter's rule-of-thumb that 'two on-the-record official sources is ideal, and it'll beat one on-the-record, which will beat a known punter, which will beat an unofficial, unknown punter', and the Somerset journalist's inclination to 'put out a few feelers first', like 'a friendly word with the police', to 'gauge' if 'someone [who] has approached us with something they want us to follow up' is 'legit'. There is a fine line, though, between viewing official sources as more credible than untried, untested citizens because of their access to privileged knowledge (and willingness to speak openly) and developing such cosy reciprocal relationships that journalists become unwitting 'handmaidens of the powerful' (Paletz & Entman, 1981). Some face such intense hour-by-hour pressures – combined with lack of opportunity to leave the office in search of a wider range of stories/sources – that they become over-reliant on spoon-fed leads from well-placed elite contacts. The Sunday specialist who could not justify time out of the newsroom meeting sources unlikely to guarantee stories confessed that the experts he routinely consulted were 'kind of mates' he had 'known for years'. 'Most of my work is on the phone, text messages', he explained, defending this practice thus:

> Very rarely do government departments I deal with blatantly *lie* ...
> A lot of your sources and freelancers go, 'oh, that government depart-
> ment – they never admit *anything*', but way more often than not it's
> the *source* that's actually wrong.

Notwithstanding such remarks, it would be over-generalizing to infer that journalists' pragmatic day-to-day dependency on readily reachable official sources blinds them to the potential for such contacts to obfuscate or mislead. Contradicting the Sunday specialist, the weekend news editor observed that 'government departments lie', while the editorial director of a family-owned newspaper group based in the south-east lamented one legacy of the Leveson Inquiry into Press Standards (The Leveson Inquiry, 2012) was 'a real fear among police officers and other "traditional" contacts of sharing information with journalists' – forcing reporters to rely more on 'tightly controlled' formal channels orchestrated by 'media liaison teams'. He was one of several interviewees to argue that the speed and ease of using social media to 'crowd-source' information and quotes from citizens meant that papers could increasingly *bypass* official channels that would only mention 'things they choose to highlight' if left to 'proactively' provide 'details of breaking news'. The retired crime reporter, meanwhile, reflected on a wave of scandals involving police dishonesty – notably revelations about corrupt payments made to Scotland Yard officers by national reporters (O'Carroll, 2012) and the fabrication of events surrounding the deaths of 96 football fans at Hillsborough stadium in 1989 that fed into misguided press reports (McSmith, 2012). Though he maintained official sources generally lent stories 'more weight' and 'trust', he added a 'codicil about Hillsborough' and the 'appalling way' the *Sun* had been deceived by the police. Matching their scepticism about the integrity of (some) official sources, journalists also retain an ingrained, normative aversion to the limited newsworthiness of stories based on official press statements. Though employed by a local weekly that requires strong working relations with the police to keep its website bubbling between print editions, a trainee reporter on a south-east London weekly noted that, 'while these are our most reliable sources' and ones 'always' used to 'verify information', they would 'never' produce 'many really good stories'. His argument that 'the best stories always come from the general public' was echoed by the Sunday tabloid specialists, who (unlike their daily counterparts) faced constant pressure to produce *exclusives*. One dismissed any idea that his stories would ever *originate* with 'Whitehall, government' – their 'only usefulness' being to provide a 'response'.

Nonetheless, many off-the-record sources that journalists rely on for quotes and unattributable tip-offs are themselves key 'knowers' (Fishman, 1980): as professed experts, they tend to be either funded, commissioned or otherwise related to the establishment, or the occupants of official positions themselves (even if divulging information *unofficially*). For example, both aforementioned specialists referred to using lawyers as unnamed sources for off-diary exclusives. A broadsheet legal affairs correspondent said his 'unofficial' sources were usually those 'practising the law', while the retired crime reporter mentioned barristers, head teachers and the NSPCC as key contacts besides police officers. Significantly, all these sources have vested interests in promoting issues related to law enforcement and child protection. Journalists' heavy reliance on these sources might be put down to the same combination of pragmatism, force of habit and hard-nosed profit-seeking at the expense of investment in costly off-diary investigations that has led this increasingly commercially driven press to cut corners, churn out more pre-packaged, PR-generated 'pseudo-events' (Boorstin, 1971) and become risk-averse (especially legally). More significant here is the fact that the cumulative *effect* of this dependency on elite sources is to further reinforce the dominance of news narratives reflecting their own institutional concerns and priorities, such as crime and law enforcement – subjects conducive to dramatizing the position of children in society. In so doing, papers position themselves, by accident or design, as prisms reflecting 'bureaucratic idealizations of the world' that police, judges, firefighters, civil servants, politicians and (state-sponsored) 'experts' – from government advisors to university-based criminologists – have vested interests in 'disseminating' (Fishman, 1980, p. 154).

Commodification of news 'on the page'

One outcome of this, discernible in newsrooms on a daily basis, is that news is increasingly treated as a mass-produced commercial commodity that must be sufficiently free-flowing and packageable to fill space (in print and online) to ever-tighter, more numerous deadlines – which are themselves the products of a relentless drive to hit newsstands and update websites ahead of competitors in the unremitting pursuit of more (and more engaged) readers. And with most papers now employing (in the words of one Sunday specialist) *'way* fewer reporters' than previously, and replacing seasoned hands with trainees, those remaining feel ever 'more pressure' to deliver the goods. Hence the demands placed on the Somerset reporter to write 10 stories a day, of which 'at least one' must be uploaded online, along with 'any breaking news that filters in off the police/fire websites' – and the expectation that the Devon-based crime specialist would produce four to eight 'leads of 350 to 500 words' on a 'typical day'. This production-line culture translates into anxiety among reporters to ensure that they are always in a position to churn out immediate, publishable copy for both print and online, *wherever* they are – in turn, fostering a reluctance to leave the office (or their computers) for fear of missing calls or failing to file on time, and fuelling dependency on official sources and their communications departments. Despite recently relocating to the 'city-centre', the Devon crime specialist described the opportunity to 'go out on a job' as 'a one or two-times-a-week affair at best', while the Somerset reporter's job was 'almost entirely desk-bound', meaning she could only meet personal contacts in her spare time – unless *certain* of 'coming back to the office with something'. Moreover, the over-reliance on official sources that such workplace cultures promote was exacerbated by a creeping *de-professionalization* of newsroom staff profiles, resulting from cuts in permanent posts and over-reliance on trainees, interns and reporters on casual contracts – according to several interviewees, including the mid-market weekend news editor. The gradual sapping away of professional expertise caused by the failure (or inability) of editors to replace experienced reporters who moved on with similarly qualified successors led to a loss of both institutional memory and 'older staffers' capable of serving, in Breed's words (1955, p. 330), 'as models for newcomers'. The increased pressure consequently heaped on the reduced number of veterans who survived meant they had little time between rattling out daily quotas of regurgitated press releases and official policy announcements to mentor new trainees and interns. Not only that: the example they set was that of 'churnalists' (Davies, 2008) or effectively stenographers for officialdom (hardly a model of public-interest journalism).

And, in this new age of rolling 24/7, web-first newspaper deadlines – in which it is never too early to file a story – *editors'* primary motivation was fear of falling behind their rivals, rather than beating them to exclusives. The culture of discouraging reporters from spending time out of the office digging for off-diary leads was intrinsically related to hardwired anxieties about missing something someone else had (no matter how inconsequential). So highly prioritized was the continuous churn of content that, on days when it was their turn to cover early or late shifts, it was considered more important for even specialists to attend to the multiple (highly mechanized) ways in which *routine* information channels were monitored than work on their *specialisms*. This entailed being 'glued' to a chair and 'frantic', complained the Devon crime reporter, as he made 'round after round of calls to fire and police', waded through online press releases, answered incoming calls, monitored Twitter feeds and checked rival news sites. And this incessant demand for 24-hour news production – fuelling an over-reliance on steady streams of pre-packaged raw material – emanated directly from papers' nerve centres: their editors' offices. The editorial director of a family-owned newspaper business that had mushroomed to encompass eight paid-for weekly papers, six freesheets, 10 websites, seven radio stations and various specialist publications described his multimedia company as 'web and radio-first' – stressing 'the vast majority' of stories were uploaded to at least two websites and broadcast on air before appearing in print (the 'exception' being 'an off-diary exclusive'). Even then, decisions to hold articles back for print were commercially driven: based on individual editors' judgments that they 'will put on additional sales'. Asked how often reporters were expected to file for the web and use social media to research, write and promote stories, he outlined the following head-spinning routine:

> Reporters file all week for online. We have rotas that take us from 5 am to 10 pm each day, but in reality if something broke outside those hours I'd fully expect our reporters to be covering it. All have Twitter feeds, and we print their @names [Twitter contact details] in the paper. If something big breaks, the process is tweet one par (which will automatically appear on the site homepage) then file two or three pars for the web, with constant updates as and when we get them. Then, depending on deadlines and the story, re-nose for print.

From his position at the coalface, the Devon reporter described a similar food chain: a new-found obsession with corralling readers towards his paper's website driven 'by the editor and news eds, who will say, "can we have this for the web, now" and then expect you to rewrite it later for the paper'. A genuine 'breaking story', meanwhile, was like 'an armed siege', being 'Twitter and online-led until it is over' – when it would be rewritten for print, in distilled form, 'with "new" angles if possible'. Speaking for many others, he described a routine 'battle to explain you cannot file both at the same time and a story cannot be completed – or properly written – until you've finalized the calls and research', adding, 'we're still in that, "aarrgh – I'm not a bloody octopus" era, trying to do everything at once'. For weekly reporters, the step-change had been more dramatic, with once-a-week print deadlines supplanted by daily (or hourly) demands to upload copy – and added pressure to decide which stories to put online and which to reserve for print. The south-least London freesheet placed 'big emphasis' on the web, with 'all stories … expected to go up as soon as possible', while a senior reporter on a more traditional, family-owned group of north London weeklies had witnessed an even more dramatic shift to 'web-first' (albeit vicariously). Criticizing the 'mobile newsroom' approach favoured by her rival paper, whose reporters work out of the office on laptops, she described a culture so constrained by the straitjacket of hourly online deadlines that journalists were powerless to react when unexpected stories broke. 'They have to update their website seven times a day', she relayed, adding that when '[Prime Minister] David Cameron came to our area' the paper's chief reporter was 'under so much pressure to upload to her website she misses out on questioning Cameron!'. Even on nationals – where websites are largely staffed by dedicated teams – print reporters worried about inevitably being expected to write more for their websites in future. While the weekend tabloid news editor insisted 'the online thing makes no difference' at his paper, as it was 'a different operation', the broadsheet legal affairs correspondent said the pressure of 'constantly trying to justify' his paper's charges for accessing articles online was routinely 'communicated' by superiors, who would 'put some stuff online and flag it in the paper' to 'drive people towards' the site. Meanwhile, a Sunday tabloid security correspondent predicted that his paper was 'sure' to follow the lead of 'the whole *Mail Online* spectre', which was 'taking over, *driving*' Associated Newspapers (publisher of the *Daily Mail* and *Mail on Sunday*). Copy he filed for his weekly paper was already routinely transformed by online reporters, who added 'gloss' to make it more web-friendly.

Pressure to generate dramatic, entertaining and 'interactive' stories

If the frenetic routines of digital-era news-making leave journalists ever more reliant on particular *sources* – notably readily accessible officials and other elite knowers considered reliable and legally safe – this is only one factor conspiring to skew their focus towards specific types of *story*. If one outcome of the expansion of newspaper production into limit-less online publishing spaces has been to increase pressure on reporters to generate vast quantities of (often bite-sized) pseudo-news to fill it, another has been to stoke editors' appetites for bigger, bolder, more *dramatic* stories – replete with eye-catching headlines and pictures. An increasingly systematic feature of the process by which news judgment is exercised is the use of cold, hard data on newspaper sales figures and hit rates to measure the relative popularity of one genre over another. The implication of this trend is that, regardless of what might be objectively happening in the world and the relative importance of competing stories, reporters now face constant pressure to serve up content to prescriptive recipes designed to lure in readers and advertisers. While this may seem only a logical next step from the age-old truism that newspapers knowingly write for target audiences, the effect of wilfully pursuing certain stories – and giving them disproportionate prominence to maximize income – marks a new, more nakedly commercial, driver at the heart of the news-gathering process. Not only does it undermine the integrity of journalists' professional news judgment, but it positions newspapers as a distorting prism which, by excluding or marginalizing less popular subjects and over-emphasizing commercial ones, presents a version of social reality that is generalized, over-dramatic and lacking in nuance and variety. It is in the context of these efforts to chase market share above all else that newspapers place ever more emphasis on pushing alarmist, unrepresentative narratives over others – including dramatic stories about children. Data designed to focus news workers' minds on generating sellable stories is disseminated to journalists at all levels – from national news editors to junior weekly reporters. The local editorial director's daily routine is steeped in the business of analysing audience figures: starting at 8 a.m., he scrutinizes the 'overnight calls log' provided by his duty radio newsreader, before 'scouring' a list of potential leads for the day ahead and ensuring 'social media platforms are sufficiently busy – Twitter to tease upcoming web stories, Facebook to harvest feedback on live issues'. He then checks the company's main website 'to gauge interest levels on current stories – which can in turn determine stories' placement in [the] paper'. Information on the commercial performance of individual stories already online cascades down to the newsroom via memos emailed to every reporter each morning, detailing the number of hits their latest stories have achieved. This leads to a 'huge amount of healthy internal competition', on the basis that 'if a story is generating a lot of interest, it will move up the running order' on the website and 'inform the thinking' about whether (or how prominently) it appears in print.

Using such tactics to foster healthy internal competition seems to have had the desired trickle-down effect: the Somerset-based journalist would 'put stuff up I think will attract hits', based on 'daily reports' she received by email detailing 'which stories have attracted the most'. It was 'constantly drummed into' her which types of news were most popular – principally celebrity, travel, weather and (significantly, given the subject of this book) crime. The North London reporter faced similar pressures: with figures from Google Analytics sent round by her news editor displaying a 'massive spike' in web traffic for articles about 'crime, stabbing, young people doing bad things'. 'Because we [reporters] are quite young, it's very competitive about web traffic', she added, describing how she would consciously 'try to do something ... bigger' than her 'young counterpart' in another office if she knew he had 'got lots of hits'. Not every reporter seemed comfortable with this increasingly demand-led approach to news-making, however. As with the increased dependency on official sources, there were modest signs of resistance from older hands. Though even the deputy editor of an atypical North London paper, known for its liberal politics, conceded crime stories were 'in demand', he rationalized this as reflecting people's desire 'to know what's happening on their doorstep'. And, while the Devon crime reporter likened his paper's formula for prioritizing web stories to 'the theory used to determine what goes on the front page, what goes on page two, three, four, five and six', he cautioned that recognizing 'some stories ... attract more attention than others' could ultimately lead to an 'only-cover-stories-that-get-big-hits-online' approach.

Though she stopped short of endorsing such practices, the local daily web editor quoted in Chapter 3 admitted basing the choice of stories she uploaded online at different times of day on 'three peaks' in traffic coinciding with key points when office workers browsed online – the rationale being that she was serving a demand for 'what do I need to know this morning?' and 'what do I want to know as I'm winding down', with 'funny stories for people to read over lunch' sandwiched in between. The overwhelming example set by nationals, too, appeared to indicate that audience-driven news practices are here to stay. One Sunday tabloid specialist described disapprovingly how his paper's pace of production had been '*massively* cranked up' since it began embracing digital, adding that mention of its print circulation figures and online performance constantly 'seep into general conversation'. A colleague recalled the growing onus placed on journalists to find sellable stories on the *Independent* (a paper he had recently left), where editors 'take it really seriously'. He recalled 'chatting to the guy who was in charge of digital production', who 'had all these figures at his fingertips' illustrating which stories 'generated x amount of hits' and which 'were ... less interesting'. Although the weekend news editor saw print sales as more important – reflecting his paper's older (less web-savvy) readership – he acknowledged encouraging reporters to write stories about subjects like pensions and health, that 'get lots of interest from our readers', and fretting about 'what are we doing wrong?' whenever sales fell. Similarly, for a reporter on the *Sun* – Britain's biggest-selling daily newspaper – and the assistant news editor of a mid-market tabloid, the litmus test of audience engagement with particular stories (or types of story) was a combination of print sales and feedback received through physical (and virtual) postbags. The former emphasized his paper's use of focus groups to gauge readers' preferences for different story types, and said of its predilection for dramatic crimes involving children:

> We can't *make* crimes happen ... I'm not going to say that ... in the morning we're praying for some big murder, because I certainly don't work that way. If something happens, I'm as shocked as everyone else, but at the same time your journalistic mind is going, 'that's going to be a big story' ... To say to the public, 'we're always looking out for the macabre and the shocking' is quite grim, isn't it? It's quite cynical. Yet we know that's what people are interested in.

Likewise, while the mid-market assistant news editor denied 'searching the net' for grim news, he conceded his 'eyes' were 'looking for stories ... involving adversity' while trawling newswires. Describing his paper's readers as 'an immediate focus group' that told it what 'sells', he said his editors would 'forget about' an issue if 'it dies a death after two days', because 'we are ... trying to sell a paper'. The same bottom line-driven approach to monitoring the likes/dislikes of 'reader focus groups' – these days traceable as much through online discussion threads and social media as print sales or web hits – was applied in local newsrooms, where it consistently led to a morbid fascination with dramatic juvenile narratives. Age-old editorial decisions about where to place certain stories in the paper, according to the Somerset reporter, now involved the 'sales manager', who advised on the basis of 'previous sales' of issues with particular front pages. 'Choosing stories that sell papers' for prominent positions was 'definitely a factor' in determining what 'to put on the front', she said, adding, 'we know crime sells well, as do family tributes to dead people'. The editorial director agreed 'dramatic stories' about children were 'more newsworthy' than 'traditional "cute kids" supplements', which, while providing 'steady sales increases', could not compete with 'far higher increases' sparked by murders and kidnappings.

He said the two 'most-read' stories on his group's website 'both feature attempted child abductions' – echoing the retired crime reporter's memory of how 'sales would rocket' when his paper ran such tales.

In the first instance, then, the ability to analyse web traffic appeared to induce editors to track *how many* readers (or users) their stories attracted – and, significantly, use these measures to inform both the kinds of stories they selected from the 'news net' (Tuchman, 1978) and the sources they used to frame them. But more enthusiastic online converts had moved beyond this, in the belief that the key to profiting from the web was not so much the *quantity* of passing trade that newspapers drew in as the *quality* of relationships they developed with audience members to persuade them to return for more – and even participate in editorial processes. One national broadsheet with a sophisticated method for monitoring online readership and participation used this less as a way of guiding reporters to generate crowd-pleasing *future* stories than to enhance those already running, by developing a 'conversation' with informed readers. The paper's community manager explained:

> We're looking at what are people talking about on our site. What are they interacting on elsewhere? Should we be covering it? We find ourselves approaching journalists on the paper saying, 'we have this website: we have this huge shop window. How can we further your reporting?'

But, while there were some signs that more web-centric local papers wanted to develop similarly qualitative approaches – the local daily's web editor used its 'own analytics' to track 'uniques' (numbers of individual visitors) while also monitoring the time they spent on the site, where they were 'from', whether they were 'new' to it, and even 'how they moved through' it while browsing – the major driving force remained data tracking user *numbers*. So, while her 'default position' was to make discussion threads available beneath 'every story' online, in the hope that readers might linger long enough to debate them, she conceded that her first daily routine was to 'put on stories I think will generate the biggest hits'. Inevitably, this continual bombardment of data demonstrating the commercial appeal of certain categories of news piled enormous strain on reporters, as they simultaneously kept their radars primed for popular story types while churning their required daily quotas of content. And on occasions when they *did* stumble on leads with perceived commercial potential, they could face almost unbearable pressure from their news editors to turn these into marketable stories – regardless of whether the facts supported them. 'They [news-desk] almost *want* it to happen', explained an *Argus* reporter, adding, 'once something is a story it's quite hard to knock it down: it *suits* everyone for it to be a story'. There is clear anecdotal evidence, then, to explain why the pursuit/prioritization of stories judged to have commercial appeal based on past sales figures and hit rates leads to papers disproportionately foregrounding dramatic narratives about children – whether positioned as victims or threats. The deeper question of *why* such an appetite for these forbidding tales exists is explored later in this chapter.

Pressure to present stories in dramatic and entertaining ways

Commercial pressure on journalists to *produce* articles that feed a perceived public appetite for juvenile drama also manifests itself in the language and imagery they choose to *frame* narratives – the aim being, first, to catch readers' attention, and then to hold it long enough to persuade them to interact with stories. These efforts to engage audiences are, in most cases, intrinsically commercially motivated. The rationale is that the longer readers engage with a story, the more time they spend reading the paper (instead of doing other things) – and the more likely they are to browse other content, discuss it and, perhaps, tweet a hyperlink or share or post it elsewhere. Though journalists generally dismissed suggestions that they knowingly dramatized (let alone sensationalized) stories, they acknowledged a desire to make them 'compelling' – even 'entertaining'. As a leading feature writer on a Sunday broadsheet reflected, 'you are aware you are competing in a crowded market: you are aware they [readers] don't have time. All the while you are trying to snag and keep the readers'. Others were more brazen: the mid-market assistant news editor conceded that, in striving to 'sell a product', he was 'completely conscious' of exaggerating certain elements of stories to affect readers. 'An instinct kicks in: you *know* what to do. You *do* have a sense of, "how far can I take it?" You want to take it as far as you can', he said, adding, 'why you choose to do one thing or another ... reflects ... what you see, who you're selling it to, who will read it, and you know certain facts written in the intro or written in the headline ... make a good story – or perhaps *don't*, and that's what you leave out'.

Indeed, the idea of playing up certain aspects of a story – and playing down others – for dramatic effect is hardwired into day-to-day reporting across the sector, with journalists encouraged to frame stories in ways calculated to strike emotional chords with readers and hold their interest. Though, like many interviewees, the Somerset reporter insisted she tried to 'play it straight' and let stories 'speak for themselves', she admitted using emotive tones in tragic tales to nudge readers towards particular responses; picking the 'most dramatic element of the story for the intro', and favouring 'words such as "horror" [or] "shock" ... when writing health pieces – i.e. sick children'. 'I'll definitely write it with the aim of making the reader feel sympathy', she added. Similarly, the North London senior reporter recalled her paper's decision to 'exploit the fact that people were horrified' by a story about 'young people stabbing each other ... at three o'clock in the afternoon' because of 'a comment made about somebody's girlfriend'. Describing this story as 'a gift', she said the paper was 'very aware' of exploiting the opportunity 'to generate more copy', including features and opinion pieces, as well as straight news stories. The inclination to 'pull out the thesaurus' (as the Devon-based reporter put it) when covering incidents that are 'worse, more awful, more traumatic, more distressing than others' is becoming increasingly normative, as journalists are pressurized to 'snag and keep' readers (broadsheet feature writer). Recalling extensive reports and background features he wrote about Vanessa George, the Plymouth nursery worker who photographed herself abusing children in her care (a horror story recalled by Chapter 3's focus group mothers), the Devon reporter admitted having 'got all literary' to 'get across the horror of what happened'. 'The idea is still to keep the reader reading to the very end and if I have to make it more "readable" then I won't beat myself up about it', he argued, adding that 'what's wrong is being sensationalist when it's not needed'. And, while the group editorial director rejected any suggestion that his journalists would 'dramatize' stories – arguing that it implied 'exaggeration or embellishment, which isn't something we do' – he acknowledged giving alarming juvenile stories extensive coverage, with 'eye-catching headlines and pictures', for commercial reasons, explaining it was 'really important to be entertaining as well as informative'. As the plethora of online news outlets means that local papers are rarely the sources of 'breaking news' these days, his team had to give people 'compelling reasons ... to continue to buy' – chiefly by 'digging beneath the skin of a story and finding fresh, interesting angles'. Given that 'casual sales' to 'the supermarket shopper' increasingly 'make up a fair chunk of our readership', he conceded his 'front pages are no longer as sober as in years past'.

What this editor described as 'digging beneath' a story's 'skin' – giving it in-depth coverage that might have the *effect* (if not intention) of enhancing its dramatic impact – was echoed by the broadsheet feature writer, who reflected on the changing role of papers in a world in which, long before the next morning's editions, the 'facts' of most stories had often been picked over online and/or by 24-hour news channels. 'You get the facts – or even a live running interpretation of them – from [BBC] News 24 or the website, so what you are looking for is *understanding*: you are looking for what it all *means*', he said. A former assistant editor of another national broadsheet – where he was directly involved in decisions about how to structure the paper with the 'imperative' aim of boosting readership – said he habitually took 'an inordinate amount of time' coming up with 'an arresting image that will make people stop and want to read that page when they are going through the paper'. Though he would 'reject the word "entertainment"' to describe this process, he agreed that he tried to present his stories 'in a compelling way' – in his case, by locking into a continuum of storytelling traditions stretching back through time, whether 'around the fireside or down the pub'. More prosaically, journalists also play on *present-day* continuums by deliberately plugging *new* stories into *ongoing* societal narratives – drawing on dramatic symbolism and archetypes with which audiences will be familiar, echoing the tendency towards 'continuity' or 'follow-up' observed by, respectively, Galtung and Ruge (1965) and Harcup and O'Neill (2001). In this way, they engage in a process of conscious distortion, by generalizing events and caricaturing their protagonists for maximum narrative impact. So public perceptions of the menace posed by 'feral youth' or 'hoodies' were, argued the mid-market assistant news editor, 'reinforced' by the nature/scale of press focus on this group – with the effect that 'older generations' now complained about the threat they posed despite 'never having seen them, never having met them' and knowing about them solely 'through the prism of the media'. Admitting that his paper had consciously drawn on the hoodie motif when covering England's 2011 riots, he said it 'of course' decided to 'emphasize' the involvement of 'disaffected youth: the bored, lazy youth'. It 'almost doesn't matter if they're technically outnumbered by over-25s', because 'a disproportionate number' of youths took part. Given the same journalist's admission that he scanned newswires for 'adversity', it is clear that decisions to *construct* individual narratives in black-and-white terms are matched by similar distortions in initial news *selection*. The net *effect* of this twofold distortion is that papers culpably misrepresent reality for profit. As the feature writer put it, the tendency to give blanket coverage to 'child abduction and disappearances' – sidelining other major stories in the process – creates 'the impression that it happens more often than it does'.

Journalists as door-to-door salespeople

The pressure on today's newspaper journalists to proactively sell their stories does not begin and end with story selection and framing. The commercialization of reporting has now gone far beyond this – to the extent that reporters' jobs are not done until they have taken more *direct* steps to market their wares to the public. 'Now you know you've got to beat the opposition and there's a new way of doing this: you can tweet your line', lamented the Sunday tabloid security correspondent. Describing the regimes at other nationals, he said tweeting had become almost mandatory at his former paper, the *Independent*, while 'the last edict' at the *Telegraph* stipulated that reporters 'must tweet 10 times a day'. Indeed, direct marketing – or virtual door-to-door selling – of papers' news lines using social media has become such a standard part of daily reporting routines for many that the Devon crime reporter felt it was 'not a lot to expect' him to tweet about his (and colleagues') articles, while much of the local web editor's time was spent 'managing' her paper's Twitter and Facebook profiles. And social media use goes beyond using it as a mere marketing tool: it is also increasingly aiding the process of news-gathering itself, with audience members encouraged to contribute user-generated content that might produce follow-up stories and/or add value (and readers) to those already running. The web editor said this happened 'all the time', especially with 'child victim' stories focusing on 'kids who have died in car crashes'. Whereas 'before you would have had to wait for police to release the name' of the deceased, today 'family and friends' tweet pictures, tributes and biographical details, or 'come onto discussion threads'. The broadsheet community manager said her reporters 'use the comments around their articles and hash-tags' to 'enhance what they are writing'. But, while she insisted her paper harnessed such contributions to improve the quality of its reporting, for most others any *editorial* value of UGC was trumped by its commercial benefits. The hope was that participating audience members could create virtuous circles, drawing in yet more (and more active) readers – and, with them, advertisers. As the editorial director conceded, in relation to a wider point about the industry's pursuit of online audiences, 'an advertiser will buy a certain number of page impressions … and once the site has received that number of visitors his ad disappears – so it's in our interests to drive as much traffic as possible to present maximum commercial opportunities'.

Journalists' rationales for the narrative resonance of dramatic juvenile stories

Of perhaps greatest significance here is the fact that, in constructing their dramatized representations of social reality, journalists confess to knowingly drawing on the narrative tropes and conventions of literary and cinematic fiction. Their use of such framing devices reflects an implicit understanding that, in serving a perceived public appetite for cautionary tales involving children, they are – like gothic novelists and genre screenwriters – drawing on horror traditions stretching back centuries. A common term used by interviewees across the spectrum to rationalize the appeal of stories revolving around unresolved child abductions or murders was 'mystery'. 'There is a nub of stories that are universal to *all* newspapers ... and that is *partly* because ... they are great stories: they're stories people will be talking about in the pub', reflected the broadsheet crime correspondent, adding that 'in the *crime* context' readers were 'always intrigued by mystery'. For the *Sun* reporter, the essence of commercially popular tales was their particular mix of 'ingredients' – and the abduction of blonde-haired, blue-eyed Madeleine McCann from a Portuguese holiday resort 'had them all – it had ... every parent's worst nightmare – the ... very well-to-do family, a beautiful child and ... a very innocent circumstance'. In an explicit evocation of both the popular appeal of crime fiction and the deep-seated tendency of readers (and journalists) to project plausible scenarios back on to themselves – a 'people like us' instinct that emerged in the focus group discussions – he said:

> You can imagine the conversations ... '*we* did that, we leave our kids, remember that time we left little Johnnie and went down for a drink in the hotel?' And then you throw in the foreign element ... It was almost a murder mystery: you know, 'what happens next? What *might* have happened?'

While the crime genre looms large in the storytelling techniques used by journalists to convey dramatic incidents involving juveniles – not least because many involve abuse, murder or abduction – equally prevalent is the imagery of fairy-tales and horror movies. For the feature writer – whose 'reputation' rested on his ability to write 'entertaining, compelling' articles that were 'more of a "read"' than straightforward stories – the 'archetype of the missing child' provided a perfect locus for haunting narratives straight out of 'the Brothers Grimm' with which parents everywhere could identify. Referring to the disproportionate emphasis that papers placed on reporting such stories when they occurred against respectable middle-class/idyllic backdrops, rather than socially dysfunctional/crime-ridden ones – a 'worthy/unworthy' distinction to which we return below – he, too, evoked the 'people like us' theme:

> All these things are based on this idea, 'could it happen here? Could it happen to me?' If you get a place that looks beautiful it's perfect for that ancient narrative, in a story-telling way. That's probably part of the reason you don't get so much emphasis on things happening to kids against chaotic backgrounds: people are going to go, 'that's what happens in those awful places, isn't it?'

While this writer described the potency of stories revolving around a 'serpent in paradise' motif – a clear evocation of the idea of malign familiar strangers lurking in our midst – the retired crime specialist drew on imagery from Franz Kafka's *Metamorphosis* in recalling a macabre court story about a couple who choked their babies to death. Describing a reporter's role as being to both 'convey a story' and 'touch nerves', he recalled comparing the sight of the baby 'rocking' in a cradle in a squalid, fly-infested room 'in the middle of summer' to 'a scene from Kafka'. And, though the feature writer rejected any suggestion that journalists would exploit nightmare scenarios as 'entertainment' – insisting any parallels between the outputs of Hollywood and the newspaper industry were based on art imitating life, not the reverse – he conceded that papers might sometimes *tap into* the popular appeal of horror movies. While arguing this was primarily an 'issue' for the 'entertainment industry', rather than the news media, he reflected that 'people like to be scared ... that's why they've made six *Saw* movies' (an intriguing echo of one working-class mother's admission that she and her husband 'love our horrors'). 'They [Hollywood] create hyper-real fictions on the basis of what happens. *They* copy *us*: we don't copy them', he remarked, adding, 'it may be that out of that compulsion we produce stories that resonate' and 'have something in common with Hollywood and other forms of entertainment'. The suggestion that papers *knowingly* play up audiences' (presumed) anxieties to attract – and engage – readers was accepted with fewer caveats by others. Despite arguing that tales of fear and distrust favoured by his mid-market tabloid were, in part, driven by the 'bizarre psychosis' that attracts British audiences to 'negative' stories, its assistant news editor conceded his paper promoted a worldview that 'this country has gone to the dogs' and 'everything is in decline', including 'school' and 'the family'. For this reason, it was 'with some justification' seen as 'having quite a negative, misanthropic view of Britain [and] the world'.

Constructing a 'worthy' versus 'unworthy' discourse

Just as the 'serpent in paradise' and 'gone to the dogs'[4] metaphors evoke loss of innocence *over time*, so too do newspapers consistently distinguish between more and less innocent children (and families) in the *present*, when deciding how much (and what manner of) coverage to give otherwise comparable stories. In so doing, they implicitly reinforce a socially constructed opposition between deviance and respectability: them and us. Britain's press, argued the mid-market assistant news editor, is biased 'across the board' in 'valuing' a 'white, upper middle-class person' over either working-class or 'non-white' individuals, with 'the social class' or 'sometimes the ethnicity' of a child elevating one story and downgrading another – so 'white, respectable, middle-class will get above black working-class'. To this end, his reporters routinely checked the level of social worthiness of a child/family by typing their postcodes into (geographical visualization program) Google Street View before deciding whether to cover a story and how extensively. 'If there's a murder, "what's the postcode"?' he said, admitting that cases invariably received more coverage if their victims came from 'big five-bedroomed, detached' houses rather than council flats. Similarly, the broadsheet legal correspondent said it was 'all about the middle-class angle', with stories about 'tug-of-war in divorce' or one parent taking 'a child abroad' trumping all others – provided they involved well-heeled families. And a Sunday tabloid defence correspondent said he gained more kudos with his news desk for generating human interest stories involving the military if children, rather than soldiers, could be positioned as victims. In a further indication of the onus placed on finding dramatic stories about juveniles in general – and those from respectable households in particular – he reflected that, with soldiers regarded as 'society's sacred cows', their offspring were treated as 'society's sacred *calves*'. 'You can't get better than a story about ... this poor child of a soldier. Wow!', he said, reflecting, 'in any genre, if you can get a child into the story it becomes big news'.

For the feature writer, the middle-versus-working-class distinction was never more manifest than in the wildly contrasting coverage of, respectively, Madeleine McCann and nine-year-old Shannon Matthews, who disappeared from her home on a deprived estate in Dewsbury, West

Yorkshire, only a few months later. Despite disapproving of this prejudice, he argued that the immediate and blanket press interest in the
McCanns' plight had another commercial dimension related to measures of worthiness, besides social class: the relative attractiveness (and
articulacy) of the girls' mothers. 'You will get acres of Maddie because
her mum was beautiful, whereas not so many acres and some really
unpleasant stuff on Shannon's family because her mum wasn't', he said.
By foregrounding one victim over another – rather than giving comparable coverage to *all* such cases – newspapers were distorting reality still
further, by making the case of the middle-class, photogenic child appear
even 'more important than it actually is'. The flipside of newspapers'
bias towards affluent, physically attractive, respectable families in 'child
victim' cases is the disproportionate attention lavished on stories positioning the children of down-at-heel, unprepossessing, dysfunctional
households as 'threats'. According to the *Argus* reporter, this press stereotype has become ingrained for pragmatic reasons, as the introduction
of antisocial behaviour orders (ASBOs) – civil penalties used to target
types of low-level disorder historically 'concentrated in deprived urban
areas' (Millie et al., 2005) – enables journalists to name and shame errant
juveniles without legal redress, in a way that was impossible when such
cases only came to light through criminal proceedings in youth courts,
under which they were banned from identifying them (Great Britain.
Children and Young Persons Act 1933). 'The ASBO thing comes to life',
he said, because papers are allowed to print 'the child's name, the street
where he is'. Yet, even if we accept the argument that press interest in
ASBOs is primarily driven by pragmatic (not ideological) considerations,
one outcome of its disproportionate focus on middle-class families in
'victim' cases and working-class (or underclass) ones when writing about
'threats' is an implicit narrative distinction not only between imagined
halcyon days past and a similarly fictive present in which (to quote the
feature writer) 'everything's broken' and 'we need it fixed', but also the
relative levels of 'worthiness' of *today's* children – and their 'broken' or
'fixed' families. In this sense, newspaper discourse of the present – and
the simmering *public* anxieties it magnifies in pursuit of ever bigger,
more active audiences – displays the same cultural amnesia that Pearson
(1983) observed in his historical analysis of recurring moral panics
about child 'hooligans'. Like today's juvenile panics, all these 'outbreaks'
of delinquency were depicted by the newspapers of their times as (more
or less) decisive *breaks* with a more ordered, disciplined past. And, just as
today's public moralists – from the *Daily Mail's* Melanie Phillips (2011)
to Mr Cameron (Great Britain. Cabinet Office and Prime Minister's

Office, 10 Downing Street, 2011) – distinguish between 'worthy' and 'unworthy' children (and the 'deserving' and 'undeserving' offspring of the poor) in their discourse about 'feral' or 'troubled' families, the Victorians happily pitted the 'sacralised' (Zelizer, 1985, pp. 184–5) against the 'delinquent' child (King, 1998).

Case study: juvenile panic as urban myth

Perhaps the starkest illustration of how commercially attractive juvenile panic narratives can spiral out of control – as the viral nature of today's social mediation conspires with the hyperactive, publicity-seeking activities of primary definers and the profit-driven motives of secondary ones – emerged from analysis of the construction of a running story already touched on in Chapter 3. This was the unfolding July 2011 saga involving a supposed spate of stalking and attempted abductions by the driver of a 'black car' in various locations around Sussex. As one of the journalists responsible for chronicling this tangled tale conceded, the feverish atmosphere it engendered among members of the public – and the tense, at times hostile, exchanges it spawned online – were, in the end, entirely unjustified, as the truth of the story (to the extent it ever fully emerged) was that there almost certainly wasn't one. The following short extract, from the 16 July edition of the *Argus*, gives a flavour of the way the succession of alleged incidents was first framed on the page. In the intro of a page-lead story entitled 'Man seen loitering near schools' (Loomes, 2011a), Naomi Loomes reported:

> POLICE are looking for a man seen hanging around schools in a black car after a ten-year-old was offered a lift by a stranger.

All three core elements of this recurring story were introduced here: the concept of a 'stranger', the suggestion he had been loitering and/or offering children lifts to and from school, and the ominous 'black car' motif. The use of the word 'police' repeatedly in the story's opening paragraphs added legitimacy to the paper's assertion that these were authentic incidents. The intro was also noteworthy for its failure to specify the location where the 'stranger' made his approach (vagueness likely to have fuelled unnecessary speculation among readers about whether the incident had happened in their own neighbourhoods). In the first alleged incident, a 10-year-old girl had reported 'feeling' she was 'being followed by a black Mini', before its 'male driver' asked her if she wanted a lift, while the second revolved around the sighting of a man who 'stared at two children' while driving past them as they walked to a different school. Interestingly, the clear inconsistency in the descriptions of the two vehicles (the first a 'Mini', the second 'a black saloon car') was glossed over. Five days later, on a more prominent page (7, rather than 12), another headline informed anxious parents of a 'third child' (Loomes, 2011b) who had been 'offered [a] lift by a stranger'. Readers learnt that 'the 11-year-old girl was walking by herself' when 'a man in a black car' offered her a lift. Though yet another type of vehicle was mentioned (a Ford), consistent with the threatening familiarity paradigm (as in previous stories) was the ordinariness of its description. Perhaps most notable, however – and for very different reasons – was a piece the *Argus* ran on 26 July. So firm a grip did the unfolding mystery apparently have by this point that the paper published a full-page background feature under the headline 'Right to be aware and to educate ...' (Parsons, 2011). Unlike similar pieces, this article strained to promote calm – cautioning against overreaction by concerned citizens. While careful to avoid alienating anxious readers – it began with the truism 'nothing is more important to a parent than the safety of their children', reflecting it was 'not surprising' reports of 'strange men in black cars' caused alarm – it introduced the term 'panic' in its second paragraph. By its fourth, the piece had become even more questioning:

> Are we, therefore, surrounded by paedophiles? Are the streets of the county being stalked by predators, waiting to snatch a child the minute its parents' backs are turned?

In similarly balanced vein, the feature went on to caution readers that, though it was 'fair to say a tiny handful of people in society are practising predatory paedophiles', it was 'of great concern' that the degree of alarmism had reached the point 'where drivers and dog-walkers are being confronted with baseless accusations'. A further warning was implicit in the use of a large photograph above the headline depicting a banner reading 'Get the paedophiles out', strung from the balcony of a flat in Paulsgrove, Portsmouth, where (the paper reminded readers) there had been 'mob attacks after a newspaper campaign' – namely the *News of the World*'s pursuit of 'Sarah's Law' (Blacker & Griffin, 2010). Moreover, in a line that might have been written precisely to address the folly of panicking unnecessarily about familiar strangers – a sentiment echoing the way the hysterical public reaction to this story was recounted by working-class mothers in Chapter 3.5 – the *Argus* added, 'woe betide the man who goes to pick his child up in a black car' or dares 'say hello to one of his child's friends or offer them a lift'.

Evidence of the extent to which concerned audience members became involved in not only *responding* to the story, as reported, but in *reinforcing* its construction could be found on the lengthy discussion thread generated by the 21 July report into the alleged 'third' abduction attempt. Though the 58-post thread became the scene of an, at times unsettling, debate as two unabashed sceptics – using the aliases 'Billy Bones' and 'papa_melons' – repeatedly ridiculed parents alarmed by the alleged incidents, the overwhelming majority of posters not only accepted the reports at face value but read into the story a message about the need for constant vigilance against stranger-danger. Moreover, as with all the most extensively discussed articles in the sample, a number of posters went further, adding *information of their own* to the mix that effectively consolidated the story on which they were commenting. Among these were self-styled 'fred claus', who told fellow readers 'the same thing' had been tried by 'this sicko' that morning. Similarly, 'Tippy Toes' dismissed Billy Bones's contention that the police did not believe the various reported incidents were 'linked' or worth 'doing much about' by revealing that 'my daughter's school were informed by the police' so 'I am guessing that they do think there is a problem'.

Interviewed about this story months later, one *Argus* journalist candidly conceded that, in hindsight, it almost certainly 'wasn't true'. In a telling insight into the multi-directional way in which today's news narratives are constructed and negotiated, he described the wave of supposed incidents as a self-fulfilling prophecy emanating initially from a stranger-danger 'awareness event' that led to a succession of children reporting adults behaving suspiciously – and a resulting explosion of claims, counter-claims and Chinese rumours on social media. As an illustration, he recalled how a report from one schoolgirl sparked a local council to activate an 'early warning system' which, in turn, led to everybody 'going round saying there's been an attack, or an *approach*, which they "read" as an attack'. Confusion caused by the subsequent viral spread of rumours on social media led to people 'thinking they were getting fresh reports' when, in fact, their friends were misinterpreting (and re-posting) the same incidents as new ones. The result, he argued, was an unjustified 'panic' fuelled by a febrile combination of gossip, school pep-talks and the fact that – at least partly for commercial reasons – his editors felt compelled to include 'something in the paper' to cover themselves. However, despite reflecting that the alleged incidents 'pretty much stopped at the end of term', without police managing to confirm 'a single one' of 30-odd reports – the most dramatic supposedly involving a 'a kid fighting someone off with a tennis racket' – the reporter continued to defend his paper's decision to publicize them. The particular role of the local press as a (trusted) source of public information meant that it *had* 'to treat it like news', he argued, in case 'somebody *did* attack a young person and the police say, "well, we did tell the press"'.

In the next chapter, we unpick in detail how juvenile panics play out *in practice*, in the context of a contemporaneous case study of a textbook live news story about a 'worthy' child victim and the lost innocence of a close-knit, seemingly safe, community. By combining analysis of newspaper texts and discussion threads, parent focus groups and interviews with journalists who covered this story, we explore how juvenile panics are crystallized in the public sphere through a dynamic transaction between primary definers, the press, its audience(s) and other players. The case study will demonstrate how, far from merely *reflecting* society's anxieties, papers have the power to *activate* and/or *reinforce* them – by exploiting and repackaging deep-rooted neuroses about misplaced trust as commercial entertainment.

5
'Every Parent's Worst Nightmare': The Abduction of April Jones

On Monday 1 October 2012, at approximately 10.30 p.m., Dyfed-Powys Police tweeted a short statement, describing how it was 'increasingly concerned for the whereabouts of a five-year-old girl' from the small Welsh town of Machynlleth. Early the next day it confirmed that April Jones had been abducted at around 7 p.m., after apparently climbing into a car which had pulled up close to where she was playing with friends. The story was immediately elevated to number one headline status across British national radio, television, online and print news. Over the ensuing week the police search for April received rolling coverage and dominated national (and many regional) newspaper front pages. Every twist was examined in minute detail – from the revelation that she needed medication for cerebral palsy to the tragic irony that she had been allowed to play out on the night she was taken as a treat for receiving a glowing school report. The day after April's abduction, Mark Bridger, 46, was arrested in connection with her abduction. By Saturday, he had been charged with her murder. On Sunday it emerged that, far from being only vaguely familiar with each other, April and Bridger were indirectly related.

If the press and public reactions to the disappearance of five-year-old April Jones shared one common characteristic it was their magnification of key elements of the story that plugged into the recurring narratives about child vulnerability explored in Chapters 3 and 4. In particular, what emerged from popular discourse around this 'single sensational case' (Cohen, 2002, p. xxiii) was a generalized sense of juvenile panic positioning children as continually susceptible to the predations of malevolent adults, especially familiar strangers. The following sections unpick how this quintessential abduction narrative played out in the public sphere in the seven-day period beginning with the initial police statement confirming that April was missing – and the broader lessons we might draw from the episode. We begin by analysing how the incident was identified, conceived and pursued, based on interviews with 10 national press journalists who worked on the story, before unpicking how it was framed on the page, both by professional newswriters and through the dialogue that active audience members entered into on newspaper discussion threads. We then consider what can be learnt from the general public *reaction* to news of the abduction, as articulated both on discussion threads and in face-to-face conversations between members of the parent focus groups, which were reconvened within weeks of April's murder to discuss their responses to the case. As we shall see, journalists, their sources, their articles and members of the public all drew on the same key imagery to make sense of (and distil meaning from) April's story. And it was the convergence of focus on these common tropes – unsupervised outdoor play, mystery vehicles and abduction by (familiar) strangers – at every interface in the communication process that conspired to crystallize the simmering juvenile panic discourse.

Commercializing April: harnessing and exploiting the empathy factor

Interviews with journalists who reported April's abduction for 10 national daily and Sunday newspapers demonstrate extraordinary levels of across-the-board editorial interest in the story – from daily red-tops to Sunday broadsheets. They also help *explain* this intense focus – and, by extension, the wider newsworthiness ascribed to stories positioning children at the mercy of nefarious adults – by reflecting on its qualities as both a projection of anxieties about risk and misplaced trust shared by audience members and journalists and a classic late-modern gothic fairy-tale ideally placed to exploit these insecurities for commercial gain. Given its strong human interest dimension – a missing five-year-old girl, distraught parents and the all-too-identifiable scenario of unsupervised outdoor play against which it unfolded – it is hardly surprising that the story swiftly captured press attention. Nonetheless, the sheer scale of reporting operations launched by certain news desks, notably those of two conservative tabloids (one red-top, the other mid-market), surprised even some of their own staff. The latter's exhaustive response was vividly recalled by the journalist who made its first phone enquiries into April's disappearance after spotting a police tweet while working a late shift the night she vanished:

> We sent one reporter, who's based in Birmingham – just said, 'go first thing in the morning'. Then, by the time I came into work the next day, it was on Sky News – the full rolling Sky News coverage – and we had about six reporters down there, specialists, like our crime specialist, a colour writer ... They [the news desk] just throw so many ... bodies at it ...

The same journalist described how, even days later, 'everyone' in the newsroom was still working on the story – with the paper bolstering its 'ground staff' in Wales by assigning several reporters to spend 'day and night' in Surrey, chasing up background information about suspected abductor Mark Bridger, after it emerged that he hailed from that county. Describing the forensic attention lavished by her paper on every aspect of the story, she recalled being ordered to request a copy of Bridger's birth certificate, in search of any previously unreported biographical details, and to 'look up all the addresses' of 'hundreds of friends' on his Facebook profile, so 'people on the ground could go round and see them'. The red-top was equally exhaustive, keeping one reporter stationed in mid-Wales until seven days after April's abduction – and only withdrawing him after Bridger's initial court appearance on Monday 8 October. Towards the end of the week, the paper parachuted in reinforcements to supplement two reporters initially sent from Manchester to attend the twice-daily police press conferences and 'doorstep' April's family, friends and neighbours and a veteran journalist who was anchoring the Machynlleth operation from a local hotel. Its main bases covered, another senior reporter was dispatched from London to (as he put it) 'come up with something different' by mopping up details missed by rivals and re-interviewing peripheral individuals, including neighbours that Bridger had recently left behind on moving house. Describing the anchor's role as 'just making calls, monitoring the wires, looking at websites, bringing everything together', he said his own was motivated by the commercial question, 'what are we going to do to make it [the paper's coverage] different to everyone else?'

Far from being confined to conservative and/or tabloid papers, moreover, this disproportionate journalistic response was reflected sector-wide. Despite being less well-staffed, another, more liberal, tabloid already had three reporters and three full-time photographers at the scene by 8 a.m. the day after April's disappearance. One of its reporters described a military-style offensive, recalling how 'the most important thing was we were well organized', with everyone knowing what their 'specific tasks' were each day, barring any 'dramatic developments'. Similarly, quality newspapers were as quick to pour their (more limited) resources into the town, and nearby Aberystwyth, where police news conferences were held. One senior reporter on a liberal broadsheet spent two weeks in Machynlleth, establishing an early routine of filing 'a story first thing, one at lunchtime and others whenever something happened'. Reflecting his paper's prioritization of web coverage, he also posted 'regular iPhone videos and tweets' via a 'live blog', before emailing his editors 'what they wanted for the paper' later the same day. And, despite having a smaller editorial budget, another liberal broadsheet assigned two reporters to cover the story from day one – including its sole regional reporter for northern Britain and its crime correspondent, who rang his news editor on a 'day off' to urge him to 'look at sending on this one' after stumbling across the story online. The regional correspondent described finding Machynlleth 'under siege' from satellite trucks and frenzied reporters when he arrived early on Wednesday. 'Even the *Times* had four people there', he remarked, and the overall media presence felt 'incredibly mob-handed'. One of those *Times* reporters concurred with this view of overkill – remarking that 'TV crews were really getting in the way in the end' and 'police were going, "what exactly are you going to do? Live coverage of us finding a body?"'.

Sunday papers – whose next editions would be published nearly seven days after April's disappearance, at a point when (barring a last-minute murder charge on their eve of publication) major story developments were likely to have evaporated – also invested significant resources throughout the week in keeping watching briefs in mid-Wales. A leading Sunday broadsheet feature writer, whose joint by-line appeared on a page-lead the following weekend, recalled his news desk's determination to make something of the case by 'throwing some people at it', including its 'best door-stepper'. His bosses 'wanted a spread from the very beginning', plus a comment piece and 'almost certainly' a 'front-page story' with a 'minimum two pages, maybe three or four' dedicated to it. Again, the Sunday papers' early commitment to covering the story as extensively as possible was reflected universally – from bigger-selling to less popular titles; broadsheets to tabloids. Like other newspaper publishers, instead of pooling its papers' resources, Express Newspapers mounted two separate operations in Machynlleth – one each for its daily and Sunday titles – according to one of its reporters. Set alongside the red-top's desire to 'get something no one else has got' and the liberal tabloid reporter's observation that 'there is always pressure to get exclusive lines on these stories', the idea that journalists working for the *same* newspaper group were competing against *each other* for new angles and information on April and Bridger offers yet more evidence of the extreme commercial appeal editors ascribed to the story. Asked whether they had ever been involved in such large-scale reporting operations before, the red-top journalist could only name the McCann case, while the mid-market tabloid reporter listed three others: the 2011 shooting of five-year-old Thusha Kamaleswaran, London's youngest ever gun crime victim; the 2012 assassination of the al-Hilli family in the French Alps; and (weeks before April's murder) the alleged abduction of 15-year-old Megan Stammers by her schoolteacher, Jeremy Forrest. Tellingly, all focused on juvenile 'victims' of dramatic events.

The disproportionate priority that newspapers accorded the case over other news events is illustrated by more than just the *scale* of their reporting operations. The *Times* reporter was diverted from an assignment linked to a highly newsworthy ongoing public debate about deaths in police custody – an issue conforming to the oft-demonstrated news values of 'continuity' or 'follow-up' (Galtung & Ruge, 1965; Harcup & O'Neill, 2001). He recalled being 'phoned up ... at about seven o'clock in the morning, and told, "get to Machynlleth"' – a redeployment requiring him to 'hire a car', as he had taken a train to his previous job (in Warrington). April's abduction, he said, had 'very much' eclipsed everything else. Similarly, the liberal tabloid journalist recalled his editors' 'massive emphasis on the April Jones story in that first week' – putting this down to a judgment about 'what issues affect normal people more than others'. Even set against two other big rolling stories that week – an emerging scandal over allegations of historic child sexual abuse by the late television presenter Jimmy Savile and the annual conference of the Labour Party, of which his paper was a supporter – April's disappearance was felt to merit most attention. 'There is little doubt', he reasoned, 'that the abduction of a little girl from a normal working-class estate in Wales was much more relevant to people than the breaking Savile scandal or politics'. Indeed, only one interviewee (the live tweeting broadsheet reporter) disputed the notion that April's story was the most newsworthy of the week. Despite committing several journalists to it, including its Manchester reporter, crime correspondent and a live blogger, he insisted his paper probably 'put more resources into the Savile and Labour Party conferences' – stories it viewed as equally big, 'or bigger'. The *consensus* view of April as number one news priority was summed up by the mid-market reporter who picked up the story on her late shift. She attributed the intense press interest to the fact that April 'was a real person' and 'we had lots of pictures of a nice British family' – a source of appeal to a paper that 'wants to get a real face and a real person attached to' stories. By contrast, 'with the Savile case, it was anonymous people ... you can't name because of Operation Yewtree [police investigation]'.

A cursory glance at discussion threads published beneath early online newspaper reports of April's disappearance (a breakdown of which is given in Figure 5.1) confirms that it was not just journalists who viewed the case as extremely newsworthy. Many of the 580 posts on the most animated site, *www.mailonline.co.uk*, castigated the paper for not reporting April's story even *more* prominently. Typically, the 20-plus posters who criticized the site for initially failing to make the story its splash couched their comments as disbelieving questions. 'DM ... why is this story not currently at the top of your page?' whined 'jax, Essex', while 'soon to be ex pat [thank God]' queried 'why is this not the first story? Clearly a lot more important than Jimmy Saville'[1] and 'Loubymlou, Liverpool' asked 'what does it take for stories like this to be the main headline'. The most extreme example of this collective call from frustrated readers for the *Daily Mail* to rethink its priorities, however, was this near-hysterical hyperbole from 'John, Nottingham':

THIS STORY SHOULD BE THE TOP NEW[S] IN THE WORLD, you the people of the world this is your time to help we need to find this girl.

Similar sentiments were voiced by focus group members. The shy working-class mother, who admitted becoming instantly hooked by media coverage of April's abduction, expressed her irritation at the fact that it died down after a few days – the point at which Bridger was charged with murder and editors had to avoid prejudicing court proceedings (Great Britain. *Contempt of Court Act 1981*). In a revealing critique of professional news practices, she complained that TV and newspaper reports 'just sort of ended', leaving her thinking, 'hang on a minute – why ain't it still broadcasting when she's still *out* there?' An extension of these disproportionate gut reactions was the several-times-repeated concern that Britain should introduce a national alarm system to notify authorities/ communities nationwide the moment a young child disappeared, to maximize the chances of finding him/her. Among those calling for 'an automatic alert, with a picture if possible, going out to EVERY mobile phone in the country' was 'bridal 234, Portsmouth, United Kingdom'.

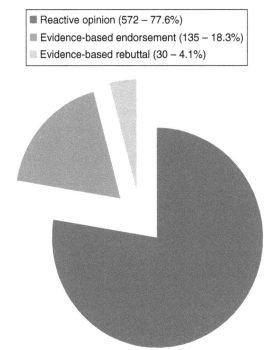

Figure 5.1 Breakdown of discussion posts

As it transpired (and the following day's print edition reported), April's abduction actually marked the first occasion when a then recently launched Child Rescue Alert system *was* activated in Britain (Laville, 2012). Indeed, the fact this US-style alarm system had been introduced at all (in 2010) – and utilized so soon afterwards – arguably reflected escalating sensitization to the prospect of child abduction indicative of a simmering juvenile panic.

The most unequivocal evidence of disproportion in discussion thread responses, though, can be discerned from a straightforward breakdown of the balance between comments *affirming* the hegemonic narrative and those adopting more 'negotiated' or 'oppositional' standpoints (Hall, 1980). For legal reasons, discussion threads on websites that ran them were largely withdrawn or shut down by the evening of 2 October – the point at which Bridger had been arrested and editors would have risked contempt of court proceedings had they continued publishing potentially prejudicial remarks. However, of 737 posts left by that point on the *Daily Mail*, *Sun*, *Daily Express* and *Times* websites – the only sampled publications to run threads – more than three-quarters (572) were straightforward reactions, of which 96 per cent (550) affirmed (or failed to challenge) dominant reading(s) of the story, as reported. The overwhelming consensus among readers contributing to these discussions, then, endorsed the underlying 'parental panic' discourse promoted by the reporting frenzy April's disappearance had provoked: namely the cautionary tale that, if left to play out unsupervised, even among friends and in familiar surroundings, young children were susceptible to being poached by predators. As Figure 5.3 illustrates, nearly 82 per cent of *evidence-based* posts endorsed the panicky consensus, with most of those contributing them boasting first-hand child-rearing experience – adding the weight of their own parenting expertise to enhance the persuasiveness of the dominant newspaper discourse. A typical endorsement from a *Daily Mail* reader upholding the dominant 'scary world' paradigm *without* directly condemning April's parents was 'cheryl, basingstoke's' statement that her 'thoughts are with the parents', as she 'would be going out of my mind' if this had happened to her five-year-old granddaughter. By contrast, 'family5, Bromley' adopted a position typical of those critical of the Joneses' parenting (explicitly or by inference) by questioning why, 'in this day & age where things are getting worse' – a clear evocation of the recurring idea that today's world is *less safe* than previously – some families were 'getting more relaxed'. Likewise, 'Clara, Dublin' stated there was 'no way I would have my 5 year old niece or any 5 year old playing outside at that time', before displaying textbook anecdotal evidence of the priming power of news narratives:

Do people not read what happens on the news!???

The most powerful evidence-based endorsement of this 'gone to the dogs'[2] paradigm, however, was 'bar, notts'' evocation of the fairy-tale motifs harnessed to polarize angelic April and demonic Bridger in newspaper coverage to dismiss the 'make-believe' attitudes of latter-day parents whose children were 'kept in an innocence that is not really safe'. In a rose-tinted allusion to a near-mythic past, (s)he wrote that, while children could play out safely in villages 'in the late fifties', when 'everyone looked after everyone elses children', there was 'not so much car ownership' and 'creepy men that lived in your area were generally known about', today's child abusers could 'travel around' easily. Besides drawing on fairy-tale tropes harnessed in news discourse, this contribution was significant in explicitly conflating two day-to-day concerns about child safety repeatedly voiced in focus groups – traffic and predatory paedophiles – by conjuring up images of a world in which 'creepy men' cruised around preying on unsuspecting children. Another revealing endorsement came from the wistfully self-christened 'somewhereovertherainbow, bucks', who referred to her fears emanating (at least partly) from the media, in saying she 'wouldn't let my 5 year old out to play with friends at 7.30 on a school night' because 'all you read recently is bad things in the news about children'.

Yet this borderline hysteria – and journalists' matter-of-fact assertions about the normative newsworthiness of April's story – only superficially explain why this single incident was held to justify such *disproportionate* investments of time, manpower and money that might otherwise have been harnessed to cover other events, and why it so singularly captured the collective imagination. The week of April's abduction witnessed not only Labour's conference and the start of a tsunami of allegations against Savile, but a tightening of the race to secure the US presidency between Barack Obama and Mitt Romney and the latest twist in a long-running saga over the British government's frustrated attempts to deport Muslim preacher Abu Hamza to Jordan. Yet, far from according one or more of these, between them, a comparable investment of scarce resources, newspapers instead chose to marshal their troops, on a mammoth scale, to provide saturation coverage of the frantic search for a missing five-year-old girl. If one mark of a moral panic is the degree of 'disproportion' (Goode & Ben-Yehuda, 1994) with which news organizations react to dramatic events that speak to widespread societal concerns – first selecting them over other stories, then framing them as dramatically as possible – the British press's response to April's abduction was a textbook illustration of this process in action. So what reasons did journalists themselves give for this overkill? Rationales they offered as to why they/their editors found April's story *quite* so newsworthy included:

- The presence of a victim from a respectable ('worthy') household/ neighbourhood with which readers might easily identify
- Empathy with the family felt by readers and journalists who were parents themselves
- The unexpected, dramatic and unambiguous nature of April's abduction

- Snowballing commercial pressures to compete for angles once the story kicked off
- Novelty factors particular to this story – the use of social media by police/family to publicize April's disappearance and the coincidence of timing with the Savile scandal

'People like us': innocent children, respectable families and 'worthy' victims

As we shall see from the coming analysis of news coverage itself and the responses it generated, April's abduction embodied several key elements of the classic 'child victim' paradigm identified by focus group participants and journalists and in Chapter 4's textual analysis. Chief among these was the perceived innocence of not only April herself but her manifestly devastated parents – and, significantly, the relative *level* of worthiness that many papers ascribed to April's ('respectable' working-class) family as a consequence. This contrasted markedly with the more suspicious attitudes that some journalists recalled their editors adopting in relation to ('dysfunctional' working-class) households at the centre of other then-recent missing child cases, including those of Shannon Matthews (Moreton, 2008) and Tia Sharp (Chesshyre, 2012). The importance that papers placed on establishing *levels* of worthiness in April's case was illustrated by an instruction that the mid-market late-shift reporter received from her night editor after alerting him to the tweeted police appeal to use Google Maps to check out the appearance and character of April's estate, in case her family was 'too "rough" to be of interest' to the paper. 'We looked and it was, "ah, it's a council estate, but it looks ... quite nice", and the mayor, the local councillor, was, like, "oh yeah, they're a really nice family"', she recalled, adding, 'it was a Welsh village: it wasn't as bad as an inner [city] and it was a place that was considered safe enough for a five-year-old to play out ... and nothing had ever happened there for over 100 years!'. Similarly, the red-top reporter emphasized his editors' keenness to establish that the Joneses were 'our kind of people' before plunging into the story. Should 'this exact situation – "a child gets kidnapped"' reoccur, but 'the mum is a prostitute and the dad has been unemployed', with 'a criminal record as long as your arm', there would be 'a lot of red flags' to dissuade papers from covering it so extensively. While acknowledging that such attempts to determine levels of worthiness amounted to class prejudice, the broadsheet feature writer said his paper had implicitly distinguished between the Joneses' story as a 'worthy' McCann-style tale, rather than an 'unworthy' Matthews case, in which Karen's disappearance from her council home a few months after Madeleine 'got a different *kind* of coverage ... a *hostile* coverage', as if to say 'of *course* a child would go missing, 'cos these people [on Shannon's estate] don't know how to care for children'. Similarly, both the red-top reporter and liberal broadsheet crime correspondent explicitly distinguished between the apparent stability (and, by inference, respectability) of April's background and the problematic family situation from which Tia had vanished months earlier. Having covered both stories, the latter described April as a 'child that was loved, looked after, cared for', in contrast to Tia's 'complex family story', which produced 'a very early suspect ... whose story didn't ... stack up' (Stuart Hazell, partner of her maternal grandmother). His regional reporter colleague concurred that, from early on, it was 'pretty much established that she (April) was a deserving victim', in that 'there was nothing to suggest there was any parental involvement'. Contrasting this with Tia's case, the red-top reporter argued that, though 'a prime example' of 'a shocking story ... that ... ticked all the boxes''', any clear-cut 'worthy victim' status began 'unravelling' as soon as journalists examined 'the parents and the family'.

Aside from her social status and family background, several reporters noted how April ticked other 'worthy' boxes, citing her tender age, gender, cute appearance, blonde hair and even race – clear echoes of the 'missing white girl syndrome' identified by Stillman as a facet of numerous high-profile child abduction stories, including the McCann, Payne and Soham cases (Stillman, 2007). Several drew attention to the historic media prominence of 'child victim' stories focusing on girls, rather than boys: almost all alluded repeatedly to the fact April was 'a girl' (with the broadsheet feature writer commenting that, other than James Bulger, he could not recall an abduction story concerning a boy as high-profile as April's or 'Maddie's'). The mid-market late-shift reporter emphasized the importance of April's looks – describing the advantage that the story gained, in perceived reader appeal, when she stumbled on photos the girl's cousins had posted on Twitter confirming she was a 'cute child'. As we shall see, pictures emphasizing April's angelic looks played a crucial role in framing her narrative in almost all papers – particularly when juxtaposed with a widely used maniacal portrait of Bridger. For the feature writer, the importance of pictures as framing devices – and rationales for selecting and magnifying some stories over others – was as much about establishing the 'people like us' status of families affected by tragedy as the vulnerability of victims. Recalling early 'positive' coverage of the McCanns with the disparaging portrayals that the Matthews household garnered long before Shannon's mother was implicated in her daughter's disappearance, he argued Maddie's story 'got so many inches of coverage because she [Madeleine's mother, Kate McCann] was good-looking, because pictures ... of the anguished mother, looking gorgeous, with the teddy bear in her hand and a summer top on, could easily fill three-quarters of a page'. This was a manifestation of 'the extent to which the parents are seen to be like us – or like we *see* ourselves to be'. By contrast, the red-top reporter returned to *his* 'people like us' theme by arguing that his readers would struggle to sympathize with a story about children (and, by extension, parents) from different cultural/ethnic backgrounds to their own – particularly if these could be related to lowly social positions. Describing grieving parents who 'can't string three words together' as a 'complete switch-off', and contrasting such people with April's mother and father, he argued there were 'things that people empathize with and other things that they don't'. As we shall see from the textual analysis, the process of othering outlined by these two journalists in relation to news values used to distinguish between more and less worthy families was applied even more rigorously in framing Bridger.

Readers and journalists as parents: universalizing April

Another key factor contributing to the importance attached to the story, according to several journalists, was the degree of empathy that they and colleagues felt for April's family as parents *themselves* – and, by extension, the chord that editors felt her disappearance would strike with readers. As we shall see in the next section, this empathy factor manifested itself in published news discourse – and online reader responses – as a generalized impression that stranger-danger and other extra-familial threats presented *ubiquitous* risks to any parents loosening their children's reins, and a similarly universalized sense of loss at April's disappearance. Relating April's story to the wider issue of why 'child victim' stories are accorded such high editorial priority, the feature writer rationalized this empathy factor as, in part, a reflection of the 'age of the people who make decisions about news'. 'Editors tend to be people who've got teenage kids, news editors tend to be people who've got younger kids, reporters tend to be people who are just having kids – so we're all *primed*, we will automatically think that what we care about is what everybody cares about', he explained. As for the *commercial* appeal of such narratives, when Maddie disappeared 'people *did* turn on their televisions hour after hour, day after day, 'cos they were interested'. A father of three, he was one of several interviewees who confessed to having been personally distressed by missing children incidents he had covered – describing 'the Holly [Wells] thing, Jessica [Chapman] thing' and the abduction and murder of 'Milly Dowler in particular' as stories that 'really burned deep into my conscience as a … father'. His view was echoed by the liberal broadsheet regional correspondent (who had two daughters). Describing incidents like April's disappearance as 'the most disturbing story types … to cover and also to read about', he suggested journalists' 'attitude to stories about children changes dramatically' when they become parents. But it was the crime editor of a conservative broadsheet who offered the most sophisticated analysis of how the relationship between the 'reporter-parent' and 'reader-parent' played out in the news-making process. Referring to his own circumstances, and drawing on what might be described as a paradigm of *universalized parenthood*, he suggested 'we all have the same fears … When Sarah [Payne] happened my daughter was nine, and now I've got two other children, aged two and six. On a human level, you basically *feel* it yourself and you know that all other parents are going to feel the same'. The empathy factor, then, is a *triangular* process: it is directed, firstly, through the emotional connection many editors/reporters feel with the plight of parents experiencing such horror stories and, secondly, their expectation that *audience members* (or those with their own children/ grandchildren) will be similarly affected. But there is also another way of interpreting this circuit of news construction/framing and processing/response: value-judgments applied by professionals weighing up the newsworthiness of 'child victim' stories against others they might have selected from the 'news net' (Tuchman, 1978) during a given day or week is, in part, a process of translating empathy for tragedy victims into a cold-blooded, commercial assessment of the *saleability* of such tales, based on their predicted audience impact.

This idea that dramatic stories about children promote a deeper engagement between audience and newspaper – and/or 'reader' and 'reporter' – than other news is explored in more detail as a commercial concept in the next-but-one section. Returning to it as a primarily *empathetic* notion, however, the broadsheet crime editor summed up the three-way discourse linking victim to reporter to reader in such cases as 'the awful cliché' that incidents like April's abduction manifest 'every parent's worst nightmare'. No coincidence, perhaps, that this cliché recurred – as if culturally hard-wired – in three other journalists' testimonies, and repeatedly in both the news discourse and posts on discussion threads analysed later in this chapter. Though almost all interviewees alluded (if often obliquely) to the empathy factor, mention of it was noticeably more marked among those with their own children. To the feature writer, the power of April's story was the sense that the apparently rare (stranger-danger) scenario it initially presented quickly transformed into a *familiar* stranger incident that could plausibly befall *any* parent, once the chief suspect was established as a family friend. Transposing the idea of April's abduction as an identifiable scenario – a variation on the fear of abuse by familiars that even official statistics tell us is *relatively* commonplace compared to stranger attacks (e.g. Krugman, 1995) – with the previously discussed notion that journalists and readers alike identify with 'people like us', he reflected:

> The question I think editors are asking as they look at the facts of a case is, you know, 'to what extent could this happen to any of us?' And with April, there's very clearly a chance that it *could* ...' cos if somebody with no background whatsoever [of crimes against children] steps out of our friendship circle, and abducts a child, you know that could happen anywhere ...

News values reaffirmed: 'unexpectedness', 'surprise' and an 'unambiguous' abduction

Another aspect of newsworthiness April's story boasted over those of Tia, Shannon and even Madeleine was the *unambiguous* nature of her disappearance – a quality equated with a core news value identified by Galtung and Ruge (1965). If there was one factor besides her solid family background confirming her as a worthy victim (with the accent on the *latter* word) it was the unequivocal way the case was reported from early on, by police and press alike, as abduction. As the feature writer summed up:

> April was a classic case of the missing child: good-looking, young child goes all of a sudden ... Every parent's nightmare but ... actually every *citizen's* nightmare, in a way.

Though not a father himself, the liberal broadsheet crime reporter viewed the story similarly, distinguishing between April's case as 'a classic ... snatch' and the fact that there 'will always be missing people' – not all of whom are deemed worthy of comparable attention. 'Sometimes these things are slow-burners, but this was very obviously abduction ... and she was *five*', he reflected, adding, 'the age of the child and the nature of her disappearance' resonated particularly with editors. The *Express* group reporter also cited the story's 'classic' abduction tropes as keys to its newsworthiness. These tropes – unsupervised outdoor play, mystery car and predatory (familiar) stranger – recalled many of the strongest fears voiced by focus group participants. As we shall see, they also recurred consistently in both the framing of April's narrative in print and responses to the story from focus groups and those contributing to discussion threads. 'The fact she was only five years old and ... was seen in a vehicle and then driven off' were, this reporter argued, elements that rang early alarm bells – as was the fact 'the police put a message out straight away, and it didn't look like a family member'. There was 'a *feel*' that it was 'more serious', he added, referring to the twist that Bridger 'lived not far from the mum and dad'. Establishing that April's disappearance was being treated as a crime involving someone without her immediate family also proved vital for the mid-market late-shift reporter. Verifying this with the police was another preliminary check she was ordered to conduct before writing anything. 'The news editor was like, "right, can you just check it out? It's a missing girl, but she's probably just ... been picked up by her stepdad"', she recalled, alluding to a procedure routinely used by journalists to distinguish between genuine kidnappings and 'runaways' or children 'abducted by the parents' during custody disputes. Similarly, the liberal tabloid reporter argued 'context plays a role' in news judgments about whether to treat a child's disappearance as a story, because 'children go missing almost every day from all kinds of backgrounds', often turning up 'safe and sound'. Significantly, both reporters raised the importance that news desks attached to gauging the *level* of seriousness with which police view an incident before committing themselves to high-stakes investments in a story. Stating 'you can usually take a cue about the nature of the disappearance by the police reaction', the liberal tabloid reporter demonstrated how much trust journalists routinely invest in such cases in official sources with their own institutional agendas – in this instance, to appeal for witnesses to a serious live incident and, in so doing, sensitize public awareness about the possibility of such crimes occurring, and the vital role they play in combating them. This reflects the pattern of newsgathering observed in other studies of the construction of panic narratives (e.g. Hall et al., 1978; Fishman, 1978), and is a theme we return to in coming sections.

The rare and 'unambiguous' nature of the abduction scenario (Galtung & Ruge, 1965) that unfolded swiftly after April's disappearance clearly helped dramatize the story – and justify rapid investment of scarce journalistic resources – in *general* terms. However, the level of 'unexpectedness' (ibid.) or 'surprise' (Harcup & O'Neill, 2001) arising from this *particular* incident was magnified by the fact the location where it occurred, Machynlleth, had (to those aware of it) a long-held reputation for community spirit and low crime rates. Acknowledging the added newsworthiness this fact lent the story, the red-top reporter recalled journeying to an 'idyllic part of the world', while the broadsheet regional correspondent described Machynlleth as a 'little hippy idyll' and the *Express* group journalist the sense of 'going back in time' as he drove into the Welsh countryside – impressions that (as we shall see) leant a further dimension to the evocative narratives reporters conveyed in their writing. Careful to distinguish between April's unusually isolated yet community-oriented council estate and (less worthy) neighbourhoods of a more ghettoized, dysfunctional kind – a distinction insinuated in some published coverage – the red-top reporter described Machynlleth as 'a largely working-class town' where 'people tend to know everyone' and there is 'hardly any crime', apart from 'the occasional fight outside a pub'. The sense that one baleful act had stolen not only *her* innocence but her *community's* became another integral ingredient of how the story was dramatized. For the feature writer, though, the combination of *general* 'classic' abduction tropes discussed earlier with the unique setting in which this particular crime took place also lent it a literary dimension. Likening the story to a dark, late-modern 'Hansel and Gretel' – a throwback to certain themes explored in relation to historical representations of children in Chapter 2 – he described the 'deep, dark, mysterious part of the country' where it occurred as somewhere you might find yourself if you 'keep going for a couple of hours' beyond 'the edge of nowhere'. 'There is an elemental aspect to the landscape, too, with the mountains and the woodlands and the forest – so there is a ... kind of dark poetry about it in a way', he reflected, emphasizing the evocative appeal of 'a nice-looking young kid who goes missing suddenly in this mysterious, elemental, fairy-tale-type space'. Yet, while emphasizing the story's fabular qualities, he also attributed its potency to the fact it fed into a continuum of latter-day cautionary tales about 'the archetype' of 'the missing child' preyed on while out of her parents' sight – another example of the 'continuity' often identified as a consistent news value of western journalism (Galtung & Ruge, 1965; Harcup & O'Neill, 2001). 'We *know* this story', he said, '*I've* covered this story: this is Milly ... this is Holly and Jessica'.

Selling papers: the commercial appeal and snowball effect of missing children stories

As mentioned earlier, a flipside of the genuine sense of *empathy* underpinning the rationales that journalists gave for April's perceived worthiness as a news subject – her youth, angelic looks, stable family background and perceived similarity to readers' (and reporters') own children – was the *commercial* appeal they attached to her story. Interviewees cited a mix of personal impressions and anecdote to support the notion that one consideration editors took on board when judging how much to invest in such stories was their potential to attract more readers, engage them more meaningfully and, by extension, generate higher profits. For the feature writer, the measure of a story's commercial appeal was its ability to produce not only quantitative gains like newspaper sales or web hits, but a (qualitative) *depth* of involvement with readers. By playing up its symbolism and mystery, editors hoped to immerse readers hard-wired to societal concerns about risk and trust as *active participants*, rather than passive consumers. The commercial element was predicated on a recognition that tales like April's were 'the ultimate *interactive* stories' – ones seen as a boon by newspapers that 'want everybody to *participate* … in the multimedia sense … *across* the platforms, and get on the forums'. 'What you're asking people to do', he added, 'is not just to say, "oh there's a poor little girl gone missing", but to *think* about her: "where could she be? Could she be in your back garden?"'. Implicit here was an intriguing suggestion that the viral nature of (online) rumour-mongering about such tales – a source of confusion debated at length by parent focus groups – is something of which editors are fully cognizant as they conspire to create (commercially driven) conversations around them.

Just as some journalists interviewed in Chapter 4 spoke of their news editors circulating data on their papers' sales figures and hit-rates, the red-top reporter raised the importance of focus groups as a determinant of the gatekeeping decisions that news teams took when lavishing such attention on stories like April's. 'We have focus groups of our readers who come and sit down in a room and say what they're interested in', he said, adding that, from 'an entirely commercial perspective', executives would greet some stories with the hard-nosed business response, 'hold on a minute, we don't want to be doing stories on this because we've already seen from focus groups that this is a complete turn-off for readers'. Another primer fuelling this commercial mind-set, according to several interviewees, was the snowball effect beginning with the initial decisions by some outlets to go big on such stories – and the inducement this gave competitors afraid of losing out on audience-generated income to follow suit. Rather like the process of 'continuity' observed in newspapers' coverage of certain events and issues by Galtung and Ruge (1965), Harcup and O'Neill (2001) and others, once a story like April's has got off the ground, and there appears to be a public appetite for regular updates, competition between rival publications for new details/angles – and the level of importance that news desks attach to these – intensifies. For the red-top journalist, the April snowball effect was driven by 24-hour television news channels, which had the advantage of being able to report the story as a live unfolding drama from Monday evening onwards – a day-and-a-half before most papers had a chance to splash it in print. Inferring evidence of demand for updates from the relentless nature and extent of TV coverage *supplied*, he said, 'if TV think it's a good story and there's "events" – there's a search going on and it's on Sky all day and night, and everyone wants more – that kind of ramps up the ... necessity to produce the coverage on *your* part'. Nonetheless, even more important than edging *ahead* of one's competitors was the need to *keep up* with every newsworthy development they covered – an expression of the 'pack' mentality so often observed in newsroom ethnographies and interviews with journalists carried out for earlier studies (e.g. Tuchman, 1978). The red-top journalist illustrated this point by conjuring up an imagined quote from April's mother which would have appealed to journalists' commercial instincts as they raced to outwit each other to write the most involving story:

> If ... you know that all your competitors are looking at this line that ... the mum has ... described her daughter as an 'angel from above', then, you know, that's very powerful, so ... everyone kind of ... *follows* each other.

The intense competition newspapers faced to *keep up* with rivals out of pathological fear of missing any minor development (and the potential sales/web hits flowing from it) tells only one side of the story. As the red-top reporter and others argued, what the print press ceded to rolling news channels and online outlets in terms of *timeliness* they were expected to make up for in *synthesis* – and exclusive 'extras'. For him, this gave papers willing to commit sufficient resources a competitive advantage: while the police search of 'quarries and caves' and the presence of 'divers in rivers' made for 'great, gripping TV' that stoked viewers' 'emotions' (and fuelled their appetite for further coverage), the largely *descriptive* nature of these visuals appeared, after a time, 'very dry and very straight'. By contrast, the press were freer to speculate and explore the 'theories' or latest 'line of inquiry' around April's disappearance, allowing them to 'run a story that, you know, police are searching this quarry system' that is 'full of ... mine shafts and holes, where you can leave a body'. Intense competition for new angles was also alluded to by the *Express* group journalist, who recalled striking lucky by bumping into one of April's few relatives not to have given interviews prior to the weekend (her maternal grandmother) and persuading her to speak to him. This was a line he was 'keen on getting' high up in his published story 'because we had that exclusively'. Similarly, the late-shift mid-market reporter said of her paper's day-to-day pursuit of additional angles beyond those revealed through the numerous police press conferences – the source of much of the coverage printed in less well-staffed titles, according to interviewees – that papers 'needed multiple lines' to stand out, because 'there was so much coverage'. Evidence of intense competition for news lines and efforts to keep up with the pack – especially in relation to biographical background on Bridger and his connections to April's family – were both visible in the textual analysis of print coverage explored later in this chapter.

Social media, citizen searchers and Savile: the April Jones case as perfect storm

Most of the factors that journalists saw as justifying the degree of newsworthiness attached to April's story – and the nature and scale of its coverage – appeared to reflect normative (if commercially driven) news values that they/editors would apply to most dramatic tales involving child victims. However, as several interviewees reflected, additional elements came into play in this case which conspired to further elevate the story's profile. One influential factor was the role that technology (especially social media) played in facilitating many aspects of the coverage – from the tweeted police statement and newly instated Child Rescue Alert system used to raise the alarm nationwide to the frenzy of Twitter and Facebook activity that followed from family, friends, celebrities and concerned citizens. Technology both accelerated the process of disseminating press statements and news updates to media organizations from official channels and frequently became *part of the story* itself – with April's family harnessing social media to post images of the five-year-old immediately after her disappearance and webcast their appeals (and the related 'pink ribbon' awareness campaign) over ensuing days (Lawton, 2012a). Moreover, social media also proved crucial to the process of audience meaning-making, as shown by responses the story generated from focus groups and discussion threads (analysed later). Of all the influences that technology exerted on the *news-making* process, however, it was the use of social media to publicize the incident initially that was most unique to this story – with a small local constabulary, Dyfed-Powys Police, issuing its witness appeal via Twitter and becoming the first UK force to activate a then-new US-style national alert system for missing children introduced in 2010 by the Child Exploitation and Online Protection Centre. While the latter fact became the subject of coverage in itself (*Times*, 2012a), journalists reporting the story in its early stages recalled how crucial social media were in helping them source and verify information – at a much faster rate than would otherwise have been possible. The reporter who wrote the first press agency snap alerting news desks to the story recalled frustratedly struggling to access the Dyfed-Powys Police website for confirmation of April's disappearance after her night editor asked her to investigate the source of a rumour trending on Twitter. Only by *excavating* back through a long succession of viral tweets and re-tweets posted by members of the public was she able to establish 'the cops were on Twitter and that's where it was coming from'. While she used more traditional reporting skills to develop the story further, at every turn she was aided by technology – using Google Maps to locate a local pub and service station from whose owners she obtained quotes and a 'reverse phonebook' to contact April's godmother in Aberystwyth. The mid-market reporter, working a parallel late shift, also cited Twitter as her primary tool for confirming both basic details of the story and its suitability for her paper. This enabled her to add momentum to the unfolding tale by writing a hurried report for the following day's late editions – something no other paper managed:

> It was big on Twitter – people kept on re-tweeting about it. I went on Facebook. We didn't have her [April's] name. Well, we did have the name Jones – but *Jones*, in *Wales* ... I think we quite quickly found her parents on Twitter ... and a cousin, I think, and they both had pictures of her.

Another key factor that enhanced the story's perceived newsworthiness – fuelled by the flurry of dialogue and Chinese whispers on social media – was the unprecedented scale of public involvement in the manhunt. So huge was this operation, mounted the night April disappeared, that the service station the agency reporter contacted stayed open so that volunteers could refuel their vehicles and the pub landlord told her that all his customers had left to join in. The search's continuation over coming days led to the story splitting into what the liberal broadsheet regional correspondent described as 'two parts': the investigation and 'the town's reaction'. Indeed, so extensive and persistent was the level of public participation (at times defying police appeals for volunteers to leave it to the emergency services, as weather conditions worsened and the prospect of finding April alive receded) that growing tensions between professionals and amateurs spilled over into a major strand of later coverage.

If one factor above all others enhanced the story's perceived newsworthiness, though, it was the fact that April's abduction occurred in the same week as the first trickle of a relentless tide of allegations of child abuse against Jimmy Savile. As juxtaposed headlines about (and images of) April and the deceased TV star attested in the coming days, the coincidence of timing of these two disparate stories amounted to a perfect storm conducive to *crystallizing* the simmering panic about child vulnerability in late-modern Britain identified in earlier chapters. As the liberal broadsheet crime reporter observed, such explosions of publicity tend to come about in circumstances where there is some additional 'backdrop' – besides the drama of the actual incident – to elevate it above everything else. For Wells and Chapman, abducted and killed by Ian Huntley in Soham almost exactly a decade before, the scale of coverage had been influenced by the rhythms of the news calendar and the fact they vanished during a 'quiet summer'. For April, it was the fact 'the Savile thing kicked in' at almost exactly the same time. The *Express* group reporter concurred, rationalizing the *Sunday Express's* determination to put April on page one – despite the gradual slowdown of developments later in the week – as, in part, a consequence of general sensitization to 'child victim' narratives resulting from the parallel unravelling of the Savile scandal. 'I think we all kind of knew that it was going to be front-page news because it had been such a big story – the timing of it, him being charged [and] it was that week of the Savile allegations breaking', he reflected. For the mid-market late-shift reporter, however, Savile was only part of the equation. In fact, April's abduction took place against an *already* febrile atmosphere generated by not just the drip-drip of revelations about Savile, but a succession of dramatic tales that had unfolded over preceding weeks, involving the victimization of minors by predatory adults. This continuum had begun in late summer with the disappearance of 12-year-old Tia, followed by Megan's alleged abduction. Though she confused the order of these stories while recounting them, the reporter recalled going 'straight from that [April] onto ... the girl who was kidnapped by her teacher, within weeks – and then ... straight onto Savile' – bracketing the string of dramas as 'four, you know, paedo stories in a row' and describing how all were treated as so important that 'everyone' on the paper was requisitioned to work on them. In fact, so dominated was its agenda by such stories by the time the April and Savile coverage appeared that 'editorial staff ... seemed worried there were too many paedophiles in the paper' – suggesting that (notwithstanding their intrinsic commercial appeal) it might encounter a law of diminishing returns if its pages became *too* saturated by this grim 'child victim' discourse. Journalists' concerns that they were contributing to a feeding frenzy of alarmism about children's vulnerability to the predations of dangerous adults were not without foundation, as we shall see from the textual analysis.

Keeping up with the Joneses: sourcing April's story

If a single factor shaped the way journalists framed April's story while committing it to the page – besides a shared sense of the inherent newsworthiness of key imagery it conjured up – it was their choice of sources. Most interviewees confessed to relying on the police even more than usual – a fact they blamed on Machynlleth's remote location and the absence of other obvious contacts, bar April's friends and family and various (expert) emergency services recruited to coordinate searches of mountains and rivers. In choosing (or being forced) to rely so heavily on the police, though, newspapers allowed themselves to be led by a statutory law enforcement agency motivated by an agenda to promote the value and effectiveness of its work – a case founded, in part, on portraying the world as threatening and prone to sudden, dramatic crimes. While it might be a step too far to evoke Hall et al.'s (1978) idea of crime as a consciously 'ideological' construction in this particular context, the economic backdrop of the times and, by extension, pressures facing the police as a publicly funded institution were arguably very similar to those of the early 1970s explored in *Policing the Crisis* – with individual forces fighting to assert their importance in the face of swingeing austerity cuts (*www.bbc.co.uk*, 2010b). Several interviewees went out of their way to praise the professionalism displayed by police officers overseeing this case, with the liberal tabloid reporter describing them as 'in control of the story from day one' and 'extremely helpful'. Likewise, the liberal broadsheet regional correspondent suggested officers were 'very good' at 'deliberately drip-feeding information to keep new lines bubbling'. Though he described this, critically, as calculated news management – a technique used to keep stories in the public eye by issuing a steady stream of information geared to media deadlines – he recognized its usefulness to him personally. As his paper's lone reporter in Machynlleth, he would otherwise have been over-stretched trying to find new lines for each day's paper, compared to the multiple journalists sent by rival titles. His London-based colleague was similarly impressed by officers' command of the situation, recalling 'the really good job' they did in 'answering journalists' queries'. One aspect of this 'good job', besides offering 'bubbling' updates on the progress of the search, was the running commentary they provided on their investigation into the mysterious Bridger. The broadsheet crime editor remarked on the 'really unusual and quite legally controversial' deci-sion detectives took to 'stick his [Bridger's] name out' prior to charging him – six days before the suspected abduction was formally elevated to murder. The very fact that such moves were 'unusual' rendered them all the more newsworthy to journalists, while the police's provision of striking photos of everything from a wild-eyed Bridger to his (seized) Land Rover lent the story an irresistible visual impact.

Although more pragmatically than ideologically driven, in the first instance, reporters' professed dependency on the police echoes the find-ings of numerous earlier studies, in which academics have warned that journalists' over-reliance on official sources whose systems are geared to providing them with reliable channels of oven-ready information can have the (perhaps unintentional) *knock-on effect* of framing news narratives in terms reflecting not only societal norms, but elite agendas (Tuchman, 1972; Chibnall, 1975, 1977 and 1981; Gans, 1979; Fishman, 1980; Bantz, 1985; Schlesinger, 1987). The most vivid illustration of the shared consensus between news media and police influencing the construction of this particular story was the broadsheet crime editor's revealing remark that, when reporting dramatic stories such as 'live' missing children cases, he had come to think of himself as fulfilling a 'public service'. It was not only acceptable but routine for journalists to dispense with editorial conventions in such cases by agreeing to publish – and 'nowadays to tweet' – numbers that the public should call if they had information that might help solve them. In a comment that appeared to point towards a degree of *active* ideological complic-ity between the press and the establishment, with shades of Herman and Chomsky's 'propaganda model' (1988), he conceded that crime stories like April's abduction were 'as high a priority for us as they are for the cops', and 'for pretty much the same reasons: to get the message out there'. And the dominance of establishment definers in framing

April's story went beyond journalists' reliance on the police. It was notable how many early tributes gathered by reporters on the ground (and via social media) came not from her family but other official, or semi-official, sources, including elected councillors, the local mayor, a vicar and her teachers – the latter representing a profession with vested interests in promoting child protection. Given the close-knit nature of Machynlleth's community, it may have seemed logical to journalists to contact such individuals, in the expectation that they would be familiar with the Joneses (not to say easier to track down in the earliest stages, when reporters were frantically trying to establish the facts of the case, confirm it as abduction, and liven up their copy by obtaining quotes from people who knew April). Nonetheless, it is significant that the mid-market late-shift reporter – in stressing the practical problem of locating the Joneses – set such store on the fact that the 'mayor' or 'councillor' (note the vagueness) she managed to contact the night April vanished confirmed they were 'really nice' (and thus worthy of her paper's sympathy).

Besides officials, the key sources pursued by journalists were primarily April's relatives, friends and neighbours – as reflected in much of their testimony (and print coverage analysed later). The most common reason given for doorstepping these individuals was to lend the story a human interest dimension that would heighten readers' empathy towards the family – something not so easily provided by official sources. The broadsheet regional correspondent's explanation of the division of labour between himself in Machynlleth and his London-based colleague was that he was tasked with 'focusing on the human side' by reporting the 'town's reaction'. Meanwhile, the deskbound agency reporter explained her night editor's urgency in getting a regional reporter to the scene as a desire to 'talk to local people' and 'humanize the story'. A vivid example of how sensitive handling of friends and neighbours could potentially pay off with sought-after exclusives came from the red-top reporter, who recalled a colleague persuading 'a friend of the family' to part with a photo of April riding her pink bicycle. This image ended up a front-page splash – reflecting its poignancy, given the widely reported fact that she had been playing on the same bike the night she vanished. But the journalists were unanimous that the prize human interest contacts were April's own family – and, with Machynlleth and its environs besieged by reporters within hours of the story breaking, it is hardly surprising that everyone, from both sets of grandparents to her godmother, were swiftly subject to feverish press attention. As the week wore on, the intense competition between papers for quotes from family members who had not yet been interviewed elsewhere is reflected in the *Express* group reporter's anecdote (cited earlier) about his determination to frame his story around his exclusive (if fleeting) chat with April's maternal grandmother.

From the interviews alone, then, it is clear that journalists relied on two principal types of source in their efforts first to keep up to speed with the manhunt and second to project human faces onto the unfolding drama: official contacts (principally police, April's school and councillors) and the Joneses, their friends and neighbours. The fact that both investigators and April's parents were making coordinated use of press conferences, tweets and Facebook appeals to keep her name and image in the public eye, even as hopes of her safe return faded, rendered the press ever more *dependent* on these sources – and, by extension, wary of deviating from official portrayals of the story as they deliberated how to frame articles. The only way any exclusive – therefore, *individual* – angles generally emerged was through a reporter occasionally striking 'lucky' (to quote the *Express* group journalist) by obtaining quotes or photos not seen elsewhere. But even when this occurred, the overwhelming object of speaking to new sources – once the worthiness of April's parents had been established – was to humanize the story by first *generalizing* it to symbolize incidents that could befall *any* family and, second, framing Bridger as a sinister familiar stranger, in opposition to the virtuous 'people like us' signified by the grief-stricken Joneses and their community. The question of how journalists' choice of sources contributed to the framing of April's abduction on the page is one to which we now turn.

Constructing a crime: panic and the 'serpent in paradise'

The lavish manpower and resources newspapers invested in covering April's story in the week following her disappearance was reflected in blanket coverage in their pages – another classic illustration of the 'disproportion' associated with moral panics (Goode & Ben-Yehuda, 1994). In the week commencing with the first full day of print coverage (Wednesday 3 October), the nine dailies and 10 Sundays sampled ran 157 separate articles on April between them, spread over 156 pages – many devoted entirely to the subject.[3] While the *Sun* and *Daily Mail* printed the most pieces (20 and 18 respectively), close behind was a broadsheet, the *Times* (16) – a mark of the overwhelming consensus about the story's newsworthiness. And, though geographically distant from Machynlleth, the Brighton *Argus* reflected this universal appeal by leading its sole national news page with it on day one (*Argus*, 2012, p. 2). Significantly, its two other biggest national stories were the latest twist in the Savile saga and teacher Forrest's appearance before an extradition hearing in France over Megan's alleged abduction.

A key measure of the disproportionate prominence April's story achieved was the extent to which its reporting eclipsed that of other, arguably equally newsworthy, subjects. Various stories that might normally have benefited from extensive column inches went largely unreported – or under-reported. A vivid illustration of this can be glimpsed by contrasting the limited range of subjects covered in the nationals on Wednesday 3 October with the more extensive menu of potential leads listed on the previous morning's news schedule published by PA (Press Association Mediapoint Newswire, 2012). Though far from prescriptive, these schedules are circulated at least twice daily to every national newspaper and other subscribing organization, and list the main events that the agency's editors are assigning their own reporters to cover on subscribers' behalf on a given day. As Manning White (1950) observed more than six decades ago in his classic study of the different levels of gatekeeping filter represented by wire agencies and, in turn, editors who select stories from their output, there is usually some variation between the choice of events prioritized by newswires and those selected to appear in the next day's newspapers. However, the disparity between the 7 a.m. 'PA Headlines' published to subscribers on 2 October and the balance of coverage given to competing stories in print the following morning was stark.[4] While the top story listed on PA's schedule after April – Labour leader Ed Miliband's keynote speech to his party conference – was widely reported on 3 October, several of its other leads featured minimally or not at all. These included two stories conforming to long-recognized news values of 'continuity' (Galtung & Ruge, 1965) or 'follow-up' (Harcup & O'Neill, 2001), by representing the latest developments in high-profile sagas: the latest twist in a long-running controversy over the putative deportation of Hamza, and an appeal by the British Chambers of Commerce for Ministers to invest billions in infrastructure projects to stimulate economic growth after four years of on-off recession. The latter was ignored by every sampled paper (*ProQuest Newsstand*, 2013). By contrast, the one story that enjoyed almost equal billing with April's was the unfolding scandal of historic child abuse allegations against Savile, which generated 156 articles – stripping out the 16 pieces focusing on related claims (subsequently disproved) about another celebrity, Freddie Starr.[5] The combined effect of saturation coverage given to the April/Savile stories – the faces of their key protagonists often juxtaposed on front pages – was striking. That the Savile saga was, like April's abduction, a horror story positioning children as victims of extra-familial threats posed by (superficially benign but predatory) adults only added to the sense that the week's news agenda was dominated by a febrile and crystallizing juvenile panic discourse focusing on familiar strangers. Hardly surprising, perhaps, that colleagues of the mid-market late-shift reporter should end up grumbling about there being 'too many paedophiles' in their paper.

As if consciously tapping into this panic discourse, at the same time as they began devoting disproportionate space to analysing the circumstances of April's disappearance, speculating on her whereabouts and following every twist in the ensuing search, the papers reserved sizeable chunks of the limited room left to cover other news for *further* stories casting children as innocent victims of violence, abuse, neglect and other assorted threats. In common with other crystallizing moments of juvenile panic – whether the frenzied, campaigning coverage arising from the abduction and murder of Sarah Payne or, by contrast, the bogus youth crime wave hysteria dwelt on by Hall et al. and Fishman (both 1978) – newspapers appeared to be actively trawling the 'news net' (Tuchman, 1980) for stories that supported the dominant discourse underpinning the April and Savile cases: namely that children are helplessly beset at every turn by all manner of dangers. Among the myriad 'child victim' stories unrelated to either individual that appeared in the nationals' pages during the first three days after the girl's disappearance were the following: 'On trial for child abuse 63 years ago', 'Tot death: mum hid his injuries', and 'Girl, 2, died after swine flu blunder' (*Daily Mirror*, 3 October); 'Killer used his kids as pawns', 'Boy's car fall death' and 'Girl hit by tube train' (*Sun*, 3 October); 'Tragic tot: nursery staff held' (*Daily Express*, 4 October); 'Did having ears pierced make this teenager's heart stop?' (*Daily Mail*, 4 October); 'Brit child is ferry victim' (*Daily Mirror*, 4 October); and 'Girl bitten by friend's Collie' (*Daily Star*, 5 October). On one day alone (Friday 5 October) the *Daily Mirror* ran a side panel about the court appearance of former newspaper tycoon Eddie Shah for allegedly raping a 13-year-old girl two decades previously (a crime of which he was later acquitted); a single-column filler about a three-year-old boy who had been allowed to wander, unsupervised, out of his nursery into a road; a basement (bottom-of-page) story about a 'serial paedophile' who attempted to kidnap a boy of 10 while his mother bought groceries at a supermarket checkout; and a facing page-lead focusing on a photograph of grieving mother Erica Pederson posing happily with the two young children her estranged husband had stabbed to death the previous weekend. Moreover, of all the headline stories promoted by PA's 2 October schedule the one that achieved the highest hit rate in the following day's papers (besides April's disappearance and Mr Miliband's speech) was the abduction of schoolgirl Megan. This featured heavily in the *Sun*, *Daily Telegraph*, *Guardian* and *Independent*. In short, by lavishing saturation coverage on April and Savile, and devoting so much of their remaining space to other tales positioning children as victims – in many cases of nefarious adults – national newspapers contrived to promote a bubbling panic about juvenile vulnerability that became the overwhelmingly dominant news discourse of the week.

Threatening familiarity, stolen innocence and the collapse of trust

If the coincidence of April's abduction with the Savile allegations provided the *context* for the ensuing panic, a key way in which it *manifested* itself was through dramatization of particular aspects of the missing child story in press coverage. The headlines, intros and overall language and imagery that newspapers used to construct April's story on the page – and details they emphasized – reflected many classic framing conventions identified in Chapter 4. In so doing, they also tapped into concerns repeatedly voiced by focus group mothers who fretted about 'the dark', sinister cars and the half-familiar (ergo potentially threatening) 'man in the park'[6] – gothic fairy-tale tropes calculated to heighten readers' emotional identification and involvement with the story. By dwelling on the proximity to April's home of the abduction scene and the lack of coercion apparently used to persuade her to climb into the mystery car, papers drew heavily on the 'threatening familiarity' paradigm. In print reports from Wednesday 3 October onwards, Superintendent Ian John was quoted as saying that April had 'willingly' entered the mystery car – raising the prospect she had known her abductor. And, as more elements of the story clicked into place over the ensuing days, it was increasingly dramatized as a late-modern cautionary tale about misplaced trust and familiar strangers – with early suspect Bridger cast in the wicked uncle role. This framing of Bridger was visible from an early stage, with the *Sun* already asserting by day one of its print coverage (effectively day three of the story) that he was 'close friends' with April's father (Phillips, 2012, p. 1) and the next morning's *Daily Telegraph* informing readers that two of his children 'live yards from April' (Rayner et al., 2012c, pp. 1 and 3).

Nonetheless, there were two clear stages in the evolution of the familiar stranger narrative that eventually prevailed: the more traditional *stranger-danger* abduction scenario painted by the press, through its dialogue with the police and local community, in the first 36 hours after April's disappearance; and a subtly distinct *strangers in our midst* narrative that emerged through the slow drip-drip of biographical details linking Bridger ever more closely to her friends and family in the days following his arrest. The former paradigm was best symbolized by hazy descriptions of the phantom car into which April had unwittingly climbed in the drizzly gloom that Monday evening – a montage of often conflicting recollections attributed to her young playmates. In early reports, the vehicle would sometimes transform from a 'light-coloured van' into the blue Land Rover belonging to Bridger that detectives seized from a repair shop in the same article (Alleyne, 2012). As early as day one of the print coverage, however, the car's colour was being glossed over, as police confirmed they were looking for a left-hand drive vehicle, and the fact that only a handful of these – including Bridger's – were registered to owners in the Machynlleth area insinuated itself into stories (Chamberlain et al., 2012). Taken together with the growing body of evidence pointing towards Bridger's familiarity with April, suddenly the identity of her captor seemed to have moved much closer to home.

'Safe' spaces, deceptive faces

Beyond the familiar tropes of mystery cars and threatening familiars, newspapers chose to emphasize an added dimension in their story-telling: the sense that, unlike on other occasions when children had been snatched in comparable circumstances, in this case April herself represented only one aspect of the innocence stolen by the events of 1 October 2012. The other was the secure reputation of a neighbourly rural town long viewed as an idyllic enclave insulated from the perils and predations of more crime-ridden neighbourhoods. To this extent, April's narrative not only displayed newsworthy qualities like 'negativity' and 'personalization' but also an element of 'unexpectedness' (Galtung & Ruge, 1965) or 'surprise' (Harcup & O'Neill, 2001) beyond that associated with more commonplace 'child victim' stories. To illustrate, the *Daily Mail*'s capitalized front-page headline on the first day of sampled coverage read 'PLEASE LET OUR LITTLE APRIL COME HOME SAFE' (Wright et al., 2012, pp. 1–2), its intro quoting them directly pleading for the return of 'our beautiful little girl' (words repeated two paragraphs in). Later in the same piece (one of three the *Daily Mail* ran that day) it pointedly described her 'former' council estate as 'quiet' and its residents in 'shock', with a lengthy quote from one (Matthew

Harris) describing a neighbourhood where 'kids play out together and everyone looks after everyone else'. Alongside various tributes from relatives to the 'bubbly' girl with 'a lovely character' contained in an inside piece profiling both April and Machynlleth, reporter Rebecca Evans ran a string of quotes from family friends and neighbours describing their estate as, variously, 'a safe environment', 'a very safe place to live' and 'somewhere you don't have to worry about letting your children play outside' (Evans, R., 2012, p. 2). Indeed, this device – contrasting the sinister nature of April's disappearance with the conflated virtues of the five-year-old herself and her atypically caring community – was reflected across the spectrum. The double-page spread the *Times* devoted to the story that day opened with her family's 'desperate appeal' for the safe return of their 'beautiful little girl', in an extended quote emphasizing the 'small, close-knit' nature of their neighbourhood (O'Neill et al., 2012, p. 4). Here (as in numerous reports) Machynlleth's community spirit was underscored by a separate article focusing on the huge overnight search mounted by volunteers, initially locals, but subsequently from 'near and far', in addition to the 'official' hunt coordinated by emergency services (Jenkins & Bannerman, 2012, pp. 4–5). Similarly, the *Daily Telegraph* used the 'beautiful little girl' quote in both its front-page headline and opening paragraph (Rayner et al., 2012a, pp. 1–2). An extended version of the same quote, also on page one, again saw the parents refer to their 'close-knit community', while the second of three pieces (Rayner et al., 2012b, pp. 2–3) described April's abduction as 'barely comprehensible' to locals, relaying the agency line that, in a show of solidarity, a nearby petrol station had 'reopened its pumps', enabling volunteers to top up on fuel to aid their search, while refuse collections were temporarily 'suspended' so even bin-men could 'join in'. At the other end of the market, the *Sun* (Phillips & Wells, 2012, pp. 4–5) quoted Gwenfair Glyn, April's head teacher, praising both her 'bubbly' and 'very popular' personality and the 'close community' in which she lived. In one of his many interviews over coming days, town mayor Gareth Jones was quoted praising the 'remarkable and not unexpected' community spirit locals displayed by 'rallying together' to find April. By contrast, the headline of a *Times* colour piece on Friday (Bannerman, 2012, pp. 4–5) spoke volumes about the community's sudden loss of innocence – and trust. Its headline quoted the following chilling diagnosis by café-owner Sam Burkill: 'Maybe it's an illusion that everyone knows each other.'

This impression of Machynlleth as a peaceful, previously crime-free, idyll was reflected in testimony from several local residents who contributed to discussion threads following April's disappearance – often to rebut criticisms from readers living elsewhere that the town was unwise to lower its guard by adopting an unconventionally *laissez-faire* approach to childcare. More than this: time and again, evidence-based posters drew on their direct personal knowledge of Machynlleth, or rural Wales generally, to contest the suggestion that stranger-danger lurked everywhere. 'RhianStephanie, Cardiff' was one of several who leapt to Machynlleth's defence, asserting (albeit in the past tense) that 'serious' crime there was 'non-existent' and 'everybody knows everybody'. In so doing, she reinforced various idealized newspaper representations of the community – which, in themselves, contradicted those same papers' portrayals of the ubiquity of nefarious familiar strangers. A more illustrative approach was adopted by another Machynlleth resident who went beyond concurring with oft-repeated descriptions of 'Mach' as a place where 'everyone knows everyone' to portray it as an enduring pastoral idyll where normative protective behaviours necessary in 'a city or even a large town' were inappropriate – or, at least, had been up to this point. 'I don't think people realize how small Machynlleth is!' he/she said, describing 'big open greens, surrounded by houses' which 'nobody has ever considered ... a danger'. It was 'really normal' for 'a child to be out in front of her own home with her mates before darkfall' and anyone suggesting April 'shouldn't of been out on her own' were 'wrong' – not least because 'at 7 o clock ... it isn't even dark!'.

The notion of stolen innocence was not only expressed through depictions of Machynlleth, but also the way newspapers referred to April's family and police efforts to coax information from friends said to have witnessed it. To illustrate, the *Daily Star* (Lawton, 2012b, pp. 4–5) quoted neighbour Judy Price praising the 'very good and caring home' from which April had been taken, before noting Supt John's assurance that the little girl's playmates were 'being treated with sensitivity' by 'specialist officers trained to deal with children'. The *Independent* also stressed the 'gentle questioning' that police were undertaking with child witnesses, directly quoting Detective Superintendent Reg Bevan on the 'delicate and time-consuming' task (Peachey, 2012, p. 2). Among many compliments showered on April's family was councillor Williams' description of them in the *Sun* as 'hugely respected in the town' (Phillips & Wells, 2012, pp. 4–5). The emphasis interviewees placed on the loving, respectable character of April's family – and reporters' repeated selection of quotes reflecting this – echoed the sentiments of interviewed journalists who pointed out a distinction they noted while researching the story on the ground between her stable personal circumstances and the more dysfunctional parental setups of other high-profile (working-class) child abuse victims, like Shannon and Tia. Taken together with the overwhelmingly positive picture painted of her 'former' council estate – which some stories informed us had recently been named 'Best Kept Estate in Montgomeryshire' (*Times*, 2012b, pp. 4–5) – the overall portrayal of April's background contrasted starkly with the run-down, ghettoized sink estates familiar from those other cases. Just as newspapers routinely use postcode visualization programs like Google Maps to judge whether a story is right for their readers – and, by extension, how much effort to invest in covering it – so, too, the framing of April's versus Shannon or Tia's neighbourhoods symbolized the underlying 'deserving/undeserving' disjunction distinguishing between children from 'poor but respectable' homes and those from 'poor and unstable' ones. As both Shannon, aged nine, and Tia (15) were also considerably older than April, it could be argued that the 'young–old' measure of victim 'worthiness' was also applied by papers in these cases (Sommerville, 1990).

Framing Bridger: constructing a folk-devil

An all-too-familiar feature of even the earliest print reports was the clear contrast between the sweetness and innocence of April and the reputed shadiness (and probable malevolence) of Bridger. By the time the first 3 October editions went to bed, the 46-year-old was already in custody, and, though not yet named by officers, identified by every paper bar the *Express*, on the basis of information credited to unspecified local sources. Though these early reports were notably devoid of the more lurid labels attached to suspects in other notorious cases (albeit generally at later stages in inquiries, when foul play has been proven or described in court), from the outset Bridger was subject to the language and imagery of 'othering' (Mooney, 2009) – with background details selected to illustrate his dysfunctional private life, intimidating physicality and loner-like status in the community. And though not all papers ran photos of him on day one, most that did pointedly juxtaposed the same hazy, torso-length shot of a pumped-up man, sporting tattooed chest and goatee beard, with one of several interchangeable shots of elfin April – whether in a pink party frock, blue-and-white-checked dress or the purple coat she had worn the night of her disappearance. The most detailed early picture of Bridger appeared in the *Daily Telegraph* on 3 October (Evans, M., 2012, p. 2). Like several papers, it described him as a 'former soldier' – a claim that turned out to be false (*www.itv.com*, 2012) – who had also worked as a lifeguard, welder and slaughterhouse-worker, and fathered up to six children (Rayner et al., 2012b, pp. 2–3). Significantly, it balanced this run-down of his colourful CV and personal life with the assertion 'he is also thought to have spent large periods of time unemployed' (Evans, M., 2012, p. 2). Among anecdotes raked up about his recent past was the revelation that the 'fit and active man' had been evicted from a previous house after his landlady discovered he was keeping chickens indoors. The paper also described an alleged sighting of Bridger by local Gloria Edwards shortly before his arrest which further played up the image of a shifty ex-Army type – describing him as 'walking quickly towards the bridge that led into the town, wearing sunglasses and a khaki jacket and with his head down'. The *Times* adopted a similar focus on Bridger's chequered employment history and love life, describing his recent separation from a partner with young children and referring to his 'relationships with several women in the area' (O'Neill et al., 2012, p. 4). By the following day, Bridger's name had been confirmed by police and coverage of their investigation switched to the isolated cottage to which he had recently moved. The emphasis that reporters placed on this dwelling – the *Sun* described it being 'ripped apart' by forensic officers (Wells & Phillips, 2012, pp. 4–5) – was supplemented by suitably moody shots of its exterior, with white-suited forensic officers trooping in past recycling boxes brimming with empty beer bottles. In addition, the ongoing depiction of Bridger as a furtive figure with something to hide was enhanced by prominent use in both the *Sun* and the *Daily Mirror* (in the latter's case, on page one) of a fuzzy screenshot taken from footage filmed by *Channel 4 News* apparently showing a man scurrying along the bank of the River Dyfi (Aspinall, 2012, pp. 1 and 3). The image of Bridger as a diehard military man – perhaps used to covering his tracks – was again alluded to by several papers, through descriptions of clothes he was reportedly wearing when arrested: a green jacket and (beneath his waterproofs) 'camouflage trousers' (Chapman & Riches, 2012a, p. 5). This gung-ho image was embellished the next day, when the *Daily Telegraph* ran a piece describing him as a 'keen weapons collector', based on claims by neighbours that he 'kept samurai swords and deactivated guns' at home (Rayner, Marsden, & Silverman, 2012, p. 3). Meanwhile, Bridger's official identification encouraged certain titles, notably the *Daily Mail*, to opt for full-blown character assassination – prefiguring mention of his name with loaded adjectives like 'divorcee' and 'unemployed', and detailing how he had 'struggled to hold down a steady job' since moving to Wales and starting 'a string of relationships' with women whose children he had fathered (Evans & Bentley, 2012, p. 5).

These loaded references to Bridger's itinerant status were not confined to tabloids: even the normally sober *Independent* described him as a 'regular in local pubs', who, after splitting with his latest girlfriend, slept in his car (Brown, 2012, p. 6).

The melodramatic use of language in headlines and intros, especially in tabloids, appeared designed to set up an implicit opposition between April's desperate (therefore virtuous) parents and her unyielding (ergo heartless) abductor. On day one, the *Daily Mirror* juxtaposed the sinister image of the five-year-old being 'snatched' (Smith & Aspinall, 2012, pp. 4–5) with that of the 'distraught' parents she had left behind, while the *Sun* substituted this adjective with 'tormented' and described how Mr and Mrs Jones had 'begged' for her release (Phillips & Wells, 2012, pp. 4–5). Significantly, both papers accompanied their splashes that day with similarly oppositional portrait shots: one of tattooed Bridger, the other of innocently smiling April. But perhaps the most potent aspect of Bridger's othering occurred from day two, following the release of his official police mug-shot – which, thanks to its ubiquity in newspaper coverage over coming days, would soon become the iconic image of the suspected abductor. In it, a ghostly Bridger stared into the camera, wide-eyed, ashen-faced and unshaven – the personification of the unknowable, unhinged and/or demonic loner. This single photo accompanied nearly one in four of all 157 articles about April printed over the next six days.

From stranger to familiar

The second, decisive, phase in framing Bridger – his repositioning as familiar stranger – began unfolding in a handful of newspapers as early as our day one (3 October) and was fully established by the second full day of print coverage. Thereafter, rival titles became increasingly competitive in their efforts to root out additional – wherever possible, exclusive – titbits about the nature/extent of his links to April's family. On 3 October, even as other papers (principally the *Daily Telegraph* and the *Daily Mail*) sought to position Bridger as a shadowy, feckless loner incapable of holding down either jobs or relationships, the *Sun* was already describing him as a 'close friend' of the Joneses (Phillips, 2012, p. 1). Another key detail to emerge from the first day's print reporting was the police's insistence that April had 'willingly' climbed aboard the car/van – and, in the absence of confirmation that it was a left-hand drive vehicle, potentially into the driver's side (*www.bbc.co.uk*, 2012). This detail was amplified in the *Daily Mirror* with further nuggets of indirect witness testimony relayed by friends and neighbours, including the haunting claim that, before clambering aboard, April had reassured her anxious playmates with the words, 'it's all right: I know them' (Smith & Aspinall, 2012, pp. 4–5) – the plural raising the prospect (alluded to occasionally elsewhere over coming days) that more than one captor was involved. The paper was also the first to mention widely reported rumours that April had been playing 'in the same vehicle two or three days ago' (ibid.). Similarly, the *Daily Telegraph* claimed one of Bridger's daughters was with April at the time of her abduction (Rayner et al., 2012b, pp. 2–3). The closeness of Bridger to April's family circle, however, only began fully emerging on days two and three of print coverage. Having been the first paper to run a full profile-style article on the suspect the day before, the *Daily Telegraph* amplified readers' picture of his familiarity with April on 4 October by relaying how he had taken her and friends 'for a ride in his Land Rover' a couple of days earlier and not one but two of his children (a 10-year-old daughter and 12-year-old son) had been playing with her around the time she disappeared (Rayner et al., 2012c, pp. 1 and 3). Meanwhile, in what appeared to be a coded reference to information disclosed days later about Bridger's more direct relationship to April – notably the revelation that he was the uncle of her two half-sisters (Evans & Ford Rojas, 2012) – the *Guardian* pointedly noted how police 'refused to speculate' on 'how close Bridger was to any members of April's family' (Morris & Laville, 2012, p. 3). A day later, with the news that Bridger had been re-arrested (this time on suspicion of murder), a raft of new details emerged – including the *Daily Telegraph's* soon-to-be widely reported disclosure that he had attended the same parents' evening as the Joneses shortly before April's disappearance (Rayner et al., 2012d, p. 1) and an anecdote that the *Daily Express* and others reported that, earlier the same year, he had taken April on a crabbing expedition with two of his children (Chapman & Riches, 2012b, p. 5).

'Every parent's worst nightmare': normalizing and universalizing stranger-danger

Most of the analysis so far has focused on the disproportionate *amount* of coverage that April's abduction generated in newspapers compared to other stories during the week of her disappearance. But there is one further pattern indicative of disproportionate news framing which emerges from detailed study of these texts: the suggestion that April's disappearance was far from the isolated occurrence most independent research would indicate (Furedi, 2001) and that it represented a threat any parent might face, anywhere – at any time (Jenkins, 1992). This normalization, or *universalization*, of stranger-danger as an all-pervading, ever-present evil was expressed in various ways – most notably through papers' selection of background information to (de)contextualize the case and emphasize particular comments made by claims-makers, ranging from the police and uneasy locals to politicians and celebrities. The notion of omnipresent stranger-danger was best symbolized by a frequently quoted pronouncement of officers leading the manhunt. On Tuesday 2 October, at the first of many media conferences, Superintendent Bevan described April's disappearance as 'every family's worst nightmare' (Rankin, 2012). While this truism emphasized the extremely unusual nature of the incident – and, by extension, the unlikeliness of its happening to anyone else – it would be so widely repeated in coming days, not least in newspapers, that it came to signify something quite different: in short, a sense that *every* family should be on their guard, *at all times*. A simple Google search of the terms 'April Jones' and 'every family's worst nightmare', conducted on 15 February 2013, demonstrated the extent to which Supt Bevan's words were reported as news, and disseminated via social media, in ensuing months – throwing up 25,500 results, from all the main national newspaper websites to those of regional titles like the *Liverpool Echo* (Mullin, 2012) and news-aggregating sites such as *www.inooz.co.uk* (*www.inooz.co.uk*, 2013). In so doing, it testified to the heightened 'sensitization' (Cohen, 1972) to juvenile threats manifest in audience responses to coverage of the story, as demonstrated in posts on newspaper discussion threads and by focus group parents. Similarly, 13,700 Google results were produced by a search using the terms 'April Jones' and 'every parent's worst nightmare', also carried out on 15 February 2013. This phrase was widely reported after being used by one early contributor to a Facebook page set up by April's family and friends to raise awareness of her disappearance (coincidentally, it was also the exact tagline of *Vanishing Point*, a child abduction thriller by best-selling writer Val McDermid published a month earlier). As if to add to the simmering panic discourse, meanwhile, it took precisely two days for the words 'every family's nightmare' to be uttered by British Prime Minister David Cameron, who was widely quoted in newspapers on Friday 5 October appealing for help in finding April following the revelation that she needed medication for mild cerebral palsy (a condition suffered by his late son, Ivan). This twist had, in itself, only added to the vulnerable image popularized of the little girl (Chapman & Riches, 2012c, p. 4).

But it was not just the words that prominent claims-makers used to frame April's story that articulated a universalized sense of 'strangers in our midst' in those early days. Deliberate editorial choices newspapers took when contextualizing the story also appeared calculated to suggest child abduction/kidnapping was a pervasive, rather than isolated, phenomenon. The liberal *Guardian* played into this narrative more proactively than most, going out of its way to dramatize stranger-danger as a widespread problem – in so doing, adding weight to Meyer's (2007) conclusion that, when it comes to issues like child abuse/abduction, its discourse falls broadly in line with those adopted by tabloids. In a discrete article on the first full day of print coverage, headlined 'More than half of abductions are by a stranger' (*Guardian*, 2012, p. 2), the paper quoted a 2004 Home Office study showing that, of 798 police reports of minors being abducted in England and Wales, 56 per cent had involved strangers. Only by closely reading the full text would readers have discerned that eight out of 10 such incidents were *attempted*, rather than successful, abductions – and, of the 44 per cent of cases involving adults known to their victims, more than half were perpetrated by parents. A more typical device that newspapers used to convey the idea of pervasive stranger-danger was allusion to other high-profile recent cases. In addition to reproducing a slew of tweeted appeals from celebrities – television presenters Philip Schofield and Davina McCall, Stephen Fry and comic actor Simon Pegg among them – many papers quoted sympathetic comments from Kate and Gerry McCann, whose daughter, Madeleine, had vanished days before her fourth birthday, during a family holiday in Portugal. The *Sun*, meanwhile, ran a full-page day-one piece angled around the haunting similarities that Sara Payne supposedly saw between April's case and that of her own daughter, Sarah, who had been abducted and killed by paedophile Roy Whiting a decade earlier (Payne, 2012, pp. 6–7). The intro offered a masterclass in how disparate crimes might be speciously conflated into a wider discourse about the prevalence of particular threats:

> THE mother of murdered schoolgirl Sarah Payne has spoken of her 'devastation' after five-year-old April Jones was snatched in a chilling repeat of her own daughter's abduction. (ibid.)

Conflation of April's abduction with any number of other cases – and, more significantly, the wider suggestion, implied by much of the coverage, that stranger-danger represented an *omnipresent* threat – was a running theme of purely reactive discussion posts. Despite amounting to little more than echo chambers for the dominant narrative that they inferred from news accounts, as with many of those posted beneath articles analysed in Chapter 4 their cumulative effect was to *consolidate* the febrile juvenile panic discourse promoted by this generalized rhetoric of fear. Typical posts to this effect included a warning from 'Lizzie, London' that 'this happened in a small town and it just goes to prove it can happen anywhere' and 'Cupcake, Southeast's' baleful entreaty to parents everywhere to 'be aware of the dangers this sick world has at every turn and protect the child!'. Similarly, 'Nigel, Doncaster' – who, perhaps significantly, hailed from a town only recently the focus of national media attention over the notorious 'Doncaster boys' case (Doncaster Free Press, 2010) – despaired:

> Not another one! What's wrong with people? How has society got to this state?

Several posters also expressed horror at April's abduction by parroting the line voiced by detectives quoted in early reports that the scenario represented 'every parent's worst nightmare'. Nine people used this phrase on the *Daily Mail*'s discussion thread, with another five echoing their sentiments on the *Sun*'s. But perhaps the most extreme (and literal) universalization of April's case – and the proximity to readers everywhere of both the story itself and the threats it symbolized – was the alarmist warning from *Daily Mail* poster 'uk is finished, bath' that 'we all need to be vigilant, April was put into a van, this kid could potentially be next door to YOU'. Similarly commonplace were posts emphasizing April's youth and innocence – 'metzymems' likened her to a 'little petal' on the *Sun* website, while posters on *www.mailonline. co.uk* described her, variously, as a 'poor little angel', 'poor wee princess' and 'beautiful child' – in stark contrast to the diabolism many ascribed to her abductor. The then unknown malefactor was variously reviled by *Daily Mail* readers as a 'monster', 'sick', 'evil' and, of course, 'predator'. The habit of alluding to him as both freak of nature and feral beast – a dual trope familiar from both news narratives and discussion threads analysed in Chapter 4 – extended to the language that posters used to describe punishments they wanted him to suffer. A Hong Kong-based poster said he should be 'annihilated', 'blueheart, Torquay' demanded his 'castration' and numerous others called for the return of the death penalty. A related feature of many pro-hegemonic opinions was the sense that readers had been both emotionally and *physically* repulsed by thoughts of a child being taken – visceral responses echoing focus group mothers who spoke of their anxieties about what abductors might be 'doing to' their captives.[7] Posts in this vein included 'darlodave, darlington's' complaint about feeling 'sick to the stomach' and other readers' claims to feel, variously, 'sick reading this', 'cold and shaky' and 'ill'. One melodramatic *Daily Mail* poster, from Limerick, even claimed her 'heart literally broke'. Besides upholding a view of the world as a dangerous place where child-snatching predators lurked around every corner, the other main facet of affirming opinions was a belief that – while children should have rights *in principle* to play out independently – there was a cut-off age below which none should be allowed out alone. Countless *Daily Mail* and *Sun* readers expressed angry criticism of April's parents for letting her out of their sight. Such tirades often adopted a rhetorical approach, as illustrated by this from 'Andy, Manchester' on *www.mailonline.co.uk*:

> What kind of parents allow a five-year-old to play outside unsupervised in the evening?

Some posters even spelt out what April *should* have been doing at the time she was playing unsupervised. 'Pippye483, lancs' argued she should have been 'in the bath, having a bedtime story or fast asleep at 7.30' – images of responsible child-rearing echoed by other critics. Most punitive was 'Sam, Bradford', who called on unspecified 'authorities' to investigate April's parents and 'consider placing the [other] children in a home' after drawing an explicit opposition between the (sensible) practice of ensuring five-year-olds 'were in jamas in the warm having supper & a story at 7:30' and the idea April had been left 'roaming the streets'. Significantly, even those who stood up for her parents against such condemnations still generally distilled the same underlying *meaning* from the story: while disputing the fairness of blaming the girl's family for her disappearance, they concurred with the view that (stranger) danger lurked everywhere. Responding to the last comment, 'polo, Nottingham' castigated fellow readers for suggesting April's siblings be put into care – but implicitly endorsed their view that she had been 'left out to play later than you would let your own'. And 'nataliesabSun, kent' was one of several lamenting the level of vigilance required today. Implicitly accepting the notion that unsupervised children *were* perpetually threatened, she despaired, 'it's so sad that we can't let our children play outside where it should be safe without the fear of them getting kidnapped!' Similarly, 'taff, Wales' lamented that 'this little town' that people 'would regard as really safe' had become the latest casualty of 'Broken Britain' – echoing opinions voiced in the discussion threads and focus groups analysed in Chapters 3 and 4. Others adopted the contradictory position exemplified by a Plymouth poster that, although 'the only person to blame for this is the perpetrator', nonetheless 'some fault has to be levelled at parents who are so willing to take chances with their childs [*sic*] safety'.

As with the discussion threads explored earlier, the overwhelming pro-hegemonic consensus visible in most posts generated by April's abduction was periodically interrupted by a more nuanced, negotiated, class of comment. While most readers reluctantly agreed with the common sentiment that children should not be allowed out alone, some appeared angry and frustrated that random, exceptional crimes had induced risk-averse parents to routinely restrict their children's freedoms so severely. As 'pm123' put it on the *Sun's* site, it may have been 'a bit late for a 5 yearold [*sic*] to be out playing', but 'it is absolutely terrible that a child is not safe just a few yards from their home' – a fact that suggested 'those very few "sick" people are turning them into prisoners who cant do anything'. Perhaps unsurprisingly, outright oppositional posts were conspicuously thin on the ground so soon after the incident that provoked these discussions – with barely one per cent of the total falling into this category. One factor that might explain this is that, unlike with many of the threads analysed previously, those commenting on April's case were confined to a single day: between news breaking of her disappearance and Bridger's arrest. The overwhelming tone conveyed by these posts therefore seemed rawer and more charged than usual. Nonetheless, ranged against such an insurmountable consensus, the few dissenters brave enough to stick their heads above the parapet came out fighting, as demonstrated by this stream-of-consciousness tirade from 'jessicanye82, Morden, United Kingdom':

> ... so because of that all children should suffer you should keep them locked up from the world she was probably just enjoying the last few days of being able to play on her bike outside maybe people should stop with calling the parents evil and find the evil person that did this ...

More intriguingly, what was most compelling about the majority of oppositional posts on this occasion was the fact that eight out of 10 were *evidence-based*, rather than simply reactive. While just three out of 572 reactive posts took an oppositional standpoint (see Figure 5.2), this was true of 13 of the 165 evidence-based ones – with another 17 adopting negotiated positions (see Figure 5.3). Moreover, most evidence-based posters *contesting* the dominant framing of April's story, and latent meaning(s) inferred from it, appeared particularly well placed to do so, with several purporting to live either in Machynlleth itself or similarly

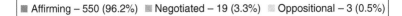

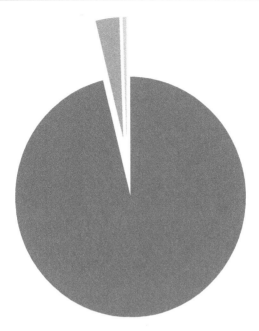

Figure 5.2 Breakdown of reactive opinions

rural locales, often also in Wales. Indeed, a recurring characteristic of many of these rebuttals was the polar distinction drawn between 'small town' or 'village' (safe) and 'city' or 'big town' (dangerous) – implicitly invoking the idea of (lost/stolen) innocence repeatedly transposed onto Machynlleth, and April's neighbourly estate, in press coverage. 'Caz, Wrexham' was one of several posters to speak up for small-scale communities everywhere – not just Machynlleth's – in refuting suggestions stranger-danger was omnipresent:

> I notice a lot of comments from places like London, Manchester and other huge connurbations asking why a 5 year-old is playing out at 7.30 pm. Well in many places in the UK parents are not constantly looking over their shoulders as they live in friendly communities where they feel safe. Children here in North wales regularly play out at this time.

■ Endorsement (135 – 81.8%) ■ Negotiated response (17 – 10.3%)
▨ Oppositional response (13 – 7.9%)

Figure 5.3 Breakdown of evidence-based responses

By drawing a polar opposition between 'friendly communities' and the rest, however, such posters made a more nuanced point than merely *challenging* the consensus about the pervasiveness of extra-familial threats to children's wellbeing. Rather, they implicitly distinguished between 'good' and 'bad' (or more and less crime-ridden) neighbourhoods – having it both ways, by acknowledging that stranger-danger was a real and present threat in *other* areas but denying this was the case in *theirs*. In so doing, they mirrored the less universalized observations about the safety or otherwise of children's 'home habitats' (Hillman et al., 1990) explored in Chapter 4, and, in a curious way, revived the deep-rooted binary distinction between *our children* and *other people's* that emerged from both focus group discussions and Chapter 2's review of historical conceptions of childhood. In addition to oppositional posters who mobilized personal knowledge/experience to challenge the dominant discourse, as in Chapter 5 there were those who simply *re-presented* facts down-played in articles to offer different readings not only of the circumstances of April's abduction, but also the underlying 'pervasive juvenile threat' narrative. 'Gill, UK' implored fellow *Daily Mail* posters to stop 'judging the parents' and 'saying "why is she out so late"', while emphasizing 'IT was only 7.30, she was with her friend and is [*sic*] SOUNDS LIKE IT WAS IN A SAFE AREA'. While comments contesting the dominant critique of April's parents generally received short shrift from those backing the consensus ('Gill, UK's' remark met a terse 'clearly not' from 'Jenny, Leicester'), pro-hegemonic voices were less nimble in parrying blows struck by oppositional posters who drew on previous media stories about lax judgment by middle-class parents to point out the double standards applied to those from different social backgrounds. Echoing sentiments expressed by the journalist who contrasted the media's swiftness to condemn Shannon Matthews' mother with the universal sympathy initially expressed for the McCanns, 'mystic 1981, newport' queried the 'responsible-versus-irresponsible parent' distinction implied by those critical of April's freedom to play out late, by reminding fellow *Daily Mail* readers 'when a doctors and a teachers child went missing from an appartment' (presumably a reference to the McCanns) they were not 'judged so much'. Others cited alternative forms of prior knowledge, including official statistics, to question popular (mis)conceptions of the prevalence of threats. 'Caz, Glasgow' recalled data showing 'children are at more risk from people they know than a stranger' (La Fontaine, 1994; Grubin, 1998; Pritchard & Bagley, 2001). While failing to specify the source of her knowledge – professional expertise or media reports – she reminded others, 'abductions like this are actually quite rare indeed, and that's if this is a stranger abduction'. As with the other discussion threads, though, the most effective evidence-based rebuttal was posted by a reader who authoritatively challenged not only the underlying discourse of the papers' April coverage but a key detail of the story itself. Rebutting a central 'fact' repeated time and again by posters critical of her parents – the suggestion that she had been playing out in the dark – 'JoJo, Swansea, United Kingdom' wrote:

I'm in Wales, it was light at 7.00 pm and still at 7.30 pm ...

But, while such insightful counter-claims offered dynamic examples of persuasive challenges by citizens to the dominant discourse – and ones with *potential* to moderate other readers' perceptions of social reality – as in Chapter 4 they were rare. In the end, 93 per cent of discussion posts (685 out of 737) supported a hegemonic reading of the signification of April's story. This bias in audience meaning-making towards a disproportionate perception of menace and risk was also reflected by parent focus groups, as the next section demonstrates.

Crystallizing concerns: April Jones, the dark, the mystery car and the familiar stranger

As with the papers' over-manning of the April story, and the resultant saturation coverage, the way in which focus group mothers responded to it was with disproportionate alarm. More significantly, the general consensus was that this cautionary tale vindicated restrictions that they already routinely imposed on their children to keep them safe – suggesting that, at the very least, news reports had *reinforced* protective parental attitudes and behaviours. The strength of concerns aired by most mothers in response to April's abduction revolved around the fact that the scenario reported by papers – and other key definers, notably the police – tapped into themes, and appeared to validate fears, that they had proactively raised in the more exploratory discussions analysed in Chapter 3. Chief among these were various signifiers which, taken together or in isolation, drew on the potent 'threatening familiarity' paradigm. From a twilit playground on a close-knit estate to mystery vehicles of indeterminate make (and, in this case, colour) to an archetypal familiar stranger (Bridger), April's tale contained all the elements of a latter-day suburban horror story – and was entirely consistent with previously articulated worries about 'the dark', 'black cars' and the shifty 'man in the park'. The fact that April was snatched by a mystery driver while playing outside with friends in encroaching darkness prompted some mothers to instinctively criticize her parents for allowing her out late unsupervised. As in many discussion posts, several participants, particularly working-class mothers, voiced disapproval – applying a rationale that *universalized* the prospect of stranger-danger, irrespective of how safe a given neighbourhood might otherwise appear. A straightforward criticism came from the teaching assistant (despite the fact she claimed to apply a *laissez-faire* approach towards her own children's outdoor movements). 'Where's the *parent?*' she said of her immediate reaction to April's disappearance, adding, 'they shouldn't be ... in their house ... while their kids are outside ... at seven o'clock at night'. Similar sentiments were expressed by a mother-of-four with a new baby, who was one of several contributors to contrast her own (responsible) approach with the (irresponsible) one of April's mother – an echo of the 'worthy/unworthy parent' discourse underpinning observations on *other people's* children to which she had contributed in earlier discussions. She described how she 'kept looking' at her own daughter, thinking, 'she's [April] younger' and 'I wouldn't even let [her] out at that time'. And, in an exchange with the nursery worker explicitly focusing on children's vulnerability to risk, the teaching assistant dismissed any suggestion that April's parents were justified in believing her safe because she was playing with older kids. When the former suggested 'friends' could 'get distracted', she replied, 'other children can be the *cause* of … accidents'.

As before, middle-class mothers adopted a more live-and-let-live attitude towards the fact April had been allowed out late – with more than one recalling the tragic irony that this was reportedly a one-off reward for a glowing school report. However, when the writer said she had been 'comforted' by the fact April was playing out with older children (rather than alone) at the time of her abduction, not all seemed convinced. Though stressing she did not 'mean to say, "oh, I'm such a good mother"', the nurse recalled how 'my children were always in bed by seven, aged five', while the midwife (a single mum) asserted that her sons 'would have been in having a bath, getting ready for bed' at April's age. Belying more critical responses, one or two mothers in each group echoed comments posted by newspaper readers defending the relative safety of rural communities by defending April's parents, on the grounds that her family lived in a more secluded community than theirs – and it was wrong to generalize that the same parental restrictions should be imposed everywhere. Even a self-confessed 'over-protective' 30-year-old working-class mother with two daughters (aged six and seven) acknowledged that, compared to the high-crime, less community-orientated neighbourhood where she lived, 'in Wales it's completely different', while the position adopted by one of two tower-block residents was modified by her childhood memory of being 'allowed out on the street at seven o'clock' because 'we lived in a close'. Here, a curious inversion seemed to be at work between the (more typical) tendency of parents to identify with *respectable* societal norms when it came to distinguishing between their own and their children's behaviour and that of other (*less* respectable) households: in reflecting on the overall neighbourhood they inhabited, the working-class mothers displayed a keen sense of self-awareness that they were unlucky enough to live in an area that was relatively more crime-ridden than rural Wales. In this respect, they clearly aligned themselves with numerous online newspaper readers who perceived potential danger around every corner (including in their own locales), rather than the handful who claimed to live in areas mercifully free of the hazards they associated with other, larger and more anonymous, places.

As in earlier meetings, working-class mothers were particularly exercised by one defining trope of the threatening familiarity scenario: the image of a young child being abducted by a mystery driver in a nondescript (and therefore universally imaginable) vehicle. At times, this menace assumed a spectral quality, fuelled by the fact that every aspect of the offending car's description had fluctuated in early reports about April's disappearance – from colour to make and model and even whether it was a right-hand or left-hand drive vehicle. The car's symbolism provided a stimulus for discussion in two respects: it acted as a catalyst for recollections of other high-profile stories focusing on child abduction and as a focal-point for exchanges of opinion about how and when parents should broach the subject of stranger-danger with their children. Of the previous news stories recalled explicitly, two surfaced prominently: the McCann case and the spate of local 'black car' incidents reported the previous year, which working-class mothers had discussed extensively in earlier meetings. Maddie's story was raised by the teaching assistant as a comparative case in the context of media speculation that Bridger's blue Land Rover was being scoured for DNA evidence by detectives – just as, for a time, Portuguese police had focused on the McCanns' car in seeking traces of her whereabouts. Tellingly, though, it was the mothers' almost mythic collective memory of the 'black car' sightings that opened up into a wider, often self-reflexive, discussion about the need to strike a balance between warning children about the *possibility* of abduction and frightening them unnecessarily. Echoing the criticisms of other people's children (and other parents) voiced in earlier discussions – and in implied recognition of her own tendency to panic at times – the 'over-protective' mother recalled how the black car sightings had left both her and her son worrying unduly, because 'everyone round here was all freaking out and running out all day, going, "there's a car outside with tinted windows – let's go!"' As a result, her son became 'completely panicky about kidnappers, believing 'everybody was a kidnapper: *everyone*'. 'He was like, "that man's a kidnapper! The man in the shop was trying to kidnap me!" And I was like, "they *weren't!*".' The elliptical exchange about the black car motif was prompted by the nursery worker's admission that April's abduction had sensitized her to questions of misplaced trust. In particular, it had prompted her to take her son aside before he attended a football match with her brother to caution him against saying hello to anyone familiar without his uncle's permission. By first relating April's case to one within her own purview (the black car sightings), then drawing lessons from the abduction incident to guide her son on his soccer outing, this mother was both *universalizing* the story's implications for every parent and *personalizing* them by projecting them onto her own circumstances. 'I didn't talk about it because of the April Jones thing as such', she insisted, before confessing, 'I just said, "make sure you check with whoever you're with before you go off – even if it's *me*"'.

As in previous meetings, the conflicted feelings with which parents openly wrestled as they exchanged (frequently self-critical) observations about the impact of April's case on their own parenting practices led to broader discussion of the contribution of social mediation – in particular, Facebook and school-gate gossip – to the prevailing panic. Responding to the 'over-protective' mother's anecdote about the black car scare panicking her son, the nursery worker relayed how April's story had a similar effect on hers, who returned from school saying, 'there's a bad man taking children *here*'. This rumour-fuelled misunderstanding forced her to explain 'it's not *here* … a girl *did* get taken – it wasn't *here*, but she was out on her own … and you don't go out on your own, [so] if you're out with an adult like me, then it's not something you've got to be worrying about'. By mentioning social media and the school-gate rumour-mill as sources of their own anxieties – and playground gossip as the wellspring of worries affecting their *children* – the mothers were returning to the issue of Chinese whispers as a conduit for promoting panics discussed in Chapter 3. Not only were parents across Brighton and Hove reacting to news of April's abduction hundreds of miles away by warning their own children about the prospect of a similar fate befalling them: the viral spread of key elements of the story (unsupervised play, mystery car, familiar stranger) had the effect of obscuring, and universalizing, its *location*. In so doing it appears to have generalized the incident's *meaning* for families everywhere. Similar evidence of a generalized discourse about child abduction – fuelled by the instantaneous nature and 'placeless proximity' (Baym, 2009; Gulbrandsen & Just, 2011) of online communications – emerged from middle-class mothers. The midwife laughed as she recalled 'friends in this [Facebook] group…going on about having this "stranger-danger" talk with their kids', 'posting the pink ribbon [campaign]' and urging others to 'click on it and share' it – despite the fact 'you're certainly not going to find her in East Sussex…'

Besides offering a disturbing symbolic image for the perceived omnipresence of stranger-danger – as exemplified by both Brighton's black car scare and April's abduction – the mystery vehicle element appears to have provided a helpfully tangible menace for those mothers minded to warn their offspring about the risks of being snatched, and an ominous, Grimmesque locus for their children's own processing of the story. To this end, the teaching assistant was one of several parents who admitted taking advantage of the opportunity to broach the subject of stranger-danger after catching one of her daughters watching a TV report about April's disappearance. 'Being seven ... she was glued to this telly, going, "mum, when's she coming home?" And we had to explain to her what had happened', she recalled. So persistent were the mothers' references to discussions that April's abduction had provoked with their children – particularly around the mystery car – that these dialogues appear to have represented a key stage (for parents *and* offspring) in their mean-ing-making around the case. Moreover, by negotiating meaning in this way, families were actively participating in the wider societal process by which the simmering panic discourse underpinning mediated repre-sentations of this story (and others like it) came to be *crystallized*, once more, in the public sphere. Worries about misplaced trust – like those articulated in the above mother–daughter exchanges – inevitably also led to consideration of the story's bogeyman element: in this case, the repeatedly invoked nightmare figure of the familiar stranger. In Bridger, the man arrested on suspicion of April's abduction and murder within 24 hours of her disappearance, there was an immediate stranger in our midst, as it emerged he lived on the same estate, had fathered several local children and invited the little girl aboard his Land Rover days ear-lier. The subsequent drip-drip of biographical details only added to the sense of his being known to April's family, yet strangely disconnected and unfathomable. We learned that, hours before she vanished, he had attended the same parents' evening as her mother – the fateful event that led to April being allowed out unsupervised – and within days it emerged that her two half-siblings were his nieces. The tangled, indirect nature of Bridger's relationship to April was lost in translation in much of the focus group discussion – with members alluding to him, vari-ously, as 'a family friend' (tower-block resident) and 'this geezer who just lived next door and kept himself to himself' (teaching assistant). But what did emerge strongly, as on previous occasions, was a widespread awareness that April was known to Bridger (and he to her), and general unease at any thought that she might have been preyed on by some-one she believed she could trust. This haunting prospect – rehearsed in earlier discussions about paedophile nursery workers and recognizable parents with whom one is on nodding terms – was as much a concern for middle-class as working-class mothers. Recalling an anecdote she had shared previously about the message promoted by a crèche where she once volunteered – namely that 'it's so unusual to have a predator, a paedophile' – the middle-class nurse described how April's story had shaken her long-held belief that children would be safe if they followed their 'gut instinct' about whether to trust someone. 'April must have trusted him in her stomach [and] what really scares me above anything else is that somebody could be deceitful', she said, projecting this scenario onto herself by considering the horrific thought that 'someone I *know* might be having really dark thoughts about murdering a child'.

Discussion about the familiar stranger dimension of April's story prompted both groups to recall another then-recent juvenile disappearance with a similar subtext that had also been extensively reported: that of 12-year-old Tia, whose body was found, wrapped in a sheet, in the loft of the home she shared with her grandmother and the latter's boyfriend a week after they had reported her missing. As with April, it was only a matter of time before the familiar stranger of the piece – in this instance, Tia's step-grandfather, Stuart Hazell – was charged with her murder. As the midwife noted, 'it's like with Tia Sharp ... The mum thinking she's with her granny, and she's got a boyfriend, and thinking, "that's my mother, and I trust my mum that this man's nice"'. This notion of malign intent lurking behind the friendly façades of familiar strangers appeared, as ever, to strike a chord most powerfully with those who could relate it to their own 'schemas' (Graber, 1984). Though she began by sounding philosophical about the risk of trusting people with whom one was only loosely acquainted, the hostel worker quickly lapsed into voicing a generalized wariness of others that recalled her previous declaration that the nature of her work attuned her to fears that the world was 'more dangerous' than 'other people think' – by reflecting on the 'very affable, very charming' façades' of 'clients' who were 'actually ... a sexual predator'. She also drew on a vicarious experience – coincidentally, from Wales – to further vindicate her concerns about familiar strangers. This concerned the case of a woman whose plea for help had been ignored after she telephoned police to report her daughter missing. Wrongly assuming the child to be with the woman's ex-partner, officers failed to 'pull out all the stops' – only to discover she had actually been abducted and abused by 'an acquaintance' who had been 'brought in by a friend into the household'. The most vivid personal projection of the familiar stranger figure, though, surfaced as a direct personal memory of the 'over-protective' mother which drew on a montage of elements related not only to April's abduction but coverage of the Savile allegations – conflating themes raised by the two stories, as newspapers had also done. As a household-name celebrity, Savile could hardly be described as a typical familiar stranger – being famous and, therefore, too distant from most people's daily lives for them to be acquainted with him personally. Yet sinister tales of this once venerated charity fundraiser misusing his avuncular public persona to win the trust of vulnerable hospital patients and children in care only to abuse them in private rooms or during country drives in his Rolls Royce reminded this mother of an uneasy experience from her own childhood that had informed her parenting:

> ... I had a similar experience ... I was quite young, and I knew – I ran out of the house and got my dad, straightaway ... This was my mum's best friend ... Man, I knew it was wrong. Nothing too far, but it was *wrong*. He shouldn't *be* in the bedroom ...

Responding to April: from reaction to action

While several parents confessed to more marked behavioural responses to April's story – giving their sons and daughters pep talks, or further limiting their outdoor freedoms (at least temporarily), because of anxieties it fuelled – most said it had strengthened their determination to maintain *existing* boundaries, rather than encouraging them to impose *new* ones. Echoing many sentiments expressed on discussion threads, the 'over-protective' mother said the story 'backs up my ... protectiveness' and 'why I don't let my kids out!'. Similarly, the nursery worker who had related her jitteriness to her single mother status in earlier sessions reflected how 'stories like this reaffirm why you *don't* want your children out or why you are protective of them', because 'it [abduction] *does* happen'. But, beyond reinforcing existing approaches to parenting, to what extent can April's story – and the heightened coverage it received in the news – be said to have had an *effect* on these mothers? To begin at the simplest level, the avid attention most mothers claimed to have paid to TV, radio, print and online news – and the degree to which some had regularly tuned into it – appeared to demonstrate levels of interest bordering (in some cases) on addiction. The tower-block resident, writer and nurse all admitted having been *affected* by the story – and obsessing about checking the headlines for any news of April's whereabouts. Like several others, the writer recalled reading up on it in the press – at one point recalling a 'family tree' that a broadsheet published illustrating the convoluted connection between April and Bridger – but her most regular source of updates was BBC Radio 4's lunchtime news programme, *PM*, to which she 'was tuning in every day … kind of waiting for news'. Both she and the nurse rationalized their intense interest by referring to the empathy they felt for Mrs Jones as mothers themselves – another example of participants' repeated projection of media narratives back onto their own schemas. The nurse gave this vivid account of how the haunting associations she drew from the story upset her emotionally:

> A few days later [after the abduction was first reported], when I heard the anguished plea of the mother saying, 'please bring my little girl back', I just absolutely broke down and cried my eyes out. I think that might be partly because … my second daughter's just left home, so … I felt like I'd lost my baby as well, and I just sort of howled in the kitchen. It was awful.

Similarly, one of two tower-block residents rationalized her interest in the story as reflecting the fact that she had her own 'little ones'. But she distinguished between the level of pep talk it prompted her to give them – which she confined to explaining the media coverage she was watching – and full-blown stranger-danger chats favoured by others. 'When I was watching it, I was saying to them, "look, a little girl's gone missing". You know, "a naughty man did it" – you always have a naughty man, don't you? – but I can't say I've had "the chat"', she said. But, in contrast to those who stayed plugged into the story, one or two mothers stressed they had pointedly *avoided* media coverage after initially hearing about it – largely *because* it had upset them (another indicator of the strong emotional responses it provoked). The retired schoolteacher – who insisted she 'barely read the papers', 'never' watched TV news and 'occasionally' heard 'Radio 4 news by accident' – described feeling disturbed about April's case but impotent to '*do* anything'. In Chapter 3's discussions this mother had mentioned her general avoidance of news and preference for 'more reliable' sources of information like 'books', during a debate about parenting practices and, in particular, the wisdom of leaving children unsupervised. Her attempted avoidance of coverage of April's abduction, and other stories embodying similar concerns, arguably owed much to her personal circumstances: as a single mother whose son had been subject to a protracted custody battle with her former partner. Significantly, she had voluntarily raised this issue several times during earlier discussions, at one point projecting a scenario onto the mystery about April's disappearance that appeared to draw heavily on her own schema. Conceding she had 'some history' to inform her theory, she said her family had been 'put through the family courts, and that's confidential', which 'means you can't know about the various characters involved'. This had led her to 'wonder if there's ... there's another parent or ... some connection ... and the guy who's charged was trying to be a "rescuer" ... and that child is out there somewhere, happier than she was'.

As demonstrated by much of the dialogue already quoted, then, most mothers appeared to have been *affected* by April's story – particularly those for whom it chimed with personal experiences. No sooner had the shy working-class mum recalled her initial reaction to hearing 'another kid's gone missing' – a response indicative, in itself, of a generalized sensitization to stranger-danger – than she began reliving concerns for the safety of her own 14-year-old sister, who 'ran away' fleetingly around the same time. Similarly, during a lengthy strand of working-class discussion focusing on several mothers' concerns about their children's tendency to disappear with friends without asking permission, the woman who had recently given birth for a fourth time recalled calling the police in a panic the previous summer after her daughter vanished while playing outside. Her alarm had been heightened by the fact that Brighton was then in the grip of the supposed 'black car' incidents repeatedly alluded to by this group. Conjuring up a nightmare scenario which drew not only on April's story but an amalgam of previous abductions, she recalled, 'what was panicking me more than anything' was the question 'what would they be *doing* to 'em?'. News representations of April's story (and others like it) clearly *affected* these mothers, then – but how far should we go in inferring *effects* from their responses? It is one thing to suggest that someone has been upset or angered by a story encountered directly or indirectly in the media: quite another to infer that this experience has changed, or even modified, their existing perceptions or behaviours. Nonetheless, based on their testimonies, for many of these mothers April's case seems to have justified, and *reinforced*, boundaries they already imposed to limit their children's independence, while (for a time) increasing their anxieties about the likelihood of abduction. This heightened 'sensitization' – long recognized as a key stage in an unfolding moral panic (Cohen, 1972; Goode & Ben-Yehuda, 2009) and cited specifically in previous writings about paedophile/abduction scares (Critcher, 2003; Meyer, 2007) – manifested itself in various actions they admitted taking after learning of the story, from giving their children stranger-danger pep talks to further tightening their reins around outdoor activities. Moreover, several of those who responded by reminding their children about the risks of talking to other adults mentioned the fact that, by the time they did so, these warnings had already been given by the child's school or nursery – an indicator of heightened *community-wide* sensitization in the classic panic mould. When the nurse began 'feeling anxious about' her eight-year-old daughter 'walking round to school by herself', she decided to 'talk to her about not getting in people's cars' – only to be told, 'oh, we know all about that: we've learnt about it at school'. A similar experience was relayed by the nursery worker, who, while on placement, overheard a teacher warning pupils not to 'go off with anyone'. This anecdote had the added dimension of reviving the discourse about *familiar* strangers, in that she recalled the teacher saying, 'what if you saw *me* in the street and I said, "come with me"? What would you say?'. Indeed, the teacher's explicit invocation of the threatening familiarity paradigm had, this mother argued, risked undermining her pupils' confidence in her by positioning *herself* as a familiar stranger. A more vicarious illustration of the way questions of trust about adults known to children appears to have surfaced in parental pep talks following April's disappearance came from the midwife, who, despite trying to avoid 'voyeuristic and gossipy' Facebook tittle-tattle, confessed to being disturbed by a forum in which mothers 'were going crazy, like, "right, we are having a stranger-danger talk tonight, blah blah blah"'. Recalling a web-link posted by one contributor to a piece by 'an American writer' urging parents to talk to children less about 'stranger-danger' than 'wary individuals', she expressed disquiet at advice suggesting that parents should 'tell your child to always seek out a *mum*' – as if 'all of a sudden, "*men are not safe*"'.

Besides giving pep talks, some mothers did assert that the story had made them more vigilant. The ex-teacher confessed she was 'more wary' about allowing her son to play outside in her cul-de-sac until his usual '7.30 cut-off', saying she had 'found myself waving' at a parent outside to check on her son's whereabouts. The hostel worker, meanwhile, said the 'effect' of the April coverage had led to her warning her 13-year-old son as she dropped him by a short-cut through a wood that morning to 'stick by another group of boys' and 'don't talk to strangers'. She conceded she was 'probably slightly more worried, yes' after reading and hearing about April, adding that 'there was definitely … an effect'. The nursery worker also reacted to the story behaviourally – finding herself 'watching' as her son slept and feeling 'really emotional, seeing him being safe'. Describing her gut response to April's abduction, she added, 'it hurts your heart' and 'makes you feel more aware of … keeping your child safe'. Similar sentiments, and indicators of apparent behavioural responses to the story, emerged from many discussion posts – with 'emma, belfast' stressing her determination to 'drum into my 3 year old about not talking to or going with strangers', and a Wolverhampton-based poster saying she had 'taken the opportunity to talk to my son and explain what has happened'. While it is impossible to be scientific about any impact April's story had on parents, then, both focus groups and discussion threads produced abundant *anecdotal* evidence to suggest that it reinforced existing attitudes towards child safety and related parenting practices, in the short term at least. More significant, though, was the sense that people had been *affected* by the story, which resonated with them primarily because of the familiar tropes on which it drew – notably unsupervised outdoor play, mystery cars and duplicitous familiar strangers.

Mediating April: the abduction story as crystallizing moment

So what do the interviews with journalists, published newspaper narratives and audience responses have to tell us, collectively, about *how* this crystallizing moment in Britain's rolling juvenile panic came about? More importantly, how can the disproportionate way in which this undoubtedly horrific case was processed and responded to at all levels in the 'circuit of mass communication' (Miller et al., 1998) help us *anatomize* the process by which panic narratives about children bubble back to the surface in the public sphere? Who were the key definers of this panic discourse, and whose influence was most decisive in shaping its terms and emphasis through the aegis of news reception, social mediation and agency: the police, other official sources, news media, moral entrepreneurs like the citizen searchers from the Machynlleth community, or ourselves (and our peers)?

As in their previous discussions about specific media stories (notably the McCann case), a common tendency among focus group mothers was to *project* the circumstances of April's abduction onto their own 'schema' (Graber, 1984). This suggested that its resonance lay principally in the fact that they could easily imagine themselves in her mother's predicament. But this empathetic response – a reflection of the 'people like us' factor that *journalists* with children observed in their own reactions to such stories – worked both ways, with those critical of April's parents drawing on it as often as those defending them. In contrasting her own practices with those of April's family, the 'overprotective' working-class mum suggested she would be more responsible in the same situation – adding that her children 'don't go out ... on their own', so 'that child shouldn't have been out'. And, despite having enjoyed similar freedoms to April when she was a child, the tower-block tenant who used to live in a close said her present home environment prevented her from permitting her own children similar leeway. Using vivid but unspecific language, indicative of a generalized concern about familiar strangers, she said she was afraid to let her daughter 'go down on the communal garden on her own, because ... there's somebody in my block that could do it'. Moreover, generalized concerns extended beyond those explicitly related to nefarious strangers – familiar or otherwise – with the nursery worker observing that parents' worries were 'not just' about fears that 'people might take 'em', but wider concerns about 'all sorts of dangers'. In so doing, she described the montage of often ill-defined threats evoked by more sensitized parents in both groups: in essence, through the prism of a single (heavily publicized but extremely rare) event, more safety-conscious mothers appeared to manifest a *generalized* sense of panic redolent of the nervy, sometimes fraught, dialogue observed on discussion threads. The collective, mutually reinforcing, process of interpersonal meaning-making in which mothers (and posters) engaged as they deliberated April's story, then, both *exemplified and encapsulated* the dynamics by which Britain's simmering juvenile panic is periodically crystallized.

But why did this single incident seize people's imaginations *so* fiercely – in so doing, bringing deep-seated anxieties about a plethora of other (real or imagined) threats bubbling to the surface? To begin with the simplest observation, April's story was – like the Moors murders, Bulger killing and any number of similarly horrific tales – a 'noisy construction' of the kind Cohen identified in his introduction to the third edition of *Folk Devils and Moral Panics*, as he ruminated on the explosive ways that simmering panic narratives periodically resurface in response to a 'single sensational case' (Cohen, 2002, p. xxiii). This was not a panic concocted out of nowhere, but an *authentic event*: one which, with its montage of threatening familiarity motifs (unsupervised neighbourhood play, mystery car, familiar stranger), conjured up a scenario terrifyingly imaginable to any parent of a young child (including many journalists writing about it). To coin the commonly used cliché, it was 'every parent's worst nightmare'. Who, though, were the primary definers of April's story? In that she vanished in a (to most) remote Welsh town and the initial alert was circulated by the local constabulary as a brief statement on its website and (rapidly re-tweeted) Twitter alert, the obvious answer is the police. This argument is also justified by working-class mothers' references to their feeling that officers appeared to have deliberately controlled the flow of information about April to maintain a steady stream of media stories – a view shared by several journalists, including the liberal broadsheet crime correspondent. For example, the teaching assistant drew attention to the fact that the disclosure that she needed medication for cerebral palsy only occurred 'three or four days' into the saga. Both groups also alluded to the crucial role her family (particularly her distraught mother) played in spreading the word about her disappearance and appealing to the public, with the 'pink ribbon' campaign she launched to sustain awareness of the search repeatedly mentioned in the context of frenzied social media discourse around the story. As the textual analysis demonstrates, however, the fact that this story contained *so many* 'every parent's worst nightmare' elements – unsupervised play, mystery car, abduction – meant that it inevitably generated vocal and immediate responses from all manner of other prominent parties, ranging from the Prime Minister to newspaper columnists and tweeting celebrities. Unusually, there were also two further factors conspiring to lend April's story even more power than other tales of its kind to crystallize underlying public concerns about child safety. The first was the unequivocal way in which, within hours of her disappearance, the incident was described (by both authorities and media) as an 'abduction' – rather than a *suspected* one, as in the McCann case. The second was the macabre coincidence that the story broke just two days after the first reports focusing on historic allegations about Savile's systematic sexual abuse of vulnerable juveniles. The uncommonly coincidental nature of this occurrence led to some mothers incorporating references to Savile in their reflections on April, as anecdotes quoted earlier show. And, as previously discussed, it encouraged many papers to juxtapose these two (distinct) stories on their front pages for days on end. In so doing, they symbolically conflated two very different cases as somehow symptomatic of a common social problem: children's vulnerability to abuse by adults, in particular untrustworthy familiar strangers. But of even greater significance to the question of 'noisy' versus 'quiet' panic 'constructions' examined by Cohen is the fact that one *effect* of the blizzard of April–Savile coverage was to encourage not only more alleged victims of abuse to come forward, but also various other organizations – from individual police forces to charities working with survivors of paedophilia – to 'newsjack' (Scott, 2011) these stories to raise awareness of their own child welfare-related activities. In this respect, what Cohen describes as a 'quiet' construction (or constructions) successfully piggybacked on the 'noisy' constructions of April's abduction and the burst of revelations about Savile's predatory past.

At the same time, the *media themselves* piggybacked on the April–Savile discourse to become even more exercised than usual by their habitual concerns about child abuse, paedophilia and other juvenile victim issues. Their receptivity towards piggybacking stories proffered by moral entrepreneurs was matched by an increasing inclination to actively *look out for* similar/related narratives in the 'news net' (Tuchman, 1978). The frenzy of coverage was contributed to, then, not only by numerous politicians, celebrities and other (secondary and tertiary) definers who sent condolences to April's family and exhorted fellow citizens to help find her, but also by piggybacking moral entrepreneurs – ranging from the NSPCC, which reported a 60 per cent surge in reports of child sexual abuse (NSPCC, 2012), to various police forces that took the opportunity to publicize (ongoing or historical) investigations into juvenile-related crimes. We see this pattern occur time and again during periods of heightened sensitization sparked by 'sensational cases' – most recently, in the slew of damning reports published by child welfare organizations into institutional abuse and neglect following the waves of convictions of men in towns ranging from Rotherham to Oxford for raping and abusing under-aged girls (e.g. Berelowitz et al., 2013; Gray & Watt, 2013; Horvath et al., 2014; Bedford, 2015; Jay, 2015).

A testament to the cumulative impact of this generalized juvenile panic discourse was the frequency with which mothers explicitly referenced other recent stories besides those of April and Savile and wider societal issues they linked to the stories – not to mention their self-reflective awareness of *their own* propensity to be spooked by such narratives. The melange of other 'child victim' cases mentioned included a renewed search for the body of 21-month-old British toddler Ben Needham, who had vanished in Greece in 1991, and two stories drawing on enduring fears about neglect by professionals in *loco parentis*, including a report from the day before the working-class focus group met to discuss April about a child choking on a dummy at nursery. For the hostel worker, the case called to mind a notorious local episode, revived (perhaps opportunistically) by the Brighton *Argus* in preceding weeks, to mark its anniversary: the unsolved 'Babes in the Wood' murders, in which two girls, aged nine and 10, had been sexually assaulted and strangled while playing out together 26 years previously. Reminding her middle-class peers of this case, she relayed how she had passed a banner screaming about the fact there was 'still no justice' in the cold case on her way to work. Extensive discussion of this story also arose, unprompted, in the working-class group – further testament to the heightened sensitization to articles about child abuse/

murder provoked by April's story. The fact that it related to events that, though distant in time, had occurred locally was also significant, as it again demonstrated the tendency of mothers (and the media) to project April's abduction onto familiar settings – *generalizing* the sense that children were subject to pervasive threats to their wellbeing, particularly various forms of stranger-danger.

As the nursery worker observed, again alluding to media influence on this jittery discourse:

> You've got old cases from years and years ago ... You know, *everything* ... everything that's being talked about ... It seems at the moment like it's non-stop. All the time there's something coming from somewhere – and that does make you jumpy ...

Again, these sentiments resonated with discussion thread posters, one of whom remarked that 'when I read of the almost daily stabbings and shootings of kids in most cities I try anything to make sure he [14-year-old son] comes home safe'.

The role of social mediation in crystallizing panic narratives

Consideration of this generalized discussion of contemporaneous news narratives about child victimhood leads to the question of how, once this crystallizing moment had been *initiated* – by primary (police) and secondary (media) definers – the ensuing discourse escalated into panic. More specifically, what forces were most instrumental in *spreading* panic? A clue to answering this question might be elided from the mothers most minded to monitor developments in April's narrative, who cited two principal sources of updates and speculation: professional media and interpersonal mediation. And, in line with Chapter 3's findings, it was the latter that appeared most influential (and unsettling) – whether channelled through the conduit of playground chatter or the viral rumour-mill of social media. As the above evidence demonstrates, active engagement with – or *avoidance of* – reports about April played a substantial part in the process of meaning-making for mothers, as they absorbed the story and deliberated its wider implications. However, while their testimonies suggest that they *did* use newspapers, websites and broadcast bulletins as key sources of information on the story's developments (and sensitization to its connotations), as in previous discussions the impact of *direct* exposure to mainstream/professional media appeared secondary to that of 'personal influence' (Roper et al., 1955). Several mothers recalled first hearing about the story from a brief mention of that early statement by Dyfed-Powys Police expressing 'growing concern' about a 'missing' girl on BBC1's *Ten O'Clock News*, and the nurse found out through a radio report the next day while driving her daughter home from Newcastle. However, most said their first exposure was through a friend or relative – normally via Facebook. Of those who heard through someone else, the hostel worker relayed how a tearful client approached her the morning after April's disappearance with the ominous words, 'there's a girl gone', while the working-class mum-of-four recalled popping round to visit her mother that day, to be greeted by the words, 'have you seen the news ... about April?' Indeed, the reference to April in first-name terms – an echo of 'Jamie' (Bulger), 'Maddie' (McCann), 'Sarah' (Payne) and other abduction victims – was a feature of several accounts. April's positioning as a *generalized familiar* whose plight could be projected onto parents' own children – an extension of their previously noted personalization of the story – arguably also draws on a trope adopted by the media's coverage. As the writer observed, 'she's already become a kind of "Maddie", hasn't she?'

Almost all the other mothers had learnt of April's abduction through social media. The retired schoolteacher said the news 'flashed at me' while she was checking her emails, but a more typical source was Facebook (cited by the midwife and three of seven working-class mums). The mothers' repeated singling out of both Facebook and school-gate gossip as sources of (often unsolicited) rumours about – and updates on – the saga point to both as primary sites of the panicky discourse which came to characterize how the story was publicly processed/ debated, as reflected in the textual analysis. As in earlier discussions, a self-reflective concern expressed by both sets of mothers was the power of social mediation to generate Chinese whispers, which in turn fuelled fear and uncertainty among themselves and, more worryingly for some, their children. The midwife voiced this anxiety vividly, explaining how a Facebook group she had previously set up for fellow mothers became obsessed with April's abduction. 'My daughter's five – the same age as April – and so I've had to kind of keep myself separate from it because they have just been all absolutely ... posting everything, reading everything and going, "oh my God ..."', she said, criticizing them for 'whipping it up between themselves' by posting links to 'a version of the news conference with the mother crying'. Like the ex-teacher, she admitted habitually avoiding newspapers and broadcast news – emphasizing how she preferred to carry on living, undisturbed, in a 'nice happy bubble'. Her admission that the story might unsettle her too much if she followed it closely was echoed by the hostel worker – albeit with the self-reflective caveat that, by occupying a 'bubble', she might be 'missing out on ... important stuff'. But, besides castigating Facebook as a source of hysterical gossip, the midwife was one of several parents to criticize the viral way articles, TV footage and information relating to appeals by police and April's family were shared between posters for projecting a dislocated (therefore unduly alarming) impression that the incident might have occurred closer to home. Making a similar point, the nursery worker (who also heard about the story through Facebook) recalled social media 'coverage' being 'confusing', because 'people were like, "have you seen this child?" and I was like reading it and going, "in *Wales*? Well, no, I haven't seen a child in Wales today"'. Criticizing those who 'just ... copied and pasted things', she said even 'people in Whitehawk' were guilty of this. As a result, she had been left worrying, disorientatedly, 'is it something, you know, round here? Is it something you need to think, "did *you* see someone?"'. The generalized sensitization to the prospect of child abduction promoted by the sharing of appeal information about April via social media, then, represented an influential extension of the narrative universalization observed in newspaper discourse/discussion threads – and the fears it manifested. But it was not only Facebook that these mothers condemned for promoting this generalized depiction of April's story – and the ensuing (generalized) air of panic. As illustrated by the lengthy exchange arising from recollections of the previous year's 'black car' incidents, they were also quick to criticize word-of-mouth Chinese whispers spread by *other* pupils (and parents), in a further manifestation of the underlying 'good/bad child/parent' opposition which repeatedly surfaced in their discussions. Concern about their children being unnecessarily alarmed by this abduction discourse was further voiced through criticism of stranger-danger pep talks given by teachers following April's abduction. For instance, the 'over-protective' working-class mother recalled her daughter coming home talking about 'stranger-danger' and 'going, "if anyone offers me a sweet I'm not allowed to take them"', while the nursery worker complained about nightmarish stories her son's teachers used to warn them about misplaced trust.

Yet the unfolding sense of panic was one to which, arguably, mothers *themselves* contributed – by engaging in socially mediated speculation about April's whereabouts. Taken together with the panicky, highly charged responses the story provoked in the hours after it was first reported (as evidenced by discussion threads), what the 'scare stories' spread by Facebook/playground gossip and teacher/parent pep talks demonstrated was the power of social mediation to manifest – and magnify – simmering concerns about childhood vulnerability. The noisy construction of April's unambiguous abduction was rendered *more* so by the concurrent emergence of early revelations about Savile. But, while this extraordinary coincidence might have lit the match, it was a combination of wildly disproportionate news coverage (of both stories) and equally hysterical audience responses that fanned the flames – *crystallizing* the tale of a missing five-year-old into full-blown juvenile panic.

6

Strangers No More: Towards Reconstructing Trust

Though we have long regarded our children as subjects of moral scrutiny and concern, rarely have they been treated with such heightened anxiety – or profound ambivalence – as they are in today's Britain. Late-modern childhood, as this book demonstrates, is perceived and portrayed as a state of both innocence and savagery, with juveniles besieged by a barrage of menaces while also presenting potential threats *themselves*. This ambivalence can be traced back through cultural deposits accumulated down the centuries – from political speeches and pedagogic tracts to folk-tales, children's fiction and visual art. Taken together, they present a continuum of oppositions in portrayals of the young that, in many respects, has remained remarkably consistent through time. As Chapter 2 showed, wide-eyed infants have *repeatedly* been distinguished from wild-eyed youths, girls from boys, middle-class from working-class (and underclass) kids and one's own from other people's. Moreover, a recurring undercurrent of all these antinomies has been an implicit moral distinction between 'worthy' and 'unworthy' children – and (more often than not) parents and families, too.

Yet, while these overlapping, at times mutually reinforcing, ambivalences may have been bubbling beneath the surface for generations, in late-modern Britain they have become sharpened and more deeply embedded, with contradictions between positive and negative perceptions of children glossed over and apparently unquestioned (even unnoticed). And key to helping us understand these conflicted conceptualizations of juveniles is our late-modern bogeyman, the familiar stranger: a near-phantasmagoric figure personifying the deep distrust and suspicion with which we increasingly regard our fellow man, woman and (crucially) child. Just as (s)he symbolizes the 'serpent in paradise'[1] who stalks our children, so, too, is (s)he made manifest in the guise of the hooded yob, the feral teenager, the 'bored, lazy youth'[2] – folk-devils that repeatedly resurface in political discourse, editorial judgments, published media narratives, the processing of news by both audience members and journalists, and everyday conversation. All are manifestations of the same societal malaise that is fuelling our neuroses about the malevolent spectres juveniles *face*. This is the insidious, slow-burn erosion – among individuals, families, neighbours and communities alike – of social trust.

The discourse of distrust explored by this book – the paradoxical positioning of children as both victims and threats – is routinely reproduced through news values applied in the selection and construction of stories on the page, with alarmist narratives involving juveniles seen by editors as a major driver of audience 'traffic'.[3] As the interviews carried out for Chapters 4 and 5 illustrate, news-makers are continually looking out for dramatic narratives about the young – with tales of child abduction and abuse, on the one hand, and outbreaks of lawlessness by feral teenagers, on the other, considered inherently more newsworthy than positive stories about young achievers. The high levels of newsworthiness ascribed to such cases, and the disproportionate allocation of scarce resources to cover them, is, as journalists themselves concede, principally 'market-driven' (McManus, 1994). At a time when newspapers are under more pressure than ever to attract and retain audiences, in the face of falling advertising revenue, intense online competition and the escalating cost of investing in digital publishing, their solution is to minimize the *cost* of producing stories while maximizing their *saleability* – by using readily available, tried-and-tested sources to generate vivid narratives that both arouse the public's interest and persuade it to 'participate'.[4] Fuelled by these on-tap primary definers with vested institutional interests in dramatizing the risks faced (and threats posed) by children, notably government, police and the courts, the outcome of this hard-nosed commercial approach to journalism is a grossly distorted newspaper discourse which mobilizes the literary tropes of the Brothers Grimm, horror movies and murder-mystery novels to exploit deep-seated insecurities about juveniles for financial gain. As Chapter 4 shows, a clear majority of press articles about children published in any given month – nearly two-thirds in July 2011 alone – position them as 'victims' or 'survivors', with by far the next biggest category portraying them as 'threats'.

The relish with which audiences lap up and, crucially, *buy into* these baleful narratives is testament to the 'salience' they clearly hold for us (Critcher, 2003). In the present context, this salience – a key feature of successful earlier panics – rests on the symbolism of recurrent tropes, notably recognizable settings and familiar strangers, as projections of wider concerns about personal insecurity and dwindling social trust. Parents, grandparents and even children interviewed for our focus groups displayed an intense fascination with dramatic stories about juveniles – notably those awakening lay anxieties about child abduction, youth disorder and, especially, the possibility of hidden terrors lurking in familiar surroundings or behind the deceptive smiles of benign-seeming acquaintances. And newspaper discussion threads analysed in Chapters 4 and 5 demonstrated not only high degrees of public engagement in (and concern about) such stories, but posters' overwhelming affirmation of the underlying message that most such narratives project: namely that Britain is becoming an ever more menacing place in which to live. Indeed, many contributors acted as little more than echo chambers for this dominant discourse, posting sweeping statements about everything from the perceived pervasiveness of stranger-danger and youth antisocial behaviour to the generally decadent state of contemporary Britain – a perception of a society 'gone to the dogs'[5] so wilfully exploited by papers. Moreover, the morbid curiosity that encouraged focus group mothers to debate incidents experienced vicariously through the media – and the unease they expressed about the possibility of such misfortunes befalling them – appeared to have the effect of *reinforcing* protective behaviours towards their own children. Asked about the degree of freedom they habitually allowed their kids, they enumerated various restrictions – justifying these by listing a montage of generalized risk anxieties, ranging from predatory paedophiles, hit-and-run drivers and cyber-bullies to TV violence, aggressive advertising and inanimate household objects like razors and breadknives. Discussion about the *sources* of these concerns invariably identified two key culprits – news coverage and peer-to-peer gossip, particularly 'Chinese whispers' spread via social media – with the narratives generating the greatest distress those involving aspects of threatening familiarity. These ranged from a widely reported (but later discredited) local story about schoolchildren being stalked by a would-be abductor in a black car to numerous national press stories about the abuse of minors by trusted adults like teachers, nursery workers or more loosely known familiar strangers.

The sensitization displayed by focus group participants to the nightmarish prospect of predatory adults lurking on the margins of *their own* social circles – and the possibility of abduction, abuse or even murder occurring in oft-visited, safe-seeming surroundings – is highly symbolic.

Beyond reviving generations-old fairy-tale tropes about wicked uncles and witchy stepmothers, its salience at this moment in history lies in the fact that it represents a *displacement* for wider social anxieties situated in the conflicted, uneasy position of parents in contemporary Britain. In airing concerns about familiar strangers, and displaying an appetite for news stories exploring this theme, focus groups voiced a generalized suspicion of other people's motives indicative of the erosion of social trust and mounting economic insecurity that numerous other studies have attributed to increased individualization arising from the marketization of UK society since the 1970s (e.g. Hall, 1999; OECD, 2001; Harper, 2001; Li et al., 2005; European Values Study Group and World Values Survey Association, 2006; Llakes, 2011). It can be no coincidence that research also shows this *same period* to have coincided with a steep decline in the levels of independence that British children have been allowed outside the home, as a result of growing fears about both stranger-danger and road safety that have arisen, in part, from an increasingly hectic and competitive social environment (e.g. Hillman et al., 1990; Shaw et al., 2013).

In the end, then, if this book is about anything it is not children, nor even panic, but trust. This priceless commodity appears to be in conspicuously short supply in today's socially fractured, economically atomized neoliberal societies – societies in which there is no shortage of other, more *material*, commodities. Britons' preoccupation with menacing narratives about the young, and those who would harm them, is arguably as much a distraction from deeper social problems as previous panic discourses that were even more cynically exploited by the press and powers-that-be, such as Hall et al.'s 'mugging' scare or Fishman's 'crimewave' (both 1978). And, while the drivers of juvenile panic narratives in the media might be principally commercial, an undeniable *effect* of journalists' over-reliance on police, politicians and bureaucrats when 'manufacturing the news' (Fishman, 1980) is to consolidate dominant elite ideologies in the public sphere – if only because the 'raw materials' these official sources supply them with are 'already ideological' (ibid.). Moreover, even if the *media's* primary motive is opportunism (rather than conscious complicity), one can't help wondering how happily our politicians and law enforcers manipulate our suspicions and uncertainties in order to distract us with 'the wrong things' (Hall et al., 1978, p. vii) – as they simultaneously justify ever more authoritarian judicial crackdowns, and ever greater liberalization and erosion of our public services and social security system. If this book had not been concerned with exploring the growth of distrust towards people in *general*, through the prism of juvenile panic, it might well have focused on any number of other present-day (panic) discourses that elites and the media mobilize to divide us from deviant/unworthy groups of our fellow 'citizens', in so doing exploiting and further undermining our dwindling social trust – from the demonization of benefit claimants to successive waves of hysteria about asylum seekers and economic migrants.

As it is, the discourse studied here concerns a disproportionate preoccupation with juvenile risk that has become hardwired into every level of today's news-making process: in newspaper narratives themselves; the professional (and personal) values of journalists producing them; and their dialogue with audience members, including those who publicly respond to stories (and largely affirm their agendas) on discussion threads. This clear consensus between news-makers, sources and public – and the distorted discourse resulting from it – bears all the hallmarks of an endemic juvenile panic. But, while similar in many respects to classic 'moral' panics (e.g. Cohen, 1972; Hall et al., 1978), the ongoing and (at times) nebulous nature of this *particular* discourse makes it harder to classify. In tapping into fears about familiar strangers and other predatory figures, from prowling paedophiles to hooded hooligans – a malevolent rogues' gallery one might readily describe as folk-devils – it clearly resembles the panics of old. But by embracing a melange of disparate menaces (some personified, others not) it bears closer resemblance to the generalized, less tangible anxieties that have emerged from the post-1980s 'risk society' (Beck, 1986; Giddens, 1990) and the ensuing age of 'liquid modernity' (Bauman, 2000), in tandem with the wider social, economic and technological changes described above. What it shares in common with *both* more situated panics and ongoing risk anxieties, however, is a tendency to manifest itself at times when a collision of factors conspires to crystallize it in the public sphere. These *crystallizing moments* – pinch-points at which the simmering juvenile panic bubbles to the boil – can be provoked by alarming individual incidents, eye-catching policy announcements, campaigns/initiatives or (most often) combinations of any two or more of these. As the April Jones case study demonstrates, coincidences of timing – in that case, with the Jimmy Savile revelations and various piggybacking 'pseudo-events' (Boorstin, 1971) flowing from them – help establish and consolidate panic narratives in the media, with the news values of 'continuity' (Galtung & Ruge, 1965) or 'follow-up' (Harcup & O'Neill, 2001) locking us, with sad inevitability, into vicious cycles of more (and more febrile) coverage and debate. In his 2002 introduction to the third edition of *Folk Devils and Moral Panics*, Cohen distinguished between *'noisy* constructions', in which explosions of public opprobrium and panicky behaviour stem from 'a single sensational case', and *'quiet* constructions', when social problems are 'identified' by professionals, experts or bureaucrats 'with no public or mass media exposure' (Cohen, 2002, p. xxiii). And to these he added a third category alluded to in his original (1972) thesis: that of the periodic, or rolling, panic that resurfaces repeatedly, as creeping narratives about particular risks and/or forms of deviancy become slowly more socially embedded. It is this kind of *simmering* panic, bubbling back to the boil at moments of singular drama, which forms the locus for this book, as it most clearly describes the particular nature of the collective mind-set which best characterizes late-modern Britain.

Of course, simmering panics require their ignition points, or crystallizing moments, like any other – and (as in this particular instance) 'quiet' constructions can piggyback on 'noisy' ones or 'noisy' constructions on 'quiet' ones. But whatever sequence of events lights the match, the key to the ignition process, today as ever, is the news media – which, eager to ensnare and engage audiences, knowingly tap into (and play up) these latent societal sensitivities in explosive, highly symbolic, ways. Moreover, whereas one-off panics of the past, like those over Mods and Rockers or the MMR vaccine, might only have reached boiling-point once before slowly fading away, today's juvenile panic appears to linger *continuously*, ready to bubble back to the boil at any time. The upshot is that, once any short-term hysteria has subsided, the longer-term effect of these recurrent crystallizing moments is to *keep the panic simmering*. As Cohen observed, a panic sometimes 'passes over and is forgotten', whereas on other occasions 'it has more serious and long-lasting repercussions' – even producing 'changes' in the way 'society conceives itself' (Cohen, 1972, p. 1). This book argues that it is precisely this quality which defines the nature of today's juvenile panic: the 'changes', in this case, being a deepening and acceleration of our already growing distrust towards one another.

Positioning this study in the literature

In identifying the *existence* of an endemic panic surrounding the positioning of children in contemporary Britain, this book does little more, on the face of it, than follow the well-trodden paths of previous studies. Like Cohen (1972), Fishman (1978) or Hall et al. (1978), it justifies using the term 'panic' by contrasting the blanket news coverage of dramatic stories involving juveniles not only with the lesser media emphasis on other newsworthy subjects, but the *rarity* of such extreme incidents in real life. The process of distortion at work in these representations of reality is exposed by a combination of textual analysis of newspaper articles and citation of prior academic research and official statistics debunking popular myths about the prevalence of stranger-danger, domestic child abuse and youth antisocial behaviour (Hillman et al., 1990; La Fontaine, 1994; Grubin, 1998; Corby, 2000; Pritchard & Bagley, 2001; Furedi, 2001; Shaw et al., 2013). In highlighting both these disjunctions, though, the book follows long-established convention, by honing in on the 'exaggeration' and 'disproportion' seen as fundamental features of (moral) panic discourse (Goode & Ben-Yehuda, 2009). However, while drawing on all-too-familiar precedents to define the *parameters* of a juvenile panic, it offers a fresh take on the phenomenon itself. Rather than looking at young people primarily as the *cause* of panics – as in classic studies of media-stoked flaps about drug-taking hippies (Young, 1971), Mods and Rockers (Cohen, 1972) and black teenage muggers (Hall et al., 1978) – it conceives of them, primarily, as their *subject(s)*. Specifically, it fuses the running theme common to many seminal works – the idea that youth *itself* is deviant – with the more recent trend towards focusing on panics over the young's vulnerability to the deviancy of *others* (e.g. McNeish & Roberts, 1995; Valentine, 1996a, 1996b, and 1997; Kitzinger, 1999; Gallagher et al., 2002; Meyer, 2007). Few scholars, bar Valentine, have recognized this paradoxical positioning of juveniles as 'angels and devils' (Valentine, 1996a, pp. 581–2), and, as a geographer, her study was primarily an exploration of parental controls on children's public spaces, rather than panics *per se* – let alone the media's role in fuelling them. In alighting on this ambivalence about the conceptualization of children in the *present*, the thesis also opens up the question of how this state of affairs arose – and whether it is peculiar to *late-modern* Britain or is rooted in conflicted ideas about childhood that can be traced historically. Where other studies of discrete panics stop short of addressing this question, this is among a small number – notably *Images of Welfare* (Golding & Middleton, 1982) – to locate its subject in a wider socio-historical context. And, barring certain sections of Pearson's insightful (1983) critique of the periodic panics about hooliganism, it is perhaps the first substantive piece of media research to do so in relation to the problematization of *children*. More significantly, in setting out to explore changes (and continuities) in how juveniles have been conceptualized through time, it arguably goes further than even Golding and Middleton: far from relying solely on a survey of secondary literature on the historical positioning of the young, it uses *intergenerational* focus groups to illuminate the ways in which parenting attitudes/behaviours and risk perceptions have shifted in recent decades. In so doing, it provides a test-bed of data that both reflects and illuminates the escalating seats of parental anxieties that have informed ever more stringent controls imposed on children's independent activities outside the home, as previously identified (but only partially explained) by Hillman et al. (1990) and Shaw et al. (2013).

The original take that this book brings to the study of panics about the young also has another aspect: by focusing on the way children *themselves* are problematized (both as victims and threats), it adopts a subtly different emphasis to earlier studies. Other than the aforementioned works on 1970s youth panics, most research examining panicky discourses about children has dwelt less on the problematization of *juveniles* than that of multifarious *deviants* (and other risks) threatening them. The foci of Meyer's study of media-stoked neuroses about predatory paedophiles and Boyce's of the 'health panic' surrounding the MMR vaccine (both 2007) are distorted news representations and parental perceptions of paedophiles and a government-backed inoculation campaign respectively – *not* the accompanying portrayals/perceptions of children. A further dimension this book adds to the study of juvenile panic is its attempt to pinpoint its precise *nature* – by plugging into academic debates about the spectrum of different social phenomena that have (accurately or erroneously) been tagged with this label. Far from merely describing the 'victim or threat' positioning of children as a 'moral' panic and leaving it at that, it draws on the corpus of theoretical literature published since Cohen popularized this term to cast its *particular* panic in the nebulous mould of the continuous/all-embracing panics that Hier (2003) and others see as symptomatic of atomized late-modern societies – and Beck (1986), Giddens (1990, 1991) and Bauman (2000) attribute to rapid and disquieting technological and environmental change. Moreover, in considering the possible *causes* of this climate of 'permanent' panic (Waiton, 2008), it casts the net beyond conventional academic literature, to examine the growing evidence gathered by NGOs showing a clear correlation between the embedding of neoliberal ideologies, financial insecurity and declining social trust.

Processing panics: from news-making to meaning-making

As well as being more intellectually *situated* than previous panic studies – by relating its purview to unfolding debates in both historical and theoretical literature – this book strives to be more empirically comprehensive, by adopting a 'three-dimensional' approach to investigating the news-making and reception process. In particular, it draws on ground-breaking focus group work by the Glasgow University Media Group illuminating the interplay between personal experience, social processing and news narratives, and the triangulated methodologies of the most effective studies (notably Golding & Middleton, 1982) to interrogate *all* levels of the communication process: from journalist/source to text to audience. Taking the latter point first, as Chapter 1 argued, most empirical research adopts either an *outside-in* or *inside-out* approach to gathering and analysing data. In the same year as Hall et al. (1978) published a classic deconstruction of the media-fuelled panic about an all-but non-existent mugging epidemic by contrasting hyperbolic news coverage and public pronouncements by judges and politicians with official statistics disputing their basis, Fishman exposed a similarly fictitious 'crime-wave' constructed by the American media (again in collusion with officials) *from inside*, by demonstrating how journalists became unwitting propagandists for elite ideological bias by allowing commercial pressures to render them over-reliant on official sources. Both studies, though important, failed to examine more than one or two tiers of the communication process. Hall et al. inferred journalists' (ideological) intentions by analysing their published words, but without interviewing them, and relied on a smattering of readers' letters to newspapers to illuminate their impact on audiences, rather than interviews or focus groups. Conversely, Fishman studied a newsroom ethnographically, but failed to analyse the texts that emerged from the news process – or, empirically, how audience members responded to them. Even the most three-dimensional studies of panics to date – those one might justifiably describe as 'anatomies' – have limitations in their *volume* of primary research. While Golding and Middleton's study of popular discourse around benefit claimants saw them both analysing news texts and interviewing journalists and audience members, the amount of textual analysis conducted for this book (almost all national newspapers analysed at five-day intervals over a month) and the number of people interviewed (30 journalists and six intergenerational focus groups spread over 10 meetings) was greater. That the scope of this research also embraces the new dimension of web-based discussion threads lends it further weight, by recognizing that analysis of the dynamics of today's multimedia communication circuit would be incomplete without examining the online interchange between audiences and news texts/journalists. Moreover, in testing the findings of its earlier chapters against a live, unfolding case study – again involving focus groups, interviews and analysis of news texts/discussion threads – this study presents a rare example of a 'natural history of a news item' (Deacon et al., 1999).

One of the biggest debts owed by this book, though, is the inspiration it draws methodologically from ground-breaking focus group studies by Glasgow's Kitzinger (1993 and 2004), Philo (1990, 1993) and Reilly (1999) on risk perceptions – all of which recreated the naturalistic dynamics of interpersonal mediation that have long preoccupied researchers into the complexities of news reception (Lazarsfeld et al., 1944; Roper et al., 1955). In so doing, they not only illuminated how audience members process news, individually and collectively: they persuasively demonstrated that, while peer-to-peer exchanges of gossip and personal/vicarious experience may be key to the process of sense-making about social reality, the agenda-setting power of the media to stimulate debate about underlying societal concerns cannot be underestimated. By drawing together peer groups of mothers, grandmothers and children to discuss their families' parenting practices and reflect on the perceived risks (and rights) that shape them, this study, like Glasgow's before it, goes some way towards replicating the watercooler/schoolgate exchanges that inform our day-to-day processing of stories accessed either directly through the news or, perhaps more often, via friends (or friends of friends). Moreover, in reconvening the same groups of mothers to discuss April's story months after they were initially assembled for exploratory discussions, it draws on the longitudinal approach to focus group work used so effectively by Reilly (1999) to investigate changing public perceptions of particular risks (in her case, BSE). While conscious of the debt it owes to such qualitative Glasgow studies, however, this book adds a further dimension: the ever-escalating power of social mediation in the virtual (as well as physical) public sphere. It does so both by exploring the increasingly viral nature of meaning-making (and rumour-mongering) on discussion threads and, more vicariously, through focus group participants' frequent references to social media (especially Facebook) as a *primary* source of news – and the site of panicky discourse informing their ideas and behaviours.

Limitations of this study – and pointers for future research

For all these strengths, however, there are limitations to how far any one level of the communication circuit can be analysed in a single study that attempts to address all three. Specifically, the *breadth* of empirical research undertaken here – embracing news-makers, texts and

audiences – has necessitated some compromises in *depth*. There is clear
potential for each of these crucial actors, and the interplay between
them, to be explored in a more textured, meaningful way through
ethnography. While there is an undoubted ethnographic dimension to
observing and interpreting the interactions between focus group participants, this is a tool for analysing news reception *after the event* – once
people have had time to mull over stories they have read/heard about –
rather than *during* it, as in other studies (e.g. Morley, 1980). Similarly,
while qualitative interviews with newspaper journalists provide a richer
seam of anecdote and information than questionnaire responses, they
forced the researcher to rely on the fallible memories (and honesty) of
interviewees. As Fishman (1978, 1980), Gans (1979), and Ericson et al.
(1987) demonstrate, study of the news-making process yields most
when its rhythms and routines are experienced at first hand – and the
opportunity to shadow journalists in the field, watch them interact
with contacts, and attend editorial conferences in the context of the
breaking April story would undoubtedly have contributed a layer of
understanding beyond that which interviews alone could recreate.
Moreover, there has been little in the way of ethnographic fieldwork,
thus far, to bring the findings of seminal newsroom studies of the ana-
logue era up to date by factoring in the digital dimension of modern-
day newspaper production. A research project building on this study to
illuminate the mechanics of news-making in today's online newsrooms
would have much to add to the corpus of knowledge about 21st century
journalism in *general* – not just in the context of an unfolding panic
narrative. Similarly, a more inductive approach to analysing discussion threads – involving direct participation in these forums, akin to
'virtual ethnography' (Hine, 2000), rather than textual analysis – would
potentially provide a deeper, more holistic, insight into the *nature* of
the meaning-making process in which those contributing to conversations around stories engage. In addition to the empathetic advantages
of experiencing this interaction first hand (another argument in favour
of participant-observation), particular strands of audience opinion
could be more fully explored by directing the traffic like a focus group
facilitator. While care would need to be taken to ensure such research
was conducted ethically – by announcing one's presence on forums and
outlining the nature of one's work – raising particular issues and press-
ing other posters to explain/support/contextualize views they express
might facilitate a deeper understanding of the reasons why individuals
interpret and respond to narratives as they do. Moreover, just as first-
hand observation of today's newsrooms would allow comparisons and

contrasts to be drawn with how papers operated in the past, so too would participation in online discussions about published stories illuminate the similarities and differences between social mediation in the virtual and physical public spheres. Further research could also greatly enhance the findings here in relation to news *sources*. While the question of which 'claims-makers' (Cohen, 1972) and 'primary definers' (Hall et al., 1978) are most frequently used to inform today's news narratives was addressed in Chapters 3–5, resource limitations prevented the researcher from interrogating sources *directly*. Analysis of news texts and interviews with journalists offer us rudimentary insights into how sources are selected and prioritized, but are inherently limited in their ability to illuminate the motivations/agendas/ideologies of those informers themselves. A less outside-in approach to considering the role of sources in the process of news (and meaning) making would add a valuable layer of understanding to our overall picture of the dynamics of panic discourse.

Finally, this study makes only a limited contribution to our appreciation of the impact of moral panic narratives on *deviants*. In focusing on the problematic positioning of *children* in panic discourse – both as victims and threats – it does little to illuminate our understanding of the nature(s) of the folk-devils by which children are (supposedly) threatened, or indeed deviant juveniles, let alone whether popular debate about them has the effect of amplifying their deviancy (Young, 1971; Cohen, 1972). Meanwhile, the testimony of child focus group participants is principally of interest for the insight it offers us into restrictions imposed by their parents, and the rationales behind these. Further focus group work, with a different emphasis, would be needed to tease out any evidence that negative positioning of (some) children in popular discourse contributes to deviancy amplification on the part of juveniles *themselves*. As it is, this book's primary contribution to addressing the issue of amplification relates to that of the voices of panicking definers/ claims-makers and, by extension, of panic itself.

Defusing panic: towards a more rational view of children – and trust

In demonstrating the existence of a simmering, media-stoked panic about the vulnerability and unruliness of children in contemporary Britain, this book presents a quandary: what can (or should) be done to counter the hysteria and, specifically, how can journalists (professional and citizen) play their part? To address this question meaningfully we must first acknowledge some uncomfortable truths. Panics about juveniles (or anything else) are seldom without foundation. If there were no basis at all for a flurry of publicity about a particular panic discourse, stories attempting to whip them up would quickly wither on the vine – especially in this frantic 24/7 age, in which ever more would-be stories compete for our ever more finite attention-spans. It would be folly to argue that when genuine cases of child abuse or youth disorder occur they should not be reported and debated. Moreover, the most sudden and unambiguous incidents (April's abduction) and those of significant scale (the crimes of Savile) arguably merit *more and bigger* press coverage/discussion than other matters, at least immediately after news of them breaks – just as one would expect the sudden death or surprise resignation of a political leader or a train crash involving multiple casualties to briefly eclipse other (less serious/dramatic) events. In relation to juvenile panics specifically, there is also considerable justification for the argument that, were it *not* for journalists – and informed claims-makers who use them to raise awareness of social ills that we would rather not confront – many genuine, wide-scale abuse scandals of recent decades would never have been exposed. Systematic sexual exploitation of children in institutional care; the prevalence of paedophilia in some parts of the Roman Catholic Church; and, indeed, the fact that most abuse of minors takes place inside the family home, rather than at the hands of prowling strangers, are just three (previously suppressed) realities that, in their more enlightened and enlightening moments, the media has exposed to public scrutiny. As the broadsheet feature-writer interviewed here remarked, defending his oft-castigated profession, the reason we know abused children are 'almost always' the victims of 'someone they know' is precisely *because* of '20 years of reporting of these kinds of cases'. In lifting the lid on these dark truths about previously trusted institutions – children's homes, organized religion and even families themselves – the best and/or earliest of such stories arguably served the vital social function of not so much panicking people as provoking necessary periods of self-reflection and reform. This is exactly the form of 'anti-denial' approach that Habermas (1996) and Cohen himself (2010) have advocated as a way to harness 'panics' for socially progressive ends.

But, for every example of news-makers performing a genuine public service by exposing a previously denied social evil, many more testify to an irrational obsession with the problematic positioning of children out of all proportion to the levels of jeopardy they *actually* face (or pose). The main problem with this mode of reporting, as argued extensively elsewhere, is lack of *contextualization*: individual events (or pseudo-events) are inflated out of all proportion to their significance in relation to everything else, and very rarely do the acres of coverage they generate make a serious attempt to address anything more meaningful than the *details* of isolated cases, such as any underlying social, cultural or economic factors that contribute to the circumstances in which they occur. Dramatic instances of child abuse, abduction or misbehaviour are invariably subject to the worst kind of 'episodic framing' (Iyengar, 1991) – with newspapers blowing up 'concrete events' to 'illustrate issues' (in such cases, the pervasiveness of criminal activity affecting or involving juveniles), rather than using the 'collective or general evidence' of a 'thematic' frame to present a more balanced, rational picture (ibid., p. 14). When a single incident plugging into the continuum established by previous dramatic cases (however isolated and small-scale) knocks almost everything else down the running-order – or, with classic scenarios like April's abduction, *obliterates* competing events entirely – media coverage warps into a distorted impression of reality that deserves to be challenged. Not only does this saturation of the news agenda have the side-effect of downgrading other equally (or more) important stories, so that they become scarcely noticeable – but it achieves its dominance for no more noble reason than to line the pockets of media proprietors, by cynically packaging up forbidding tales about the worst of human conduct as eye-catching commercial entertainments.

Given the manifest profitability of this approach, it is unlikely that newspapers reliant on maximizing sales and online hit-rates for their income will ever voluntarily abandon it. Part of the task, then, is to find ways of cajoling them into rethinking their news values – and adopting more measured, proportionate approaches to *applying* these. Replacing the flaccid Independent Press Standards Organisation (IPSO) with a proactive, transparent and independent regulator would be a start: as long as editors are allowed to police themselves, purely reactively, and only in relation to individual cases formally brought to their attention by third parties, it is hard to imagine the industry's underlying culture, practices and norms ever being reformed. By contrast, a truly independent regulator, empowered to *actively* challenge the balance and tone of newspaper coverage *in the round* – rather than waiting for complaints to roll in and reprimanding papers for individual articles, after the event – could make a tangible difference. This is not an argument for press *censorship* – but, rather, a regulatory regime that makes no apology for engineering a cultural transformation in its agendas (and newsgathering practices), in the service of values like balance, objectivity and impartiality still ostensibly held sacrosanct by many practitioners. One way a new regulator might do this is to regularly commission independent research into the evolving nature, purpose and practices of journalism to create a space for ongoing discussion and self-reflection. Against this backdrop, it can try to avert future crises of news-making practice, primarily by appealing to the better natures of editors, proprietors – and audiences. However, it *should* also do so by issuing stricter guidelines on the handling of news topics (sensitive ones in particular) and not being afraid to publicly admonish those who transgress them. Beyond this, our best hope lies in the power of education. Instead of concentrating so fixedly on preparing trainees for the world of journalism *as it is* – by schooling them in its existing conventions and the utilitarian necessity for papers, above all, to make money – trainers should be *questioning* these as *givens*, and mapping out a future course for the profession as it might hope to be. Somewhere amid the sea of distortion and panic that characterizes much of today's news output, the *purpose* of journalism – its responsibility for 'finding out what is really going on' and 'uncovering things' that vested interests 'would prefer to leave undiscovered' (Cole, 2005, p. 22), rather than concocting and exaggerating stories with which they would happily distract us – is being sidelined. It falls to the educators of today, and the practitioners of tomorrow, to put this right.

Notes

1 Trust, Risk and Framing Contemporary Childhood

1. Mid-market assistant news editor (see p. 170).
2. Middle-class hostel worker.
3. Middle-class hostel worker.
4. Nurse.
5. Writer.
6. Nurse.

3 Our Children and Other People's: Childhood in the Age of Distrust

1. Trainee teaching assistant.
2. Discussion threads have been quoted exactly as written throughout the book, with all punctuation/spelling errors and capital letters intact, to preserve the authenticity of the original posts.
3. See p. 116.
4. Middle-class writer.
5. Mid-market assistant news editor (see p.164).
6. NB extracts have been quoted with spelling and punctuation errors intact, to authentically reflect how they were worded by focus group members.

4 Commercializing Distrust: Framing Juveniles in the News

1. NB Bibliographic references to newspaper articles analysed for Chapters 5 and 7 have been confined to those directly quoted or cited in the text.
2. Headlines and extracts from articles have been reproduced here exactly as written, with capital letters (where used) intact, in order to reflect the emphases used by papers in print.
3. Mid-market assistant news editor (see p. 132).
4. Mid-market assistant news editor (see p. 168).
5. See p. 172.

5 'Every Parent's Worst Nightmare': The Abduction of April Jones

1. NB discussion thread extracts have been quoted with spelling and punctuation errors uncorrected, to replicate exactly how they were worded by posters.
2. Mid-market assistant news editor (see p. 164).

3. As news of April's abduction broke late on Monday 1 October (Press Association Mediapoint Wire, 2012), early evening deadlines meant that only later editions of one or two newspapers were able to report the incident the next day. For this reason, the seven-day period of textual analysis commenced with the first full day of print coverage: Wednesday 3 October. The *Sun* ran the most articles on April in the first week (20), with the *Independent* carrying the fewest (10). On the single Sunday examined (7 October), the 12 national titles collectively printed 24 articles over 29 pages. Nearly a third of these (46) featured on front pages, most as leads (splashes).

4. The Abu Hamza story was reported in only three nationals: the *Guardian*, *Independent* and *Times*. Other overlooked stories that day included a fatal crash between a pleasure boat and ferry off the Hong Kong coast. Though this appeared in every paper bar the *Times*, in the *Sun* and *Daily Mail* – two papers normally noted for their appetite for human tragedy – it merited only 107 and 78 words respectively (ProQuest Newsstand, accessed on 8 March 2013). Other stories 'under-reported' by newspapers during the seven days commencing with news of April's abduction included publication of a critical report by the Resolution Foundation think-tank into the British government's then controversial welfare reform programme – the subject of exhaustive media coverage at other 'pinch-points' over preceding months. On day three of its April coverage, the paper that had previously devoted the most space to the welfare debate, the *Guardian*, allocated a full page and two articles to April but only eight paragraphs to the think-tank study – on the same page as yet another lengthy report on Savile.

5. A significant number of the articles centring on Savile were to be found on comment, leader and opinion (rather than news) pages, and it seems reasonable to assume there would have been many similar pieces on the April case had writers been as free to air their personal views on this subject as they were about the growing mountain of evidence against the deceased (and legally powerless) television presenter. Given that police had already arrested a suspect in the April case even before the first print articles rolled off the presses, almost from the outset editors were constrained by the Contempt of Court Act 1981 (Great Britain. *Contempt of Court Act 1981*) and Press Complaints Commission's editors' code of practice (Press Complaints Commission, 2014) when deciding how to relay the story. Had they not been, April's abduction might well have generated even more articles – putting it further ahead of the week's other stories in terms of coverage.

6. Trainee nursery worker (see p. 65).

7. Working-class mother with new baby (see p. 243).

6   Strangers No More: Towards Reconstructing Trust

1. Broadsheet feature-writer (see p. 167).

2. Mid-market assistant news editor (see p. 164).

3. South-east news group editorial director (p. 165).

4. National broadsheet feature-writer (see p. 195).

5. Mid-market assistant news editor (see p. 168).

Bibliography

Albrecht, S. (2006) 'Whose voice is heard in online deliberation? A study of participation and representation in political debates on the Internet, *Information, Communication and Society*, 9(1), pp. 62–82, *Taylor and Francis Online* [Online] DOI: 10.1080/13691180500519548 (Accessed: 10 September 2013).

Alleyne, R. (2012) 'April Jones: did you see Mark Bridger on night five-year-old went missing?' *Daily Telegraph* [Online]. Available at: http://www.telegraph. co.uk/news/uknews/crime/9583673/April-Jones-Did-you-see-Mark-Bridger-on-night-five-year-old-went-missing.html (Accessed: 7 February 2014).

Anderson, M. (ed.) (1980) *Approaches to the history of the western family 1500–1914*. Vol. 1. Cambridge: Cambridge University Press.

The Argus (2011) 'Pilot saved our lives' *The Argus*, 1 July, p. 23.

The Argus (2012) 'Man, 46, arrested in hunt for April' *The Argus*, 3 October, p. 2.

Aries, P. (1962) [1970] *Centuries of childhood: a social history of family life*. Translated from the French by Robert Baldick. New York: Knopf.

Armstrong, J. (2011) 'Hand to handbag combat: Liz gets better of mugger' *Daily Mirror*, 1 July, p. 19.

Aspinall, A. (2012) 'Is this her kidnapper? Cops probe film of mystery man spotted near swollen river' *Daily Mirror*, 4 October, p. 1 and 3.

Bannerman, L. (2012) 'Maybe it's an illusion that everyone knows each other' *The Times*, 5 October, pp. 4–5.

Bantz, C.R. (1985) 'News organizations: conflict as a crafted cultural norm', in Tumber, H. (ed.), (1999) *News: a reader*. Oxford: Oxford University Press, pp. 134–142.

Barker, M. and Petley, J. (eds) (1997) *Ill effects: the media violence debate*. London: Routledge.

Bauman, Z. (2000) *Liquid modernity*. Cambridge: Polity Press.

Baym, N. (2009) 'Interpersonal life online', in Lievrouw, L.A. and Livingstone, S. (eds), *Handbook of new media*. London: Sage, pp. 35–54.

Beales, R. W. (1975) 'In search of the historical child: Miniature adulthood and youth in colonial New England', *American Quarterly*, 27(4), pp. 379–398, *JSTOR* [Online]. Available at: http://www.jstor.org/ (Accessed: 15 July 2011).

Beardsworth, A. (1980) 'Analysing press content: some technical and methodological issues', in Christian, H. (ed.), *Sociology of journalism and the press*. Keele: Keele University Press, pp. 371–95.

Beck, U. (1992) [1986] *Risk society: towards a new modernity*. Translated from the German by M. Ritter. London: Sage.

Becker, H. S. (1963) *Outsiders: studies in the sociology of deviance*. London: Collier-Macmillan Ltd.

Bedford, A. (2015) *Serious case review into child sexual abuse in Oxfordshire: from the experiences of children A, B, C, D, E, and F*. Oxfordshire: Oxfordshire Safeguarding Children Board.

Bednarek, M. (2006) *Evaluation of media discourse: analysis of a newspaper corpus.* New York: Continuum.

Bell, A., and Garrett, P. (eds) (1998) *Approaches to media discourse.* Hoboken, New Jersey: Wiley-Blackwell.

Bennett, W.L. and Iyengar, S. (2008) 'A new era of minimal effects? The changing foundations of political communication', *Journal of Communication* 58(4), pp. 707–731, *Wiley Online Library* [Online]. DOI: 10.1111/j.1460-2466.2008.00410.x (Accessed: 26 June 2015).

Berelowitz, S., Clifton, J., Firimin, C., Gulyurtlu, S., and Edwards, G. (2013) *'If only someone had listened': Office of the Children's Commissioner's inquiry into child sexual exploitation in gangs and groups: final report.* London: Office of the Children's Commissioner.

Berger, P.L. and Luckmann, T. (1966) *The social construction of reality.* London: Allen Lane.

Berkvam, D.D. (1983) 'Nature and norreture: a notion of medieval childhood and education', *Mediaevalia,* 9, pp. 165–80, *Regesta Imperii* [Online]. Available at: opac.regesta-imperii.de/ (Accessed: 1 February 2014).

Best, J. (1990) *Threatened children: rhetoric and concern about child victims.* Chicago: University of Chicago Press.

Bimber, B. (2012) 'Digital media and citizenship', in Semetko, H.A. and Scammell, M. (eds), *The SAGE handbook of political communication.* London: Sage Publishing, pp. 115–127.

Binns, A. (2012) 'Don't feed the trolls: managing troublemakers in magazines' online communities', *Journalism Practice* 6(4), pp. 547–62, *Taylor and Francis Online* [Online]. DOI: 10.1080/17512786.2011.648988 (Accessed: 3 July 2013).

Blacker, K. and Griffin, L. (2010) 'Megan's Law and Sarah's Law: a comparative study of sex offender community notification schemes in the United States and the United Kingdom', *Criminal Law Bulletin,* 46, pp. 987–1008, *Pace University Digital Commons* [Online]. Available at: http://digitalcommons.pace.edu/ (Accessed: 6 August 2010).

Blair, T. (2002), 'My vision for Britain' *The Observer,* 10 November [Online]. Available at: http://www.theguardian.com/politics/2002/nov/10/queensspeech2002.tonyblair (Accessed: 15 October 2010).

Blumler, J.G. and Ewbank, A.J. (1970) 'Trade unionists, the mass media, and unofficial strikes', *British Journal of Industrial Relations* (8), pp. 32–54, *Wiley Online Library* [Online]. DOI: 10.1111/j.1467-8543.1970.tb00570 (Accessed: 5 August 2010).

Boorstin, D. (1971) 'From news-gathering to news-making: a flood of pseudo-events', in Schramm, W.L. (ed.), *The process and effects of mass communication.* Urbana, Illinois: University of Illinois Press, pp. 251–270.

Borland, S. (2011) 'Mothers using nicotine gum to avoid smoking in pregnancy "put unborn babies at risk"' *Daily Mail,* 21 July, p. 13.

Boyce, T. (2007) *Health, risk and news: the MMR vaccine and the media,* London: Peter Lang.

Breed. W. (1955) 'Social control in the newsroom: a functional analysis', in Tumber, H. (ed.) (1999) *News: a reader.* Oxford: Oxford University Press, pp. 79–84.

Brown, J. (2012) 'Searching for a miracle, braced for the worst' *The Independent,* 4 October, p. 6.

Bruns, A. (2009) 'From prosumer to produser: understanding user-led content creation', *Transforming Audiences 2009*. Unpublished conference paper. London, 3–4 September.

Burgess, A. (1962) *A clockwork orange*. London: William Heinemann.

Burney, E. (2009) *Making people behave: antisocial behaviour, politics and policy*. 2nd edn. London: Willan Publishing.

Camber, R. (2011f) 'British boy of 16 held over CIA and PayPal hacking' *Daily Mail*, 21 July, p. 19.

Carter, C. (2011) 'Eight men charged with grooming girls for child prostitution in Rochdale' *The Guardian* [Online]. Available at: http://www.theguardian. com/uk/2011/jun/08/men-charged-grooming-girls-prostitution (Accessed: 20 November 2013).

Carter, H. (2003) 'Paedophile found beaten to death at home' *The Guardian*, 1 December [Online]. Available at: http://www.theguardian.com/uk/2003/ dec/01/ukcrime.helencarter (Accessed: 7 June 2010).

Centre for Learning and Life Chances in Knowledge Economies and Societies (Llakes) (2011) *Education, opportunity and social cohesion*. London: Institute of Education, University of London.

Chamberlain, A., Foster, E., Wells, T., and Phillips, R. (2012) 'Abducted April Jones's devastated elder sister today broke her silence over her disappearance saying: "I just want our beautiful princess home"' *The Sun*, 4 October [Online]. Available at: http://www.thesun.co.uk/sol/homepage/news/4570670/Tears-clues-a-man-in-custodybut-still-no-April-as-fears-grow-for-the-sick-girl.html (Accessed: 11 February 2014).

Chapman, J. and Riches, C. (2012a) 'Suspect's picture issued as police make new plea' *Daily Express*, 4 October, p. 5.

Chapman, J. and Riches, C. (2012b) 'Bridger went on fishing trips in car' *Daily Express*, 6 October, p. 5.

Chapman, J. and Riches, C. (2012c) 'April's sister: someone must know something' *Daily Express*, 5 October, p. 4.

Chesshyre, R. (2012), 'New Addington: the benighted estate Tia Sharp called home' *The Week*, 14 August [Online]. Available at: http://www.theweek.co.uk/ uk-news/tia-sharp-murder/48465/new-addington-benighted-estate-tia-sharp-called-home (Accessed: 7 February 2014).

Chibnall, S. (1975) 'The crime reporter: a study in the production of commercial knowledge', *Sociology* 9(1), pp.49-66, *Sage Journals Online* [Online] DOI: 10.1177/003803857500900103 (Accessed: 22 October 2015).

Chibnall, S. (1977) *Law and order news: an analysis of crime reporting in the British press*. London: Tavistock.

Chibnall, S. (1981) 'The production of knowledge by crime reporters', in Cohen, S. and Young, J. (eds), *The manufacture of news*. 2nd edn. London: Constable, pp. 75–97.

Children's Play Council (2006) *Playday 2006 survey* [Online]. Available at: http:// www.playday.org.uk/Upload/2121522_play-survey-summary-playday-2006. pdf (Accessed: 1 October 2010).

Children's Society (2007) *Good childhood inquiry*. London: GfK National Opinion Polls.

Chiricos, T., Eschholz, S., and Gertz, M. (1997) 'Crime, news and fear of crime: toward an identification of audience effects', *Social Problems* 44(3), pp. 342–357, *HeinOnline* [Online]. Available at: http://heinonline.org/ (Accessed: 23 June 2010).

Cipriani, D. (2009) *Children's rights and the minimum age of criminal responsibility.* Farnham, Surrey: Ashgate Publishing Ltd.

Clixby, H. (2005) 'Life sentence for 'savage' murderer' *The Journal,* 6 May [Online]. Available at: http://www.thejournal.co.uk/news/north-east-news/life-sentence-for-savage-murderer-4616566 (Accessed: 7 June 2010).

Cohen, S. (1972) *Folk devils and moral panics.* St Albans: Palladin.

Cohen, S. (2002) 'Moral panics as cultural politics: introduction to the third edition', in *Folk devils and moral panics.* 3rd edn. London: Routledge, pp. vvi–xliv.

Cohen, S. (2010) 'The political agenda of moral panic theory: constructing a sociology of importance', *Moral panics in the contemporary world.* Unpublished conference paper. Brunel University, Uxbridge, 10–12 December.

Cohen, S. and Young, J. (1973) *The manufacture of news: deviance, social problems and the mass media.* 2nd edn. London: Constable.

Cole, P. (2005) 'The structure of the print industry', in Keeble, K. (ed.), *Print journalism: a critical introduction.* London: Routledge, pp. 22–37.

Conlan, T. (2001) 'The brass neck of brass eye' *Daily Mail* [Online]. Available at: http://www.dailymail.co.uk/news/article-71158/The-brass-neck-Brass-Eye.html (Accessed: 18 October 2013).

Conrad, P. and Schneider, J.W. (1992) *Deviance and medicalization: from badness to sickness.* Philadelphia: Temple University Press.

Coppock, V. (1997) '"Families" in "crisis"?' in Scraton, P. (ed.), *Childhood in crisis?* London: UCL Press, pp. 58–74.

Corby, B. (2000) *Child abuse. Towards a knowledge base.* Milton Keynes: Open University Press.

Corner, J. (1983) 'Textuality, communication and media power', In Davis, H. and Walton, P. (eds), *Language, image, media.* London: Palgrave Macmillan, pp. 266–281.

Crick, A. (2011) 'Jordan uncle is molester' *The Sun,* 6 July, p.12.

Critcher, C. (2003) 'Monstrous ideas: paedophilia', in Critcher, C. (ed.), *Moral panics and the media.* Maidenhead: Open University Press, pp. 99–119.

Critcher, C. (2006a) 'Introduction: more questions than answers', in Critcher, C. (ed.), *Critical readings: moral panics and the media.* Maidenhead: Open University Press, pp. 1–24.

Critcher, C. (2006b) 'Cases', in Critcher, C. (ed.), *Critical readings: moral panics and the media.* Maidenhead: Open University Press, pp. 67–76.

Critcher, C. (2008) 'Moral panic analysis: past, present and future, *Sociology Compass,* 2(4), pp. 1127–1144, *Wiley Online Library* [Online]. DOI: 10.1111/j.1751-9020.2008.00122.x (Accessed: 14 July 2010).

Critcher, C. (2009) 'Widening the focus: moral panics as moral regulation', *The British Journal of Criminology* 49(1), 17–34, *Oxford Journals* [Online] DOI: 10.1093/bjc/azn040. (Accessed: 17 December 2010).

Cunningham, H. (1991) *The children of the poor.* Oxford: Blackwell.

Cunningham, H. (1998) 'Histories of childhood', *The American Historical Review* 103(4), pp. 1195–1208, *JSTOR* [Online]. Available at: http://www.jstor.org/ (Accessed on 14 July 2011).

Cunningham, H. (2006) *The invention of childhood.* London: BBC Books.

Curran, J. (1976) 'Content and structuralist analysis of mass communication', *D305 Social Psychology, Project 2: Content and Structuralist Analysis*. Milton Keynes: Open University.

Cvetkovich, G. and Lofstedt, R.E. (eds) (2013) *Social trust and the management of risk*, 2nd edn. Abingdon: Earthscan.

Daily Express (2011) 'Tragic tot: nursery staff held' *Daily Express* 4, p. 7.

Daily Mail (2011a) 'Police hunt thugs who drowned pony in lake' *Daily Mail*, 11 July, p. 19.

Daily Mail (2011b) 'Gang "deliberately drowned" pony in lake in front of horrified families' *Daily Mail*, 11 July [Online]. Available at: http://www.dailymail.co.uk/news/article-2013181/Gang-deliberately-drowned-elderly-pony-lake-horrified-families.html (Accessed: 18 August 2011).

Daily Mirror (2011) 'Bling baby dummy risk' *Daily Mirror*, 11 July, p. 28.

Daily Mirror (2012a) 'Brit child is ferry victim' *Daily Mirror*, 4 October, p. 6.

Daily Mirror (2012b) 'Kidnapper perv jailed' *Daily Mirror*, 5 October, p. 28.

Daily Star (2011a) 'Blast for toy ploy' *Daily Star*, 1 July, p. 29.

Daily Star (2011b) '4 years for fetish paedo' *Daily Star*, 6 July, p. 21.

Daily Telegraph (2011) 'Allergic reaction' *Daily Telegraph*, 11 July, p. 13.

Davies, N. (2008) *Flat Earth news: an award-winning reporter exposes falsehood, distortion and propaganda in the global media*. London: Chatto and Windus.

Davis, J. (1980) 'The London garotting panic of 1862: a moral panic and the creation of a criminal class in mid-Victorian England', in Gatrell, V.A.C., Lenman, B., and Parker, G. (eds), *Crime and the law*. London: Europa Publications, pp. 190–213.

Davis, H. and Bourhill, M. (1997) '"Crisis": the demonization of children and young people', in Scraton, P. (ed.), *Childhood in crisis?* London: UCL Press, pp. 28–57.

Day, M. (2011) 'Vatican recalls ambassador after Irish PM's attack on Church' *The Independent*, 26 July, p. 22.

Deacon, D. (2007) 'Yesterday's papers and today's technology: digital newspaper archives and "push button" content analysis', *European Journal of Communication*, 22(1), pp. 5–25, *Sage Journals Online* [Online] DOI: 10.1177/0267323107073743 (Accessed: 6 July 2011).

Deacon, D., Fenton, N. and Bryman, A. (1999) 'From inception to reception: the natural history of a news item', *Media, Culture and Society*, 21, pp. 5–31, *Sage Journals Online* [Online] DOI: 10.1177/016344399021001001 (Accessed: 14 June 2012).

Deacon, D., Pickering, M., Golding, P., Murdock, G. (2007) *Researching communications: a practical guide to methods in media and cultural analysis*. 2nd edn. New York: Arnold Publishers.

Department for Transport (2014) *Reported Road Casualties in Great Britain: Main Results 2013*, London: Department for Transport.

De Bruxelles, S. (2011) 'Life for fetish psycho: why was hair fiend free to kill?' *The Times*, 1 July, p. 21.

De Young, M. (1998) 'Another look at moral panics: the case of Satanic day care centers', in Critcher, C. (ed.) (2003) *Moral panics and the media*. Buckingham: Open University Press, pp. 270–290.

Dixon, T.L. (2008) 'Crime news and racialized beliefs: understanding the relationship between news viewing and the perceptions of African Americans and crime', *Journal of Communication*, 58(1), pp. 106–125, *Wiley Online Library* [Online] DOI: 10.1111/j.1460-2466.2007.00376.x (Accessed: 20 December 2010).

Dolan, A. (2011) 'Father fined £1,000 and found guilty of harassment for warning families about a paedophile' *Daily Mail*, 11 July, p. 25.

Doncaster Free Press (2010) 'Devil boys review to be public: background to Edlington attack to be revealed by new government' *Doncaster Free Press*, 8 June [Online]. Available at: http://www.doncasterfreepress.co.uk/news/devil-boys-review-to-be-public-1-844090 (Accessed: 7 February 2014).

Doob, A. and MacDonald, G. (1979) 'Television viewing and fear of victimization: is the relationship causal?' *Journal of Personality and Social Psychology*, 37(2), pp. 170–179, *APA PsycNET* [Online]. Available at: http://psycnet.apa.org/ (Accessed: 12 July 2010).

Dowler, K. (2003) 'Media consumption and public attitudes towards crime and justice: the relationship between fear of crime, punitive attitudes, and perceived police effectiveness', *Journal of Criminal Justice and Popular Culture*, 10(2), pp. 109–126, *JCJPC* [Online]. Available at: http://www.albany.edu/ (Accessed: 14 July 2010).

Edwards, A. (2013) '(How) do participants in online discussion forums create echo chambers? The inclusion and exclusion of dissenting voices in an online forum about climate change'. *Journal of Argumentation in Context*, 2(1), pp. 127–150, *Ingenta Connect* [Online]. Available at: http://www.ingentaconnect.com/ (Accessed: 12 September 2013).

Edwards, P. (1979) 'The awful truth about strife in our factories': a case study in the production of news', *Industrial Relations Journal*, 10(1), pp. 7–11, *Wiley Online Library* [Online] DOI: 10.1111/j.1468-2338.1979.tb00266.x (Accessed: 10 June 2010).

Eldridge, J. (1999) 'Risk, society and the media: now you see it, now you don't', in Philo, G. (ed.) *Message received*. Harlow: Longman, pp. 106–127.

Entman, R.M. (1993). 'Framing: toward clarification of a fractured paradigm', *Journal of Communication*, 43, pp. 51–58, *Wiley Online Library* [Online] DOI: 10.1111/j.1460-2466.1993.tb01304.x (Accessed: 22 October 2010).

Ericson, R.V., Baranek, P.M. and Chan, J.B.L (1987) 'Visualizing deviance: a study of news organization', in Tumber, H. (ed.) (1999) *News: a reader*. Oxford: Oxford University Press, pp. 97–101.

Ericson, R.V., Baranek, P.M. and Chan, J.B.L (1989) 'Negotiating control: a study of news sources', in Tumber, H. (ed.) (1999) *News: a reader*. Oxford: Oxford University Press, pp. 280–284.

Ettema, J. S. and Peer, L. (1996) 'Good news from a bad neighborhood: toward an alternative to the discourse of urban pathology', *Journalism and Mass Communication Quarterly*, 74(4), pp. 835–856, *Sage Journals Online* [Online] DOI: 10.1177/107769909607300406 (Accessed: 17 November 2010).

European Values Study Group and World Values Survey Association (2006) *European values survey 2006* [Online]. Available at: http://www.jdsurvey.net/evs/EVSData.jsp (Accessed: 5 March 2012).

Evans, M. (2012) 'Ex-soldier fathered six children with women from the estate' *Daily Telegraph*, 3 October, p. 2.

Evans, M. and Ford Rojas, J.P. (2012) 'The tangled family ties between Mark Bridger and April' Jones *Daily Telegraph*, 10 October [Online].

Available at: http://www.telegraph.co.uk/news/uknews/crime/9600265/The-tangled-family-ties-between-Mark-Bridger-and-April-Jones.html (Accessed: 5 November 2012).

Evans, M., Stoddart, H., Condon, L., Freeman, E., Grizzell, M., and Mullen, R. (2001) 'Parents' perspectives on the MMR immunisation: a focus group study', in *British Journal of General Practice*, 51, pp. 904–910, *NCBI* [Online]. Available at: http://www.ncbi.nlm.nih.gov/ (Accessed: 14 August 2010).

Evans, R. (2011) 'Are our parks safe for children or are they a haven for drug dealers?' *The Argus*, 21 July, pp. 30–31.

Evans, R. (2012) 'April – a bubbly little girl who's always smiling' *Daily Mail*, 3 October, p. 5.

Evans, R. and Bentley, P. (2012) 'Face of the man under suspicion' *Daily Mail*, 4 October, p. 5.

Fairclough, N. (2003) *Analyzing discourse*. London: Routledge.

Faiez, R. (2011) 'Afghan insurgents hang boy, 8' *The Independent*, 26 July, p. 31.

Franklin, B. and Petley, J. (1996) 'Killing the age of innocence: newspaper reporting of the death of James Bulger', in J. Pilcher and S. Wagg (eds), *Thatcher's children? Politics, childhood and society in the 1980s and 1990s*. London: Falmer Press.

Farrington, D.P. and Coid, J.W. (2003) *Early prevention of adult antisocial behaviour*. Cambridge: Cambridge University Press.

Fishman, M. (1978) 'Crime waves as ideology', *Social Problems*, 25(5), pp. 531–543, *JSTOR* [Online]. Available at: http://www.jstor.org/ (Accessed: 5 May 2010).

Fishman, M. (1980) *Manufacturing the news*. Austin, Texas: University of Texas Press.

Flynn, B. (2011) 'Mum of stab lad begs: no revenge' *The Sun*, 11 July, p.20.

Forsyth, I. H. (1976), 'Children in early medieval art: ninth through twelfth centuries', *Journal of Psychohistory* 4(1976), pp. 31–70, *Europe PubMed Central* [Online]. Available at: http://europepmc.org/ (Accessed: 5 July 2011).

France, A. (2011) 'Shy weeps as paedo stepdad freed early: abuse campaigner's fury' *The Sun*, 6 July, p. 12.

Fritz, N.J. and Altheide, D.L. (1987) 'The mass media and the social construction of the missing children problem', *Sociological Quarterly*, 28(4), pp. 473–92, *Wiley Online Library* [Online] DOI: 10.1111/j.1533-8525.1987.tb00307.x (Accessed: 11 July 2010).

Furedi, F. (2001) *Paranoid parenting*. London: Allen Lane.

Gallagher, B., Bradford, M. and Pease, K. (2002) 'The sexual abuse of children by strangers: its extent, nature, and victims' characteristics', *Children & Society*, 16(5), pp. 346–359, *Wiley Online Library* [Online] DOI: 10.1002/chi.724 (Accessed: 16 July 2010).

Galtung, J. and Ruge, M. (1965) 'The structure of foreign news: the presentation of the Congo, Cuba and Cyprus crises in four Norwegian newspapers', *Journal of Peace Research*, 2(1), pp. 64–91, *Sage Journals Online* [Online] DOI: 10.1177/002234336500200104 (Accessed: 2 May 2010).

Gans, H.S. (1979) *Deciding what's news: a study of CBS Evening News, NBC Nightly News, Newsweek and Time*. London: Constable.

Garner, R. (2011) 'Three in five of the poorest 11-year-olds lack basic literacy' *The Independent*, 11 July, p.11.

Gaskins, S., Miller, P.J., and Corsaro, W.A. (1992) 'Theoretical and methodological perspectives in the interpretive study of children', *New Directions for Child and Adolescent Development*, 58, pp. 5–23, *Wiley Online Library* [Online] DOI: 10.1002/cd.23219925803 (Accessed: 15 September 2013).

Gentry, C. (1988) 'The social construction of abducted children as a social problem', *Sociological Inquiry*, 58(4), pp. 413–425, *Wiley Online Library* [Online]. DOI: 10.1111/j.1475-682X.1988.tb01072.x (Accessed: 18 June 2010).

Gerbner, G., Gross, L., Morgan, M., and Signorielli, N. (1980) 'The mainstreaming of America: violence profile no.11', *Journal of Communications*, 30(3), pp. 10–29, *Wiley Online Library* [Online]. DOI: 10.1111/j.1460-2466.1980.tb01987.x (Accessed: 25 October 2010).

Gerbner, G., Gross, L., Signorielli, N., Morgan, M. and Jackson-Beeck, M. (1979) 'The demonstration of power: violence profile no.10', *Journal of Communication*, 29(3), pp. 177–196, *Wiley Online Library* [Online]. DOI: 10.1111/j.1460-2466.1979.tb01731.x (Accessed: 25 October 2010).

Giddens, A. (1990) *The consequences of modernity*. Cambridge: Polity Press.

Giddens, A. (1991) *Modernity and self-identity*. Cambridge: Polity Press.

Gillen, J. (April 2006) 'The age of criminal responsibility: "the frontier between care and justice"', *Childcare in Practice*, 12(2), pp. 129–139, *Taylor and Francis Online* [Online] DOI: 10.1080/13575270600618414 (Accessed: 8 October 2010).

Gilley, M. (2015) 'Mike Gibson unveils new look for Brighton Argus with "hard yards" ahead to slow print sales decline' *www.pressgazette.co.uk*, 17 April. Available at: http://www.pressgazette.co.uk/content/mike-gilson-unveils-new-look-brighton-argus-hard-yards-ahead-slow-print-sales-decline (Accessed: 29 June 2015).

Gitlin, T. (1980) *The whole world is watching: mass media in the making and unmaking of the New Left*. Berkeley: University of California Press.

Gleave, J. (2008) *Risk and play: a literature review*. London: Children's Play Council.

Goidel, R. K., Freeman, C.M., and Procopio, S.T. (2006) 'The impact of television viewing on perceptions of juvenile crime', *Journal of Broadcasting and Electronic Media*, 50(1), pp. 119–139, *Taylor and Francis Online* [Online] DOI: 10.1207/s15506878jobem5001_7 (Accessed: 5 August 2010).

Golding, P. and Middleton. S. (1982) *Images of welfare*, Oxford: Mark Robertson.

Golding, W. (1959) *Lord of the flies*. London: Faber and Faber.

Goldson, B. (1997) '"Childhood": an introduction to historical and theoretical analyses', in Scraton, P. (ed.), *'Childhood' in 'crisis'?* London: UCL Press, pp. 1–28.

Goode, E. and Ben-Yehuda, N. (1994) *Moral panics: the social construction of deviance*. Oxford: Blackwell.

Goode, E. and Ben-Yehuda, N. (2009) *Moral panics: the social construction of deviance*. 2nd edn. Oxford: Blackwell.

Google (2013). Available at: www.google.co.uk (Accessed: 15 February 2013).

Gordon, E.C. (1991) 'Accidents among Medieval children as seen from the miracles of six English saints and martyrs', *Medical History*, 35(2), pp. 145–163, *Cambridge Journals* [Online]. Available at: http://www.ncbi.nlm.nih.gov/ (Accessed: 11 July 2011).

Graber, D. A. (1984) *Processing the news: how people tame the information tide*. New York and London: Longman.

Gramsci, A. (1971) *Selections from the prison notebooks*. New York: International Publishers.

Gray, D. and Watt, P. (2013) *Giving victims a voice: joint report into sexual allegations made against Jimmy Savile*. London: Metropolitan Police Service and NSPCC.

Gray, L. (2011) 'Warning over sky lantern craze as family flees roof fire' *Daily Telegraph*, 11 July, p. 7.

Grayling, T., Hallam, K., Graham, D., Anderson, R. and Glaister, R. (2002) *Streets ahead: safe and liveable streets for children* [Online]. Available at: http://www.ippr.org/publication/55/1266/streets-ahead-safe-and-liveable-streets-for-children (Accessed: 5 July 2010).

Great Britain. *Children and Young Persons Act 1933: George V.* (1933) London: The Stationery Office.

Great Britain. *Contempt of Court Act 1981: Elizabeth II.* (1981) London: The Stationery Office.

Great Britain. *Crime and Disorder Act 1998: Elizabeth II. Chapter 1.* (1998) London: The Stationery Office.

Great Britain. *Antisocial Behaviour, Crime and Policing Bill 2013: Elizabeth II. Chapter 5.* (2013) London: The Stationery Office.

Great Britain. Department for Communities and Local Government (2012) *English indices of deprivation*, 13 December 2012. Available at: https://www.gov.uk/government/collections/english-indices-of-deprivation (Accessed: 31 January 2014).

Great Britain. Cabinet Office and Prime Minister's Office, 10 Downing Street (2011) *Troubled families speech*, 15 December. [Online]. Available at: https://www.gov.uk/government/speeches/troubled-families-speech (Accessed: 22 July 2013).

Groombridge, N. (1998) *The car and crime: critical perspectives*. Unpublished PhD thesis, Middlesex University. Available at: http://eprints.mdx.ac.uk/6692/ (Accessed: 1 July 2010).

Grubin, D. (1998) *Sex offending against children: understanding the risk*. London: Home Office.

The Guardian (2012) 'More than half of abductions are by a stranger' *The Guardian*, 3 October, p. 2.

Gulbrandsen, I. T. and Just, S. N. (2011) 'The collaborative paradigm: towards an invitational and participatory concept of online communication', *Media, Culture and Society*, 33(7), pp. 1095–1108, *Sage Journals Online* [Online]. DOI: 10.1177/0163443711416066 (Accessed: 5 October 2013).

Gumham, D. (2006) 'The moral narrative of criminal responsibility and the principled justification of tariffs for murder: Myra Hindley and Thompson and Venables', *Legal Studies*, 23(4), pp. 605–22, *Wiley Online Library* [Online]. DOI: 10.1111/j.1748-121X.2003.tb00230.x (Accessed: 5 September 2010).

Gustafsson, N. (2012) 'The subtle nature of Facebook politics: Swedish social network site users and political participation', *New Media and Society*, 14(7), pp. 1111–1127. [Online]. DOI: 10.1177/1461444812439551 (Accessed: 18 June 2015).

Habermas, J. (1996 [1992]) *Between facts and norms: contributions to a discourse theory of law and democracy*. Translated from the German by W. Rehg. Cambridge: Polity Press.

Hall, P. (1999) 'Social capital in Britain', *British Journal of Political Science*, 29, pp. 417–461, *Cambridge University Press* [Online]. Available at: http://journals.cambridge.org/ (Accessed: 6 March 2012).

Hall, S. (1980) 'Encoding/decoding' in Hall, S., Hobson, D., Lowe, A., and Willis, P. (eds), *Culture, media, language*. London: Hutchinson.

Hall, S., Critcher, C., Jefferson, T., Clarke, J., and Roberts, B. (1978), *Policing the crisis: mugging, the state and law and order*. London: Macmillan.

Hansen, A., Cottle, S., Negrine, R., and Newbold, C. (1998) *Mass communication research methods*. London: Palgrave Macmillan.

Harcup, T. and O'Neill, D. (2001) 'What is news? Galtung and Ruge revisited', *Journalism Studies*, 2(2), pp. 261–280, *Ingenta Connect* [Online]. DOI: 10.1080/14616700120042114 (Accessed 1 March 2010).

Harper, R. (2001) *Social capital: a review of the literature*. UK: Office for National Statistics, Social Analysis and Reporting Division.

Harris, S. (2011a) 'Rise of the violent "Little Emperors": children lashing out at parents to get own way' *Daily Mail* [Online]. Available at: http://www.dailymail.co.uk/news/article-2013293/Rise-violent-Little-Emperors-Children-lashing-parents-way.html (Accessed: 30 June 2015).

Harris, S. (2011b) 'Too much internet use "can damage teenagers' brains"' *Daily Mail*, 16 July, p. 15.

Hartmann, P. (1975) 'Industrial relations in the news media', *Industrial Relations Journal*, 6(4), pp. 4–18, *Wiley Online Library* [Online]. DOI: 10.1111/j.1468-2338.1975.tb00820.x (Accessed: 17 August 2010).

Hartmann, P. (1979) 'News and public perceptions of industrial relations', *Media, Culture and Society*, 1(3), pp. 255–270, *Sage Journals Online* [Online]. DOI: 10.1177/016344377900100303 (Accessed: 17 August 2010).

Hartmann, P. and Husband, C. (1971) 'The mass media and racial conflict', in Cohen, S. and Young, J. (eds) (1981) *The manufacture of news: deviance, social problems and the mass media*. 2nd edn. London: Constable, pp. 270–283.

Heath, L. and Gilbert, K. (1996) 'Mass media and fear of crime', *American Behavioural Scientist*, 39, pp. 379–386, *Sage Journals Online* [Online]. DOI: 10.1177/0002764296039004003 (Accessed: 28 July 2010).

Hendrick, H. (1997) *Children, childhood and English society, 1880–1990*. Cambridge: Cambridge University Press.

Herbert, I. (2005) 'Vigilante violence: death by gossip', *The Independent*, 23 March [Online]. Available at: http://www.independent.co.uk/news/uk/crime/vigilante-violence-death-by-gossip-6150008.html (Accessed: 7 June 2010).

Herman, E.S. and Chomsky, N. (1988) *Manufacturing consent: the political economy of the mass media*. New York: Pantheon.

Hermida, A. and Thurman, N. (2008) 'A clash of cultures: the integration of user-generated content within professional journalistic frameworks at British newspaper websites', *Journalism Practice*, 2(3), pp. 343–356, *Taylor and Francis Online* [Online]. DOI: 10.1080/17512780802054538 (Accessed: 15 August 2013).

Heywood, C. (2001) *A history of childhood: children and childhood in the west from medieval to modern times*. London: Polity Press.

Hier. S.P. (2003) 'Risk and panic in later modernity: implications of the converging sites of social anxiety', *British Journal of Sociology* 54(1), pp. 3–20.

Hier, S.P. (2008) 'Thinking beyond moral panic: risk, responsibility, and politics of moralization', *Theoretical Criminology* 12(2), pp. 173–190, *Sage Journals Online* [Online]. DOI: 10.1177/1362480608089239 (Accessed: 3 December 2010).

Hier, S.P., Walby, K., and Smith, A. (2011) 'Panic, regulation, and the moralization of British law and order politics', in S. Hier (ed.) (2011) *Moral panic and the politics of anxiety*. Oxford: Routledge.

Hillman, M., Adams, J., and Whitelegg, J. (1990) *One false move: a study of children's independent mobility*, London: Policy Studies Institute Publishing.

Hine, C. (2000) *Virtual ethnography*. London: Sage Publications Ltd.

Hirsch, P. (1980) 'The "scary world" of the non-viewer and other anomalies: a research analysis of Gerbner et al's findings of Cultivation Analysis', *Communication Research*, 7(4), pp. 403–456.

Hirsch, P. (1981) 'On not learning from one's own mistakes: a reanalysis of Gerbner et al's findings on Cultivation Analysis part II', *Communication Research*, 8(1), pp. 3–37.

Hollway, W. And Jefferson, T. (2000) *Doing qualitative research differently: free association, narrative, and the interview method*. London: Sage.

Hood, S., Kelley, P. and Mayall, B. (1996) *Children, parents and risk: a report on a research study*. London: Social Science Research Unit.

Horvath, M.A.H., Davidson, J.C., Grove-Hills, J., Gegoski, A., and Choak, C. (2014) *'It's a lonely journey': a rapid evidence assessment on intrafamilial child sexual abuse*. London: Middlesex University and Office of the Children's Commissioner.

Hunt, A. (1999) *Governing morals: a social history of public morals*. Cambridge: Cambridge University Press.

The Independent (2011) 'Teenagers mauled in bear attack' *The Independent*, 26 July, p. 30.

Ipsos MORI (2000) *Naming and shaming poll*. Available at: http://www.ipsos-mori.com/researchpublications/researcharchive/1619/Naming-amp-Shaming-Poll.aspx (Accessed: 7 February 2014).

Ipsos MORI (2002) *The repercussions of Soham murders*. Available at: http://www.ipsos-mori.com/researchpublications/researcharchive/1049/The-Repercussions-Of-Soham-Murders.aspx (Accessed: 7 February 2014).

Iyengar, S. (1991) *Is anyone responsible? How television frames political issues*. Chicago and London: University of Chicago Press.

Iyengar. S. and Hahn, K. S. (2009) 'Red media, blue media: evidence of ideological selectivity in media use', *Journal of Communication*, 59(1), pp. 19–39, *Wiley Online Library* [Online]. DOI: 10.1111/j.1460-2466.2008.01402.x (Accessed: 15 November 2010).

Jackson, B. (2011) 'First Africa famine in 27 years: Brits help dying kids...why can't rest of Europe do it too?' *The Sun*, 21 July, p.15.

Jago, R., Thompson, J., Page, A., Brockman, R., Cartwright, K., and Fox, K.R. (2009) 'Licence to be active: parental concerns and 10-11-year-old children's ability to be physically active', *Journal of Public Health*, 31(4), pp. 472–477, *Oxford Journals* [Online]. DOI: 10.1093/pubmed/fdp053 (Accessed: 5 May 2010).

Janssen, D. and Kies, R. (2005) Online Forums and Deliberative Democracy, *Acta Politica*, 40(3), pp. 317–335, *Ingenta Connect* [Online]. DOI: http://dx.doi.org/10.1057/palgrave.ap.5500115 (Accessed: 15 September 2013).

Jay, A. (2015) *Independent inquiry into child sexual abuse in Rotherham: 1997–2013*. Rotherham: Rotherham Metropolitan Borough Council.

Jeeves, P. (2011) 'Shocked mugger routed by ex-bouncer granny, 63' *Daily Express*, 1 July, p. 21.

Jeffs, D. (2011) 'Let him rot in hell: heartbroken family of murdered girl speak out on killer' *The People*, 31 July, pp. 16–17.

Jenkins, P. 1992. *Intimate enemies: moral panics in contemporary Great Britain.* New York: Aldine de Gruyter.

Jenkins, R. and Bannerman, L. (2012) 'All of us wanted to look for her' *The Times*, 3 October, pp. 4–5.

Jones, O. (2011) *Chavs: the demonisation of the working-class.* New York: Verso Books.

Judd, T. and Sundberg, C. (2011) 'The victims' stories: young lives cut short by a merciless killer' *The Independent*, 26 July, pp. 4–5.

Katz, E., Blumler, J., and Gurevitch, M. (1973) 'Uses and gratifications research', *The Public Opinion Quarterly*, 37(4), pp. 509–523, *JSTOR* [Online]. Available at: http://www.jstor.org/ (Accessed: 22 June 2015).

Keeble, R. (2006) *The Newspapers handbook.* 4th edn. New York: Taylor and Francis.

Kehily, M. (2010) 'Childhood in Crisis? Tracing the contours of "crisis" and its impact upon contemporary parenting practices', *Media, Culture & Society*, 32(2), pp. 171–185, The Open University [Online]. DOI: http://dx.doi.org/10.1177/0163443709355605 (Accessed: 3 January 2011).

Kelley, P., Mayall, B. and Hood, S. (1997) Children's Accounts of Risk in *Childhood* 4(3), pp. 305–324.

Kidscape (1993) *How safe are our children?* London: Kidscape.

King, P. (1998) 'The rise of juvenile delinquency in England 1780–1840: changing patterns of perception and prosecution', *Past & Present*, 160, pp. 116–166, *JSTOR* [Online]. Available at: http://www.jstor.org/ (Accessed: 24 July 2011).

Kitzinger, J. (1993) 'Understanding AIDS: researching audience perceptions of Acquired Immune Deficiency Syndrome', in Eldridge, J. (ed.), *Getting the message: news, truth, and power.* London: Routledge, pp. 271–305.

Kitzinger, J. (1999) 'The ultimate neighbour from hell? Stranger danger and the media framing of paedophiles', in B. Franklin (ed.), *Social policy, the media and misrepresentation.* Abingdon: Routledge.

Kitzinger, J. (2004) 'Audience and readership research', in Downing, J., McQuail, D., Schlesinger, P., and Wartella, E. (eds), *The Sage handbook of media studies.* London: Sage, pp. 167–181.

Krugman, R. (1995) 'The media and public awareness of child abuse and neglect: it's time for a change', *Child Abuse and Neglect*, 20(4), pp. 259–260.

Kussmaul, A. (1981) *Servants in husbandry in early modern England.* Cambridge University Press.

La Fontaine, J.S. (1994) *The extent and nature of organised and ritual abuse.* London: Her Majesty's Stationery Office.

Lansdown, G. (1994) 'Children's rights', in Mayall, B. (ed.), *Children's childhoods observed and experienced.* London: The Falmer Press, pp. 33–44.

Laville, S. (2012) 'Special hotline activated for first time in search for missing child' *The Guardian*, 3 October, p. 3.

Lawton, J. (2012a) 'Wear pink for April' *Daily Star*, 5 October, p.1.

Lawton, J. (2012b) 'April suspect knows family' *Daily Star*, 3 October, pp. 4–5.

Lazarsfeld, P., Berelson, B., and Gaudet, H. (1944) *The people's choice.* New York: Columbia University Press.

Le Grand, E. (2013) 'The "chav" as folk devil', in Critcher, C., Hughes, J., Petley, J., and Rohloff, A. (eds), *Moral panics in the contemporary world*. New York and London: Bloomsbury Academic, pp. 215–236.

Lett, D. (2010) '"Hoodies", CCTV and antisocial behaviour: linking panics to long-term moral and technical regulation', *Moral panics in the contemporary world*. Unpublished conference paper. Brunel University, Uxbridge, 10–12 December.

The Leveson Inquiry (2012) *Leveson Inquiry: culture, practice, and ethics of the press*. Available at: www.levesoninquiry.org.uk (Accessed: 30 January 2014).

Lewis, S. C. (2012) 'The tension between professional control and open participation: Journalism and its boundaries', *Information, Communication & Society*, 15(6), pp. 836–866, *Taylor and Francis Online* [Online]. DOI: 10.1080/1369118X.2012.674150 (Accessed: 23 September 2013).

Li, Y., Pickles, A., & Savage, M. (2005) 'Social capital and social trust in Britain', *European Sociological Review*, 21(2), pp. 109–123, *Oxford Journals* [Online]. Available at: http://esr.oxfordjournals.org/ (Accessed: 15 March 2012).

Liska, A.E. and Baccaglini, W. (1990) 'Feeling safe by comparison: crime in the newspapers', *Social Problems*, 37(3), pp. 360–374.

Local Government Chronicle (1996) 'Glasgow streets dry out' *Local Government Chronicle*, 8 July 1996 [Online]. Available at: http://www.lgcplus.com/glasgow-streets-dry-out/1525231.article (Accessed: 7 February 2014).

Loomes, N. (2011a) 'Man seen loitering near schools' *The Argus*, 16 July, p. 12.

Loomes, N. (2011b) 'Third child offered lift by stranger' *The Argus*, 21 July, p. 7.

Loveys, K. (2011) 'Teachers will be allowed to use force on unruly pupils as ministers lift "no touching" ban', *Daily Mail*, 10 July [Online]. Available at: http://www.dailymail.co.uk/news/article-2013288/Teachers-allowed-use-force-unruly-pupils-ministers-lift-touching-ban.html (Accessed: 10 August 2011).

Lunt, P. and Livingstone, S. (1996) 'Rethinking the focus group in media and communications research', *Journal of Communication*, 46(2), pp. 79–98, *Wiley Online Library* [Online]. DOI: 10.1111/j.1460-2466.1996.tb01475.x (Accessed: 13 July 2011).

Machin, D. (1996) 'Morbo, personhood, and the absence of a sensationalist press in Spain', *Journal of Mediterranean Studies*, 6(2), pp. 247–255.

Macgilchrist, F. (2012) 'Blogs, genes and immigration: online media and minimal politics', *Media, Culture and Society*, 34(1), pp. 83–100, *SAGE* [Online]. DOI: 10.1177/0163443711427201. Available at: http://mcs.sagepub.com (Accessed: 26 June 2015).

Mackenzie, S., Bannister, J., Flint, J., Parr, S., Millie, A. and Fleetwood, J. (2010) *The drivers of perceptions of antisocial behaviour (research report 34)*. London: Home Office.

Malthouse, K. (2011) 'Violence caused by organised gangs and feral youth', www.politicshome.com, 8 August [Online]. Available at: http://www.politicshome.com/uk/article/33387/kit_malthouse_violence_caused_by_organised_gangs_and_feral_youth.html (Accessed: 23 August 2012).

Manning White, D. (1950) 'The "gatekeeper": a case study in the selection of news', in Tumber, H. (ed.) (1999) *News: a reader*. Oxford: Oxford University Press, pp. 383–90.

Martindale, A. (1994) 'The child in the picture: a medieval perspective', in Wood, D. (ed.), *The Church and childhood (studies in Church history, vol. 31)*. Ecclesiastical History Society: Oxford, pp. 197–232.

Mason, B.W. and Donnelly, P.D. (2000) 'Impact of a local newspaper campaign on the take-up of measles, mumps and rubella vaccine', *Journal of Epidemiological Community Health*, 54, pp. 473–474, BMJ [Online]. DOI:10.1136/jech.54.6.473 (Accessed: 14 May 2010).

May, M. (1973) 'Innocence and experience: the evolution of the concept of juvenile delinquency in the mid-nineteenth century', *Victorian Studies*, 17(1), pp. 7–29, *JSTOR* [Online]. Available at: http://www.jstor.org/ (Accessed: 12 August 2011).

Mayring, P. (2000) 'Qualitative content analysis', *Forum: Qualitative Social Research*, 1(2). Available at: urn:nbn:de:0114-fqs0002204 (Accessed: 15 November 2013).

McCombs, M. (2004) *Setting the agenda: the mass media and public opinion*. Cambridge: Polity Press.

McCombs, M. and Shaw, D.L. (1972) 'The agenda-setting function of mass media', *The Public Opinion Quarterly*, 36(2), pp. 176–187, *JSTOR* [Online]. Available at: http://www.jstor.org/ (Accessed: 26 June 2015).

McCoy, M. E. (2001) 'Dark alliance: news repair and institutional authority in the age of the internet', *Journal of Communication*, 51(1), pp. 164–93, *Wiley Online Library* [Online]. DOI: 10.1111/j.1460-2466.2001.tb02877.x (Accessed: 14 August 2013).

McDevitt, S. (1996) 'The impact of news media on child abuse reporting', *Child Abuse and Neglect*, 20(4), pp. 261–274, *Science Direct* [Online]. DOI: http://dx.doi.org/10.1016/0145-2134(96)00008-7 (Accessed: 5 August 2010).

McManus, J. H. (1994) *Market driven journalism: let the citizen beware*. Thousand Oaks, California: Sage.

McNeish, D. and Roberts, H. (1995) *Playing it safe: today's children at play*. Ilford: Barnardo's.

McRobbie, A. and Thornton, S. L. (1995) 'Re-thinking "moral panic" for multi-mediated social worlds', *British Journal of Sociology*, 46(4), pp. 559–74. *JSTOR* [Online]. Available at: http://www.jstor.org/ (Accessed: 10 September 2010).

McSmith, A. (2012) 'The force that was above the law' The *Independent* [Online], 14 September. Available at: http://www.independent.co.uk/sport/football/news-and-comment/the-force-that-was-above-the-law-8135802.html (Accessed: 24 July 2013).

Meyer, A. (2007) *The child at risk: paedophiles, media responses and public opinion*. Manchester: Manchester University Press.

Miller, D., Kitzinger J., Williams, K., and Beharrell, P. (1998) *The circuit of mass communication: media strategies, representation and audience reception in the AIDS crisis*. Sage: London.

Millie, A. (2008) *Antisocial behaviour*. Buckingham: Open University Press.

Millie, A., Jacobson, J., McDonald, E. and Hough, M. (2005) *Antisocial behaviour strategies: finding a balance*. York: Joseph Rowntree Foundation.

Ministry of Justice (2014) *Statistical notice: Anti-Social Behaviour Order (ASBO) Statistics – England and Wales 2013*, London: Ministry of Justice.

Mooney, G (2009) 'The "broken society" election: class hatred and the politics of poverty and place in Glasgow East', *Social Policy and Society*,

3(4), pp. 1–14, *Cambridge Journals* [Online]. DOI: http://dx.doi.org/10.1017/S1474746409990029 (Accessed: 24 August 2010).

Moore, K. (2012) 'Girl bitten by friend's collie' *Daily Star*, 5 October, p. 8.

Moreton, C. (2008) 'Missing: the contrasting searches for Shannon and Madeleine' *The Independent*, 2 March [Online]. Available at: http://www.independent.co.uk/news/uk/crime/missing-the-contrasting-searches-for-shannon-and-madeleine-790207.html (Accessible: 7 February 2014).

Moriarty, R. (2011) '4 yrs for "asylum" sex fiend' *The Sun*, 6 July, p. 4.

Morley, D. (1976) 'Industrial conflict and the mass media', *The Sociological Review* 24(2), pp. 245–68, *Wiley Online Library* [Online]. DOI: 10.1111/j.1467-954X.1976.tb00112.x (Accessed: 18 July 2010).

Morley, D. (1980) *The 'Nationwide' audience*. London: British Film Institute.

Morris, S. (2011) 'Judge tells "depraved" Restivo he will never go free' *The Guardian*, 1 July, p. 9.

Morris, S. and Laville, S. (2012) 'Appeal for help to piece together suspect's movements as search for April widens' *The Guardian*, 4 October, p. 3.

Moss, S. (2012) *Natural childhood*. London: National Trust.

Mullin, C. (2012) 'April Jones abduction is "every family's worst nightmare"' *Liverpool Echo*, 2 October [Online]. Available at: http://www.liverpoolecho.co.uk/news/uk-world-news/april-jones-abduction-every-familys-3331284 (Accessed: 7 February 2014).

Muthukumaraswamy, K. (2010) 'When the media meets crowds of wisdom: how journalists are tapping into audience expertise and manpower for the processes of newsgathering', *Journalism Practice* 4(1), pp. 48–65, *Taylor and Francis Online* [Online]. DOI: 10.1080/17512780903068874 (Accessed: 28 September 2013).

Narain, J. and Eccles, L. (2011) 'Parents' revolt as headmaster is forced out for pinning violent boy against wall' *Daily Mail*, 26 July, p. 23.

Nash, E. (2011) 'Teen's horror' *The Sun*, 1 July, p.11.

National Centre for Social Research, *British Social Attitudes Survey, 2008* [computer file]. Colchester, Essex: UK Data Archive [distributor], March 2010. SN: 6390, http://dx.doi.org/10.5255/UKDA-SN-6390-1

National Centre for Social Research, *British Social Attitudes Survey, 2010* [computer file]. Colchester, Essex: UK Data Archive [distributor], February 2012. SN: 6969, http://dx.doi.org/10.5255/UKDA-SN-6969-1

National Trust (2008) *Wildlife alien to indoor children*. Available at: www.nationaltrust.org.uk/what-we-do/news/archive/view-page/item737221/ (Accessed: 14 July 2010).

Neraudau, J.P. (1984) *Etre enfant a Rome (Realia)*. Paris: Les Belles Lettres.

Nesbitt-Larking, P. (2007) *Politics, society and the media*. 2nd edn. New York: Broadview Press.

Nicholls, M. and Katz, L. (2004) 'Michael Howard: a life in quotes', *The Guardian*, 26 August [Online]. Available at: http://www.theguardian.com/politics/2004/aug/26/conservatives.uk (Accessed: 8 February 2014).

Nicks, G. (2011) 'Leave our kids alone: Cam's campaign on net porn' *Daily Star*, 12 October, p. 1.

Noveck, B.S. (2004) 'Unchat: democratic solution for a wired world', in Shane, P.M. (ed.), *Democracy online: the prospects for political renewal through the internet*. London: Routledge, pp. 21–34.

NSPCC (2012) 'Savile case prompts surge in calls to NSPCC about children suffering sexual abuse right now', *NSPCC*, 10 October [Online]. Available at: http://www.nspcc.org.uk/news-and-views/media-centre/press-releases/2012/12-10-savile-case-prompts-surge-in-calls/savile-case-prompts-surge-in-calls-to-nspcc_wdn92545.html (Accessed: 18 December 2012).

O'Carroll, L. (2012) 'Operation Elvedon: three arrested over alleged corrupt payments', The *Guardian*, 4 July [Online]. Available at: http://www.theguardian.com/media/2012/jul/04/operation-elveden-three-arrested (Accessed: 24 July 2013).

O'Connell, M. (1999) 'Is Irish public opinion towards crime distorted by media bias?' *European Journal of Communication*, 14(2), pp. 191–212. DOI: 10.1177/0267323199014002003 (Accessed: 15 August 2010).

O'Neill, S., Farmery, T., Jenkins, R., and Bannerman, L. (2012) 'Frantic hunt along river as parents beg for daughter's safe return' *The Times*, 3 October, p. 4.

Organisation for Economic Co-operation and Development (OECD) (2001) *The well-being of nations: the role of human and social capital*. Paris: OECD Centre for Educational Research and Innovation.

O'Shea, G. and Crick, A. (2011) 'Mum run down by daughter' *The Sun*, 21 July, p. 21.

Ost, S. (2002) 'Children at risk: legal and social perceptions of the potential threat that possession of child pornography poses to society', in Critcher, C. (ed.) (2003) *Moral panics the media*. Maidenhead: Open University Press, pp. 148–161.

Ozment, S.E. (1983) *When fathers ruled: family life in Reformation Europe*. Harvard: Harvard College.

Paletz, D. and Entman, R. (1981) *Media power politics*. New York: Free Press.

Parsons, B. (2011) 'Right to be aware and to educate...' *The Argus*, 26 July, p. 8.

Payne, S. (2012) 'Exclusive: April echoes hunt for Sarah' *The Sun*, 3 October, pp. 6–7.

Peachey, P. (2012) 'Man 'known to family' arrested over abduction of five-year-old' *The Independent*, 3 October, p. 2.

Pearson, G. (1983) *Hooligan: a history of respectable fears*. London: Palgrave Macmillan.

The People (2011) 'Boy 'killed' by goalpost' *The People*, 31 July, p. 9.

Peev, G. (2011) 'Pupils aged 10 should be given careers advice, says Lib Dem education czar' *Daily Mail* [Online]. Available at: http://www.dailymail.co.uk/news/article-2017063/Simon-Hughes-Pupils-aged-10-given-careers-advice.html (Accessed: 11 June 2015).

Perrie, R. (2011a) 'Asylum shriekers' *The Sun*, 6 July, p. 21.

Perrie, R. (2011b) '25ltr cider yob: teen's huge booze-up before attack' *The Sun*, 21 July, p. 31.

Pettifor, T. (2012a) 'On trial for child abuse 63 years ago' *Daily Mirror*, 3 October, p. 15.

Pettifor, T. (2012b) 'Tot death: mum hid his injuries' *Daily Mirror*, 3 October, p. 16.

Pettifor, T. (2012c) 'Eddie Shah sex charge' *Daily Mirror*, 5 October, p. 24.

Pfeil, P. and Zaphiris, P. (2010) 'Applying qualitative content analysis to study online support communities', *Universal access in the information society* 9(1), pp. 1–16, *Springer Link* [Online]. Available at: http://link.springer.com/ (Accessed: 15 September 2013).

Phillips, M. (2011), 'Britain's liberal intelligentsia has smashed virtually every social value' *Daily Mail*, 11 August [Online]. Available at: http://www.dailymail.

co.uk/debate/article-2024690/UK-riots-2011-Britains-liberal-intelligentsia-smashed-virtually-social-value.html (Accessed: 22 July 2013).

Phillips, R. (2012) 'Nicked: family pal arrested by April cops' *The Sun*, 3 October, p. 1.

Phillips, R. and Wells, T. (2012) 'Let our girl come home' *The Sun*, 3 October, pp. 4–5.

Philo, G. (1990) *Seeing and believing: the influence of television*. London: Routledge.

Philo, G. (1993) Getting the message: audience research in the Glasgow University Media Group', in *Getting the message: news, truth, and power*, London: Routledge, pp. 253–270.

Philo, G. (1996) (ed.) *The media and mental distress*. Addison Wesley Longman: Harlow.

Philo, G. (2007) 'Can discourse analysis successfully explain the content of media and journalistic practice?' *Journalism Studies*, 8(2), pp. 175–196, Taylor and Francis Online [Online]. DOI: 10.1080/14616700601148804 (Accessed: 12 September 2013).

Pollock, L. A. (1983) *Forgotten children: parent-child relations from 1500 to 1900*. Cambridge and New York: Cambridge University Press.

Porter, A. (2011) 'Workshy to go to back of housing queue', Daily *Telegraph*, 29 September [Online]. Available at: http://www.telegraph.co.uk/news/politics/8795729/Workshy-go-to-back-of-council-housing-queue.html (Accessed: 30 January 2014).

Press Association Mediapoint Wire (2012). Available at: *mediapoint.press.net* (Accessed: 2 October 2012).

Press Complaints Commission (2014) *Editors' code of practice*. Available at: http://www.pcc.org.uk/cop/practice.html (Accessed: 30 January 2014).

Pritchard, C. and Bagley, C. (2001) 'Suicide and murder in child murderers and child sexual abusers', *Journal of Forensic Psychiatry*, 12(2), pp. 269–286. DOI: 10.1080/09585180110057208 (Accessed: 15 July 2010).

ProQuest Newsstand (2013). Available at: http://www.proquest.co.uk/en-UK/catalogs/databases/detail/newsstand.shtml (Accessed: 5 March 2013).

Putnam, R. (2000) *Bowling alone: the collapse and renewal of American community*. Simon and Schuster: New York.

Pyatt, J. (2012) 'Killer used his kids as pawns' *The Sun*, 3 October, p. 10.

Ramsay, M.E., Yarwood, J., Lewis, D., Campbell, H., and White, J.M. (2002) 'Parental confidence in measles, mumps and rubella vaccine: evidence from vaccine coverage and attitudinal surveys', *British Journal of General Practice*, 52(484), pp. 912–916, *US National Institutes of Health* [Online]. Available at: http://www.ncbi.nlm.nih.gov/ (Accessed: 16 August 2010).

Rankin, B. (2012) '"Every family's worst nightmare": Detectives hunting for abducted April Jones reveal she got into driver's side of van and there was no sign of a struggle' *Daily Mirror* and *www.inooz.co.uk*, 2 October [Online]. Available at: http://www.mirror.co.uk/news/uk-news/april-jones-missing-detectives-hunting-1355725 and http://www.inooz.co.uk/article/view/1556111/-every-family-s-worst-nightmare-detectives-hunting-for-abducted-april-jones-reveal-she-got-into-driver-s-side-of-van-and-there-was-no-sign-of-a-struggle (Accessed: 7 February 2014).

The Daily Politics (2010), BBC2, 14 December. [Online] Available at: http://www.bbc.co.uk/iplayer/ (Accessed: 14 December 2010).

Rayner, G., Marsden, S., and Silverman, R. (2012) 'Kidnap suspect "was weapons collector"' *Daily Telegraph*, 4 October, p. 3.

Rayner, G., Marsden, S., Silverman, R., and Ward, V. (2012a) '"Let our beautiful little girl come home to us, plead April's parents" and "Detectives search river as tyre marks are found on bank"' *Daily Telegraph*, 3 October, pp. 1–2.

Rayner, G., Marsden, S., Silverman, R., and Ward, V. (2012b) 'Town unites as mood turns from hope to desperation' *Daily Telegraph*, 3 October, pp. 2–3.

Rayner, G., Marsden, S., Silverman, R., and Ward, V. (2012c) '"We are desperate for news of April. Please, please, help find her" and April "had been in arrested man's car"' *Daily Telegraph*, 4 October, p. 1 and 3.

Rayner, G., Marsden, S., Silverman, R., and Ward, V. (2012d) 'We just want April home now: someone knows where she is' *Daily Telegraph*, 5 October, p. 1.

Reilly, J. (1999) '"Just another food scare?" Public understanding and the BSE crisis', in Philo, G. (ed.), *Message received*. Harlow: Longman, pp. 128–146.

Richardson, J. E. (2008) 'Language and journalism: an expanding research agenda', *Journalism Studies*, 9(2), pp. 152–160. DOI:10.1080/14616700701848139 (Accessed: 15 September 2013).

Riches, C. (2011) 'Iranian paedophile is jailed, but won't be sent back home' *Daily Express*, 6 July, p. 7.

Roberts, A. (2011) '12-year-old boy warned for hoax yacht emergency', *The Argus*, 6 July, p. 5.

Robertson, P. (1976) 'Home as a nest: middle class childhood in nineteenth-century Europe', in deMause, L. (ed.), *The history of childhood*, pp. 405–425.

Rocheron, Y. and Linne, O. (1989) 'AIDS, moral panic and opinion polls', *European Journal of Communication*, 4(4), pp. 409–34, *Sage Journals Online* [Online]. DOI: 10.1177/0267323189004004004 (Accessed: 15 September 2013).

Rodger, J. (2008) *Criminalising social policy: antisocial behaviour and welfare in a de-civilised society*. London: Willan Publishing.

Roper, E., Katz, E., and Lazarsfeld, P. (1955) *Personal influence: the part played by people in the flow of mass communication*. New York: The Free Press.

Roshier, B. (1973) 'The selection of crime news by the press', in Cohen, S. and Young, J. (eds) (1981) *The manufacture of news: deviance, social problems and the mass media*. 2nd edn. London: Constable, pp. 28–39.

Rothstein, B. and Uslaner, E. (2005) 'All for all: equality, corruption and social trust', *World Politics* 58(1), pp. 41–72, Cambridge Journals [Online]. DOI: http://dx.doi.org/10.15/wp.2006.0022 (Accessed: 5 July 2012).

Rudolph, R. L. (1994) *The European peasant family and society. Historical studies*. Liverpool: Liverpool University Press.

Salkeld, L. (2012) 'Did having ears pierced make this teenager's heart stop?' *Daily Mail*, 4 October, p. 3.

Sanchez, R. (2011) 'Bedales School expels 13-year-olds for whisky and sandpit sex' www.telegraph.co.uk (Accessed: 31 October 2011).

Schlesinger, P. (1987) *Putting 'reality' together: BBC News*. London: Methuen.

Schlesinger, P. (1989) 'From production to propaganda?' *Media, Culture, Society*, 11(3), pp. 283–306, *Sage Journals Online* [Online]. DOI: 10.1177/016344389011003003 (Accessed: 24 June 2010).

Schlesinger, P., and Tumber, H. (1994) *Reporting crime: the media politics of criminal justice*. London: Clarendon.

Scott, D.M. (2011) *Newsjacking: how to inject your idea into a breaking news story and generate tons of media coverage*. London: John Wiley and Sons.

Scott, S. Jackson, S. and Backett-Milburn, K. (1988) 'Swings and roundabouts: risk anxiety and the everyday worlds of children', *Sociology*, 32(4), pp. 689–705, Sage Journals Online [Online]. DOI: 10.1177/0038038598032004004 (Accessed: 4 June 2010).

Scraton, P. (ed.) (1997) *Childhood in 'crisis'?* London: UCL Press.

Sears, N. (2011a) 'Pregnant at 15, daughter of Britain's most prolific single mother (And, of course, she's on benefits - just like mum)' *Daily Mail*, 11 July, p. 11.

Sears, N. (2011b) 'Assault on six–year-old girl may cost fashionable Steiner school £100,000' *Daily Mail* [Online]. Available at: http://www.dailymail.co.uk/news/article-2016998/Assault-pupil-6-cost-Steiner-school-100-000.html (Accessed: 11 June 2015).

Semetko, H.A. (1989) 'Television news and the third force in British politics: a case study of election communication', *European Journal of Communication*, 4(4), pp. 453–479, *Sage Journals Online* [Online]. DOI: 10.1177/0267323189004004006 (Accessed: 31 January 2014).

Shahar, S. (1990) *Childhood in the Middle Ages*. London and New York: Routledge.

Shaw, A. (2011) 'Strike day girl killed by branch: off school 13-yr-old hit in park', *Daily Mirror*, 1 July, p. 11.

Shaw, B., Watson, B., Frauendienst, B., Redecker, A., Jones, T., with Hillman, M. (2013) *Children's independent mobility: a comparative study in England and Germany (1971–2010)*. London: Policy Studies Institute Publishing.

Sheley, J.F. and Ashkins, C.D. (1981) 'Crime, crime news, and crime views', *Public Opinion Quarterly*, 45(4), pp. 492–506, *JSTOR* [Online]. Available at: www.jstor.org (Accessed: 3 August 2010).

Showalter, E. (1997) *Hystories: hysterical epidemics and modern media*. New York: Columbia University Press.

Sigelman, L. (1973) 'Reporting the news: an organizational analysis, *American Journal of Sociology*, 79(1), pp. 132–51, *JSTOR* [Online]. Available at: www.jstor.org (Accessed: 4 August 2010).

Slater, R. (2011) 'Why was Gemma abandoned to be murdered for fun by a gang of savages who she thought were her friends?' *Mail on Sunday*, 31 July, pp. 22–3.

Smith, L. (2012) 'Girl, 2, died after swine flu blunder' *Daily Mirror*, 3 October, p.19.

Smith, R. (2009) 'Doctors are the most trustworthy and journalists are the least, poll finds' *Daily Telegraph*, 12 February [Online]. Available at: http://www.telegraph.co.uk/health/healthnews/4591602/Doctors-are-the-most-trustworthy-and-journalists-the-least-poll-finds.html (Accessed: 20 December 2013).

Smith, R. (2011a) 'Killer mate showed me Becca body' *Daily Mirror*, 1 July, p. 24.

Smith, R. (2011b) 'Becca ex in "fake river rescue" plot' *Daily Mirror*, 6 July, p. 27.

Smith, R. (2012) 'Please please let her come home: parents' plea over missing April, 5, as man is held' *Daily Mirror*, 3 October, p. 1.

Smith, R. and Aspinall, A. (2012) '"Please don't get in the van, April": friend's warning to missing girl, five' *Daily Mirror*, 3 October, pp. 4–5.

Social Issues Research Centre (2011) *The changing face of motherhood*. Oxford: SIRC.

Solanki, A-R., Bateman, T., Boswell, G., and Hill, E. (2006) *Antisocial behaviour orders*. London: Youth Justice Board.

Sommerville, C.J. (1990) *The rise and fall of childhood* (reissue). London: Vintage.

Soothill, K. and Grover. C. (1997) 'A note on computer searches of newspapers', *Sociology* 31(3), pp. 591–596, *Sage Journals Online* [Online]. DOI: 10.1177/0038038597031003014 (Accessed: 6 July 2011).

Spencer, J.C. (1950) 'The unclubbable adolescent: a study in the prevention of juvenile delinquency', *British Journal of Delinquency*, 1, pp. 113–24, *HeinOnline* [Online]. Available at: http://heinonline.org/ (Accessed: 13 July 2010).

Squires, P. (2008) *ASBO nation: the criminalisation of nuisance*, London: Policy Press.

Squires, P. and Stephen, D. (2005) *Rougher justice: antisocial behaviour and young people*, London: Willan Publishing.

Statewatch (2014) *ASBOwatch: Monitoring the use of antisocial behaviour orders*. Available at: http://www.statewatch.org/asbo/ASBOwatch.html (Accessed: 7 February 2014).

Stillman, S. (2007) '"The missing white girl syndrome": disappeared women and media activism', *Gender and Development*, 15(3), pp. 491–502, *JSTOR* [Online]. Available at: http://www.jstor.org/ (Accessed: 3 June 2015).

Stretch, E. (2011) 'Life for fetish psycho: why was hair fiend free to kill?' *Daily Mirror*, 1 July, p. 25.

Stretch, E. (2012) 'My angels are in heaven now' *Daily Mirror*, 5 October, p. 15.

Sturcke, J. (2010). 'Police under investigation over Fiona Pilkington case, *The Guardian*, 16 March [Online]. Available at: http://www.theguardian.com/uk/2010/mar/16/police-under-investiation-fiona-pilkington (Accessed: 7 February 2014).

Sumpter, R.S. (2000) 'Daily newspaper editors' audience construction routines: a case study', *Critical Studies in Mass Media and Communication*, 17(3), pp. 334–346, Taylor and Francis Online [Online]. DOI: 10.1080/15295030009388399 (Accessed: 4 July 2010).

The Sun (2011a) 'Arrow hit lad's face' *The Sun*, 1 July, p. 38.

The Sun (2011b) 'Pal: I saw girl victim' *The Sun,* 1 July, p. 41.

The Sun (2011c) 'Car kids' 104 degree F hell' *The Sun*, 6 July, p. 12.

The Sun (2011d) 'Lad thick as plank' *The Sun*, 6 July, p. 14.

The Sun (2011e) 'Coldsore baby dies' *The Sun*, 6 July, p. 19.

The Sun (2011f) 'Wire theft boy killed' *The Sun*, 6 July, p. 19.

The Sun (2011g) 'Jigsaw op saves lad' *The Sun*, 16 July, p. 18.

The Sun (2011h) 'Sick yob blows up possums' *The Sun*, 16 July, p. 32.

The Sun (2011i) '"Kid push" sir quits' *The Sun*, 26 July, p. 30.

The Sun (2012a) 'Boy's car fall death' *The Sun*, 3 October, p. 9.

The Sun (2012b) 'Girl hit by tube train' *The Sun*, 3 October, p. 9.

Sunday Mirror (2011) 'Dumbbell teacher ban' *Sunday Mirror*, 31 July, p. 33.

Sweney, M. (2012) 'Is the worst of the advertising recession over?' *The Guardian* [Online]. Available at: http://www.theguardian.com/media/organgrinder/2009/may/13/worst-recession-over-advertising (Accessed: 24 July 2013).

Thompson, E.P. (1977) 'Happy families', *New Society*, 8, pp. 499–501.

Thornton, L. (2011a) 'You utter plank: boy, 14, risks life on rail line in web craze' *Daily Mirror*, 6 July, p. 31.

Thornton, L. (2011b) 'iPad baby is the apple of my eye: Tot born at 23 weeks home with mum' *Daily Mirror*, 26 July, p. 31.

Thornton, L. (2012) 'Mum slams nursery for tot walkout' *Daily Mirror*, 5 October, p. 28.

Thorp, A. and Kennedy, S. (2010) *The problems of British society: is Britain broken? What are the policy implications?* House of Commons Library Research: Key Issues for the New Parliament. Available at: http://www.parliament. uk/business/publications/research/key-issues-for-the-new-parliament/social-reform/broken-britain/ (Accessed: 31 January 2014).

Thurman, N. J. (2008) 'Forums for citizen journalists? Adoption of user generated content initiatives by online news media', *New Media & Society*, 10(1), pp. 139–157, *Sage Journals Online* [Online]. DOI: 10.1177/1461444807085325 (Accessed: 15 September 2013).

The Times (2012a) 'First test of national alert system yielded 700 leads: behind the story' *The Times*, 3 October, p. 5.

The Times (2012b) 'Hope tied up in pink ribbons' *The Times*, 5 October, pp. 4–5.

Today (2011), BBC Radio 4, 4 January. [Online] Available at: http://www.bbc. co.uk/iplayer/ (Accessed: 5 January 2011).

Tonry, M (2004) *Punishment and politics: evidence and emulation in the making of English crime control policy*. Cullompton: Willan.

Tozer, J. (2011) 'Foot fetishist who abused 18 girls in flat over takeaway' *Daily Mail*, 6 July, p. 27.

Tremayne, M. (2007) 'Harnessing the active audience: synthesizing blog research and lessons for the future of media', in Tremayne, M. (ed.), *Blogging, citizenship and the future of media*. New York: Routledge, pp. 261–72.

Treviranus, J. and Hockema, S. (2009) 'The value of the unpopular: counteracting the popularity echo-chamber on the web', *Science and Technology for Humanity (TIC-STH), 2009 IEEE Toronto International Conference*, pp. 603–608, *IEEE Xplore* [Online]. 10.1109/TIC-STH.2009.5444430 (Accessed: 15 September 2013).

Troyna, B. (1982) 'Reporting the National Front: British values observed', in Husband, C. (ed.), *Race in Britain*. London: Hutchinson, pp. 259–78.

Tuchman, G. (1972) 'Objectivity as strategic ritual: an examination of newsmen's notions of objectivity', in Tumber, H. (ed.) (1999) *News: a reader*. Oxford: Oxford University Press, pp. 297–307.

Tuchman, G. (1978) *Making news: a study in the construction of reality*. New York: The Free Press.

Tuchman, G. (2000) 'The production of news', in Jensen, K.B. (ed.), *A handbook of media and communication research: qualitative and quantitative methodologies*. London: Routledge, pp. 78–90.

UK Newsstands, accessed on February 15, 2013.

Ungar, S. (2001) 'Moral panic versus the risk society: the implications of the changing sites of social anxiety', *British Journal of Sociology*, 52(2), pp. 271–91. DOI: 10.1080/00071310120044980 (Accessed: 16 December 2010).

Valentine, G. (1996a) 'Angels and devils: moral landscapes of childhood', *Environment and Planning D: Society and Space*, 14(5), pp. 581–599, *EPD* [Online]. DOI:10.1068/d140581 (Accessed: 5 July 2010).

Valentine, G. (1996b) *Stranger danger: parents' fears and restrictions on children's use of space*. Sheffield: University of Sheffield Department of Geography.

Valentine, G. (1997a) '"Oh yes I can." "Oh no you can't": children and parents' understandings of kids' competence to negotiate public space safely', *Antipode*,

29(1), pp. 65–89, *Wiley Online Library* [Online]. DOI: 10.1111/1467-8330.00035 (Accessed: 5 July 2010).

Valentine, G. (1997b) 'A safe place to grow up? Parenting, perceptions of children's safety and the rural idyll', *Journal of Rural Studies*, 13(2), pp. 137–148, *Science Direct* [Online]. DOI: http://dx.doi.org/10.1016/S0743-0167(97)83094-X (Accessed: 5 June 2010).

Valentine, G. (2004) *Public space and the culture of childhood*. Aldershot: Ashgate.

Valentine, G. and McKendrick, J. (1997) 'Children's outdoor play: exploring parental concerns about children's safety and the changing nature of childhood', *Geoforum*, 28(2), pp. 219–235, *Science Direct* [Online]. DOI: http://dx.doi.org/10.1016/S0016-7185(97)00010-9 (Accessed: 5 June 2010).

Van Dijk, T. (1998) Opinions and Ideologies in the Press, in A. Bell and P. Garrett (eds), *Approaches to media discourse*. Oxford: Blackwell.

Van Dijk, T. (2000) 'New(s) racism: a discourse analytical approach', in Cottle, S. (ed) *Ethnic minorities and the media: changing cultural boundaries*, pp. 33–49.

Waiton, S. (2006) 'Antisocial behaviour: the construction of a crime', *www.spiked-online.com*, 19 January. Available at: http://www.spiked-online.com/newsite/article/5 (Accessed: 15 October 2010).

Waiton, S. (2008) *The politics of antisocial behaviour: amoral panics*. London: Routledge.

Walker, A., Kershaw, C., and Nicholas, S. (2006) *Crime in England and Wales 2005–06*. London: Home Office.

Weeks, J. (1989) 'Aids: the intellectual agenda', in Critcher, C. (ed.) (2006) *Critical readings; moral panics and the media*. Maidenhead: Open University Press, pp. 77–87.

Wells, T. and Phillips. R. (2012) 'Hunt goes on: new appeal from mum as suspect quizzed' *The Sun*, 4 October, pp. 4–5.

White, S. (2011) 'Foot fetish abuser paid for perving: he's jailed for preying on youngsters' *Daily Mirror*, 6 July, p. 3.

Wilson, G. and France, A. (2010) 'Get out of jail free' *The Sun*, 8 December [Online]. Available at: http://www.thesun.co.uk/sol/homepage/news/3265526/Fury-as-Tories-ditch-their-vow-to-get-tough-on-crime.html (Accessed: 30 December 2010).

Wilson, J.Q. and Kelling, G. (1982) 'Broken Windows', *Atlantic Monthly*, pp. 29–38.

Wisniewska, L. Harris, L. and Oliver, C. (2006) *Young people and antisocial behaviour*. London: Youth Net and British Youth Council.

Witschge, T. (2005) 'Normativity online: facing the boundaries of the boundless World Wide Web', in Consalvo, M. and O'Riordan, K. (eds), *AoIR Internet Research Annual Volume 3*. New York: Peter Lang, pp. 150–157.

Witschge, T. (2006) Representation and inclusion in the online debate: the issue of honour killings', in Carpentier, N. and Cammaerts, B. (eds), *Reclaiming the media*. Bristol, UK: Intellect, pp. 129–151.

Witschge, T. (2013) 'Digital participation in news media: "minimalist" views versus meaningful interaction', in Scullion, R., Gerodimos, R., Jackson, D., and Lilleker, D.G. (eds), *The media, political participation and empowerment*. Abingdon: Routledge, pp. 103–115.

Wright, S. (2012) 'Each one killed with a single shot to the head: family massacred in French Alps bore trademark of a professional hitman' *Daily Mail*, 6 September [Online]. Available at: http://www.dailymail.co.uk/news/

article-2199503/Lake-Annecy-shooting-Family-massacred-French-Alps-bore-trademark-professional-hitman.html (Accessed: 18 October 2013).

Wright, S., Bentley, P., and Evans, R. (2012) 'Please let our little April come home safe' *Daily Mail*, 3 October, pp. 1–2.

www.bbc.co.uk (2000a) 'Vigilante attack on innocent man' *www.bbc.co.uk*, 25 July. Available at: http://news.bbc.co.uk/1/hi/uk/848737.stm (Accessed: 30 January 2014).

www.bbc.co.uk (2000b) 'Paediatrician attacks "ignorant" vandals' www.bbc.co.uk, 30 August. Available at: http://news.bbc.co.uk/1/hi/wales/901723.stm (Accessed: 15 October 2010).

www.bbc.co.uk (2005) 'Call to boycott "hoodie" ban mall' www.bbc.co.uk, 13 May. Available at: http://news.bbc.co.uk/1/hi/england/kent/4545657.stm (Accessed: 15 October 2010).

www.bbc.co.uk (2010a) 'David Cameron warns public sector over budget cuts' www.bbc.co.uk, 19 June. Available at: http://www.bbc.co.uk/news/10356401 (Accessed: 30 January 2014).

www.bbc.co.uk (2010b) 'Police budget cuts detail revealed' www.bbc.co.uk, 13 December. Available at: http://www.bbc.co.uk/news/uk-11984841 (Accessed: 18 October 2013).

www.bbc.co.uk (2012) 'April Jones abduction: child got into van willingly say police' www.bbc.co.uk, 2 October. Available at: http://www.bbc.co.uk/news/uk-wales-19800140 (Accessed: 2 October 2012).

www.itv.com (2012) 'MoD: April murder suspect has never been in armed forces' www.itv.com, 4 October. Available at: http://www.itv.com/news/update/2012-10-04/mod-april-suspect-has-never-been-in-armed-forces/ (Accessed: 6 February 2014).

Young, J. (1971) *The drug-takers: the social meaning of drug use*, London: McGibbin and Kee.

Young, J. (2010) 'Moral panic and the sociological imagination', *Moral panics in the contemporary world*. Unpublished conference paper. Brunel University, Uxbridge, 10–12 December.

Zelizer, V.A.R. (1985) *Pricing the priceless child: the changing social value of children*. Princeton: Princeton University Press.

Index

CPSIA information can be obtained
at www.ICGtesting.com
Printed in the USA
LVHW05s0224151018
593604LV00015B/639/P